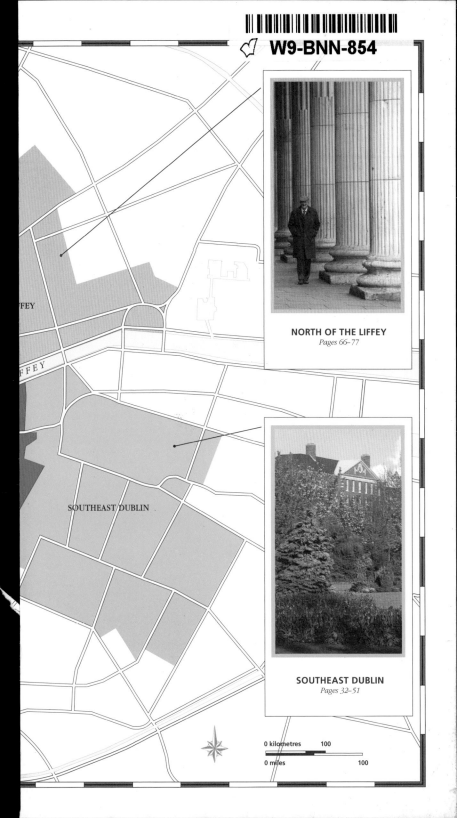

W9-BNN-854

NORTH OF THE LIFFEY
Pages 66–77

SOUTHEAST DUBLIN
Pages 32–51

LIFFEY

LIFFEY

SOUTHEAST DUBLIN

0 kilometres   100

0 miles   100

EYEWITNESS TRAVEL

DUBLIN

EYEWITNESS TRAVEL
DUBLIN

MAIN CONTRIBUTOR: TIM PERRY

OBEDIENTIA · FELICITAS
CIVIUM · URBIS

LONDON, NEW YORK,
MELBOURNE, MUNICH AND DELHI
www.dk.com

PROJECT EDITOR Claire Folkard
ART EDITOR Jo Doran
EDITOR Freddy Hamilton
DESIGNERS Paul Jackson, Nicola Rodway
DTPDESIGNERS Samantha Borland, Lee Redmond, Rachel Symons
PICTURE RESEARCH Victoria Peel

PHOTOGRAPHERS
Joe Cornish, Tim Daly, Magnus Rew, Antony Souter, Alan Williams

ILLUSTRATORS
Stephen Conlin, Gary Cross, Claire Littlejohn,
Maltings Partnership, Robbie Polley, John Woodcock

Reproduced in Singapore by Colourscan
Printed and bound by South China Printing Co. Ltd, China

First American Edition, 1999
10 11 12 13 10 9 8 7 6 5 4 3 2 1

Reprinted with revisions 2000, 2001, 2002, 2003, 2004, 2006,
2008, 2010

Published in the United States by
DK Publishing, 375 Hudson Street,
New York, New York 10014

Copyright © 1999, 2010 Dorling Kindersley Limited
London

Published in Great Britain by Dorling Kindersley Limited.
A catalog record for this book is available from the Library of Congress.

ISSN 1542-1554
ISBN 978-0-75663-221-2

FLOORS ARE REFERRED TO THROUGHOUT IN ACCORDANCE WITH EUROPEAN
USAGE; IE, THE "FIRST FLOOR" IS THE FLOOR ABOVE THE GROUND LEVEL.

*Front cover main image: Ha'Penny Bridge at sunset,
River Liffey, Dublin*

We're trying to be cleaner and greener:

- we recycle waste and switch things off
- we use paper from responsibly managed forests whenever possible
- we ask our printers to actively reduce water and energy consumption
- we check out our suppliers' working conditions – they never use child labour

Find out more about our values and best practices at www.dk.com

---

**The information in this
Dorling Kindersley Travel Guide is checked regularly.**
Every effort has been made to ensure that this book is as up-to-date
as possible at the time of going to press. Some details, however,
such as telephone numbers, opening hours, prices, gallery hanging
arrangements and travel information are liable to change. The
publishers cannot accept responsibility for any consequences arising
from the use of this book, nor for any material on third party
websites, and cannot guarantee that any website address in this
book will be a suitable source of travel information. We value the
views and suggestions of our readers very highly. Please write to:
Publisher, DK Eyewitness Travel Guides, Dorling Kindersley,
80 Strand, London, WC2R 0RL, Great Britain.

Façade of St Teresa's Church

CONTENTS

INTRODUCING DUBLIN

FOUR GREAT DAYS
IN DUBLIN **8**

PUTTING DUBLIN
ON THE MAP **10**

THE HISTORY OF
DUBLIN **12**

DUBLIN AT A GLANCE **20**

DUBLIN THROUGH
THE YEAR **26**

View across the tombstones of
Glasnevin Cemetery

DUBLIN AT A GLANCE

Although it is a fairly small city, Dublin offers a wealth of different attractions which draw in millions of visitors each year. Those in the city centre or a short way outside Dublin are covered in the *Area by Area* section of this book. Sights further out of the city include the elegant stately homes of Castletown House and Powerscourt. In central Dublin, Temple Bar offers shopping, eating and drinking and the arts in a trendy, relaxed environment. Alternatively the glittering treasures of the National Museum or the liquid treasures of the Guinness Storehouse may lure you inside. A selection of Dublin's most popular sights is given below.

DUBLIN'S TOP TEN ATTRACTIONS

Guinness Storehouse
See pp82–3

Trinity College
See pp38–9

Castletown House
See pp106–7

National Museum
See pp44–5

National Gallery
See pp48–51

St Patrick's Cathedral
See p61

Powerscourt
See pp114–15

Temple Bar
See pp58–9

Custom House
See p70

Christ Church Cathedral
See pp64–5

◁ The bell tower in Trinity College

Celebrated Visitors and Residents

For many centuries Dublin has produced some of the greatest literary names in history. However, Dubliners are also famous for music, philosophy and politics. Edmund Burke, widely considered to be the father of British Conservatism, was born to the north of the Liffey. Writers such as Yeats, Beckett and Wilde lived in the city intermittently, having been born in Ireland. Jonathan Swift began the tradition of brilliant Irish writing at around the beginning of the 18th century. Great Irish writing continues to this day, with such prize-winning authors as Seamus Heaney, William Trevor, Anne Enright, John Banville and Roddy Doyle.

The Duke of Wellington
Wellington was born in Dublin, close to what is now Wellington Quay, in 1769. He became one of the most successful generals and politicians in British history.

G F Handel
The German-born composer decided to première his most famous oratorio, the Messiah, in the new Music Hall in Fishamble Street in 1741.

NORTH OF THE LIFFEY

SOUTHWEST DUBLIN

Jonathan Swift
Famous as the author of many literary works, including Gulliver's Travels, *Swift became Dean of St Patrick's Cathedral in 1713.*

D. SWIFT

Bram Stoker
The author of Dracula, one of the most famous horror stories ever written, was born in Dublin in 1847 and lived on Harcourt Street just off St Stephen's Green.

THREE GUIDED WALKS
92

BEYOND DUBLIN **98**

TRAVELLERS' NEEDS

WHERE TO STAY **126**

RESTAURANTS, CAFÉS AND PUBS **134**

SHOPS AND MARKETS
148

ENTERTAINMENT IN DUBLIN **154**

SURVIVAL GUIDE

PRACTICAL INFORMATION **164**

TRAVEL INFORMATION
172

DUBLIN STREET FINDER
178

Interior of Avondale House, the home of Charles Stewart Parnell

GENERAL INDEX **182**

ACKNOWLEDGMENTS
191

DUBLIN AREA BY AREA

SOUTHEAST DUBLIN **32**

SOUTHWEST DUBLIN **52**

NORTH OF THE LIFFEY
66

Bookcases of rare books in Marsh's Library

FURTHER AFIELD **78**

Sheep on the farm at Newbridge Demesne, north of Dublin

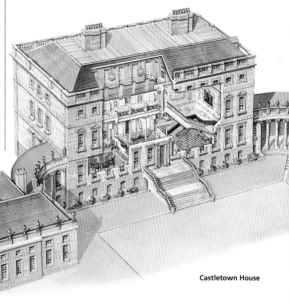

Castletown House

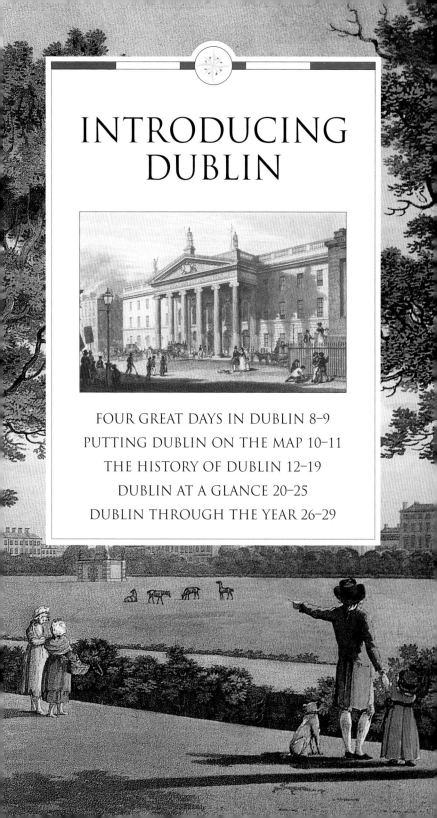

INTRODUCING
DUBLIN

FOUR GREAT DAYS IN DUBLIN 8–9

PUTTING DUBLIN ON THE MAP 10–11

THE HISTORY OF DUBLIN 12–19

DUBLIN AT A GLANCE 20–25

DUBLIN THROUGH THE YEAR 26–29

FOUR GREAT DAYS IN DUBLIN

A trip to Dublin, with its vibrant, historic city centre and the dramatic landscapes of Dublin Bay and the Wicklow Mountains in close proximity, appeals to both urbanites and wilderness lovers. What makes the Irish capital unique is its culture – a lively mix of traditional Gaelic games, music and dance and the

Celtic bronze fitting

refined pleasures of art, literature and drama, not to mention a fascinating history. These itineraries are intended to give you a taste of what Dublin has to offer, and to whet your appetite for a more in-depth experience. Costs include travel, food and admission to sights and tours. Family prices are for two adults and two children.

Baily Lighthouse at Howth Head

CELTIC LEGENDS

- A taste of ancient history
- Hurling at Croke Park
- A traditional Irish music session

TWO ADULTS allow at least €80

Morning
Start the day at **Trinity College** *(see pp38–9)*, where the Old Library houses the famous **Book of Kells** *(see p40)*. It is also worth looking at the splendid Long Room, with its barrel-vaulted ceiling and earthy smell of old books.

An early start will leave plenty of time to walk across to the nearby **National Museum** *(see pp44–5)*, with its beautiful Bronze Age collection and Iron Age bog bodies. Allow yourself at least an hour to wander through the finest collection of prehistoric gold artifacts in western Europe.

For lunch, there are a number of eateries on and around Kildare Street and Grafton Street, including

Gotham Café *(see p138)* and the tasty but pricey **La Cave** *(see p140)*, with its impressive wine selection.

Afternoon
Catch a bus to the nearby suburb of Drumcondra to watch sports legends play a top-class hurling or Gaelic football match at **Croke Park** stadium *(see p28)*. (Book tickets in advance by calling 865 8657). Matches generally take place at weekends, usually at 2pm and 4pm. The season runs from May to October; at other times of year, you can visit the lively Croke Park **GAA Museum**, and take a shot yourself with a hurley.

In the evening, head back into the city centre and on to the regenerated area of **Smithfield** *(see pp74–5)*, where the cosy and popular **Cobblestone** pub *(see p146)*, hosts regular sessions of traditional Irish music.

HOWTH

- Around Howth Head
- Seafood lunch
- Boat trip to Ireland's Eye
- An evening in Temple Bar

TWO ADULTS allow at least €80

Morning
Spend the morning walking around gorgeous **Howth Head** *(see p90)*. Dramatic cliff paths lead around the coastline, through the fishing village of Howth and its ruined abbey, and past **Baily Lighthouse**. More than half of Ireland's plant species can be found here, and there is also an abundance of wildlife, particularly birds.

On a sunny day, Howth Head is ideal for a picnic; alternatively, you can return to the village for lunch at **King Sitric** *(see p145)* or any one of the many fine restaurants along the waterfront, serving freshly caught fish and seafood.

Afternoon
From the East Pier, take a boat trip out to **Ireland's Eye** to explore the uninhabited

A hurling match at Croke Park

island, now taken over by wildlife. There are two buildings on the island: a 19th-century Martello tower and an 8th-century church ruin. The most spectacular natural feature is the huge freestanding rock called The Stack, teeming with bird life. Always stick to the paths to avoid walking on any birds' nests; great black-backed gulls will dive-bomb any intruders. It is possible to spot shags, razorbills, guillemots, kittiwakes, fulmars and even puffins.

If the weather turns bad, visit the **Howth Transport Museum**, just past the DART station. It is filled with every form of transport imaginable.

Spend the evening in one of Howth's many cosy pubs, or head back into Dublin to join the crowds and a lively scene in vibrant **Temple Bar** (see pp58–9).

CULTURED DUBLIN

- **Admiring the Irish Masters**
- **A lunchtime concert**
- **Dublin's literary heritage**
- **A play at the Abbey**

TWO ADULTS allow at least €150

Morning
Begin the day with a stroll through the **National Gallery** (see pp48–51). Allow at least an hour, and visit any special exhibitions in the new wing. At weekends, you may exit the gallery to find more art displayed on the railings around **Merrion Square** (see pp46–7).

Enjoy a lunchtime concert at the **National Concert Hall** (see p157), just south of **St Stephen's Green** (see p41). Concerts take place every Tuesday from early June to late August, and usually once a week (mostly Fridays) during the rest of the year. The music performed can be anything from classical to jazz. In summer, there are often outdoor concerts in the adjacent **Iveagh Gardens** (see p42). Stop for lunch at the **Shelbourne Hotel** (see p130).

An impressive room within the 19th-century National Gallery

Afternoon
After lunch, cross the river to the **Hugh Lane Gallery** (see p73) and the **Dublin Writers' Museum** (see p73) in Parnell Square. At weekends, the museum often offers one-man shows called Writers Entertain, on the works of Ireland's foremost writers, such as Beckett, Joyce, Wilde and Yeats (see p23). In the evening, see a play at the nearby **Gate Theatre** (see p72) or at the **Abbey** (see p70), Ireland's national theatre, a short stroll away. Alternatively, join the popular **Dublin Literary Pub Crawl** (see p156), which starts at 7:30pm from the Duke pub on Duke Street.

FAMILY FUN

- **A Viking invasion**
- **Living history at Dublinia**
- **Animal magic at Dublin Zoo**

FAMILY allow at least €150

Morning
The **Viking Splash Tour** (see p156) offers one of the liveliest – as well as wettest – ways to learn about Dublin's Viking history in special amphibious vehicles. Tours start at 10:30am from **St Patrick's Cathedral** (see p61). Tour groups will be dropped back at the cathedral from where it is a short walk to **Dublinia** (see p63). Exhibits here include life-size reconstructions of a Viking ship, medieval markets and the skeleton of a medieval woman found during excavations. Stop for fish and chips at **Leo Burdock's** (see p141).

Afternoon
After lunch, visit **Dublin Zoo** (see p81), in Phoenix Park (see p80), the largest urban park in Europe. The zoo has created a safari-like experience in the Elephant Habitat, where visitors can meet a family of elephants, including a baby born in May 2007. The zoo also has a rhino calf, born in May 2008.

A wander through the zoo can last all afternoon, but it is also worth taking some time to explore Phoenix Park itself, which opens out into woodland the further away from the city you get. It is ideal for a picnic or games – and deer spotting.

Children petting the elephants at Dublin Zoo

Putting Dublin on the Map

Dublin is the capital of the Republic of Ireland,
which takes up 85 per cent of Ireland, an island that
lies in the far northwest of Europe. Dublin sits
on the eastern coast of Ireland, on the Irish Sea, which
separates Ireland from Great Britain. The Liffey is the
main river running through the city. Dublin and its
surrounding county have a population of just over
one million, and good international communications.

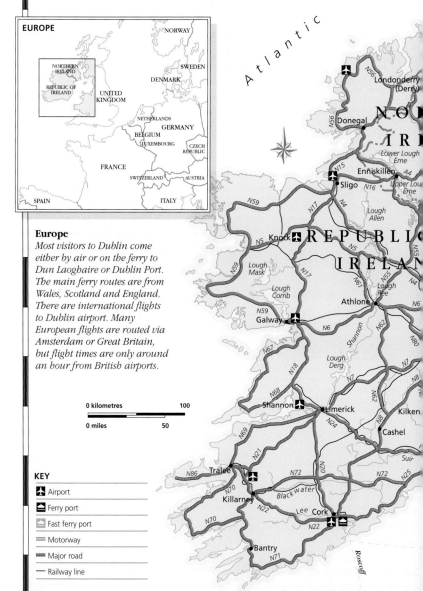

EUROPE

NORWAY

NORTHERN
IRELAND

REPUBLIC OF
IRELAND

SWEDEN

DENMARK

UNITED
KINGDOM

NETHERLANDS

GERMANY

BELGIUM

LUXEMBOURG

CZECH
REPUBLIC

FRANCE

SWITZERLAND

AUSTRIA

SPAIN

ITALY

Europe

*Most visitors to Dublin come
either by air or on the ferry to
Dun Laoghaire or Dublin Port.
The main ferry routes are from
Wales, Scotland and England.
There are international flights
to Dublin airport. Many
European flights are routed via
Amsterdam or Great Britain,
but flight times are only around
an hour from British airports.*

0 kilometres   100

0 miles   50

KEY

✈ Airport

⛴ Ferry port

⛴ Fast ferry port

▬ Motorway

▬ Major road

— Railway line

Atlantic Ocean

Londonderry
(Derry)

Donegal

N O...

I R I...

Lower Lough
Erne

Enniskillen

Upper Lou...
Erne

Sligo

N16

N56

N56

N15

A4

Lough
Allen

N59

N17

N4

Knock

R E P U B L I...

I R E L A N...

N5

Lough
Mask

N17

N61

Lough
Ree

N4

Lough
Corrib

Athlone

N6

N59

N55

N59

Galway

N6

Shannon

N62

N80

N67

N18

Lough
Derg

N7

N7

N68

N7

Shannon

Limerick

Kilken...

N69

N24

Cashel

N8

N62

N8

Suir

N86

Tralee

N72

N20

N72

N25

N70

Blackwater

Killarney

N22

Lee

Cork

N70

N22

Bantry

N71

Roscoff

GREATER DUBLIN

Swords
Malahide
Dublin Airport
Finglas
Glasnevin
Marino
Howth
Royal Canal
Liffey
Lucan
Grand Canal
Kilmainham
Ballsbridge
Dublin
Clondalkin
Rathmines
Dublin Bay
N81
Dundrum
Blackrock
Dun Laoghaire

0 km 5
0 miles 5

Greater Dublin
Nearly one third of the Republic's population lives in Dublin. Nevertheless the city is relatively uncongested and access to the centre from the ports and airport is easy.

SCOTLAND
Islay
Arran
Glasgow
Troon
North Channel
Campbeltown
Ballycastle
Coleraine
Cairnryan
Stranraer
Larne
ENGLAND
Lough Neagh
Belfast
Isle of Man
Douglas
Newry
Heysham
Dundalk
Fleetwood
Armagh
Irish Sea
Manchester
Boyne
Liverpool
DUBLIN
Mostyn
Dun Laoghaire
Holyhead
Iffey
Carlow
Slaney
Wexford
Rosslare
St George's Channel
WALES
Rosslare/Cherbourg
Waterford
Fishguard
Pembroke
Swansea
CARDIFF
Bristol
Bristol Channel

PARNELL ADDRESSING THE UNITED STATES HOUSE OF REPRESENTATIVES IN SESSION. WASHINGTON, FEB'Y 2ND 1880.

THE HISTORY OF DUBLIN

T*he city of Dublin first took form in the early 9th century when Vikings founded one of their largest settlements outside Scandinavia on the site of the present city. Since then, it has suffered wars and conflict over many centuries. In the 20th century Dublin has established its own identity and today it is a thriving, modern city, rich in history and proud of its past.*

Archaeological digs show evidence of civilization in the Dublin area as early as 7500 BC. The 4th millennium BC saw the influx of Neolithic farmers and herdsmen who built monumental tombs such as those found at Newgrange *(see pp120–21)*.

The Celts arrived around 700 BC and things changed little for 1,000 years. When St Patrick arrived in AD 432 bringing Christianity with him to Ireland, the Celts were quick to embrace the religion. During the golden age of Celtic Christianity the Dublin area was home to several churches and it is said that the present-day St Patrick's Cathedral (built in 1192) is where the saint baptized converts around AD 450. This era produced high levels of Christian scholarship, resulting in such treasures as the elaborately decorated Book of Kells *(see p40)*.

The city's modern Gaelic name of "Baile Atha Cliath" derives from a Celtic settlement on the north bank of the River Liffey. Known then as Ath Cliathe ("the ford over the hurdles") it was the only crossing over the river and lay at the junction of four major roads. It was the community at Ath Cliathe that bore the brunt of the island's first planned naval invasion by the Vikings.

Engraving showing St Patrick banishing snakes from Ireland

THE VIKINGS

Norse Vikings established their first harbour in Dublin in AD 841 and left in AD 902, under pressure from local chieftains. They returned 15 years later and built a stronghold situated between the present location of Dublin Castle and Wood Quay. It was here that the rivers Liffey and Poddle converged in a body of dark, still water which the Vikings called *Dyfflin* or *Dubh Linn* (or "black pool").

In 919 at the Battle of Dublin the Vikings fended off the King of Tara and by the mid-1100s they started to intermarry with the Celts. The Vikings were then defeated at the Battle of Clontarf in 1014 by Brian Ború, the Irish High King. Under King Sitric the Silkbeard, Dublin became a Christian vassal state. He oversaw the construction of a wooden cathedral (later rebuilt as Christ Church). By this time Dublin's population was around 5,000.

TIMELINE

7500 BC	5000	2500	0 AD	200	400	600	800	1000	1200

5000–3000 Ireland covered by dense woodland dominated by oak and elm

600 First wave of Celtic invaders

AD 80 Roman general Agricola considers invasion of Ireland from Britain

Viking silver brooch

795 First Viking invasion of coastal monasteries

1096 St Michan's Church *(see p76)* built

c.7500 BC First inhabitants of Ireland

Extinct giant deer or "Irish Elk"

2500 Building of Newgrange passage tomb *(see pp120–21)*

432 Start of St Patrick's mission to Ireland

841 A large Viking fleet passes winter in Dublin

1014 High King Brian Ború of Munster defeats joint army of Vikings and the King of Leinster at Clontarf

1147 St Mary's Abbey *(see p76)* built

◁ **Address to Charles Stewart Parnell by the Land League**

ANGLO-NORMAN CONQUEST

Feuds in Ireland led to Dermot Mac-Murrough, the King of Leinster, asking Henry II of England to send an army to aid him. This resulted in the appearance of Richard de Clare, better known as Strongbow, in 1169. Within a year he had taken control of Dublin and married MacMurrough's daughter. He was also the instigator of the construction of Christ Church Cathedral (see pp64–5).

When MacMurrough died in 1171, Strongbow was in line to succeed him. Henry II sent an army to Ireland to check his ambitions, in part by recognizing Strongbow's suzerainty over the province of Leinster. Henry then spent four months in Dublin establishing control.

The Marriage of Strongbow and Aoife, by Daniel Maclise (1854)

Under Anglo-Norman control, the structure and size of the city grew. Fortified walls and watchtowers were built, and in 1205 construction on Dublin Castle started. St Patrick's was made a cathedral in 1220 and underwent massive expansion while, in its shadows, the Liberties, the city's earliest suburbs, were growing in strength. The city became overcrowded and in 1348 was struck by the terrifying plague known as the Black Death.

TUDOR AND STUART RULE

Like the Vikings before them, the Anglo-Normans had entwined themselves in Irish society through marriage and religion. Some of them, such as the Fitzgeralds, the Butlers and the Burkes, effectively controlled dynasties. One of them, "Silken" Thomas Fitzgerald, son of the 9th Earl of Kildare, staged a revolt against London in 1534. This was defeated by King Henry VIII who, in 1541, passed the Act of Supremacy that made him King of Ireland and the head of the Church which, under the English Reformation, had broken from Rome. All land was the property of the English crown and, by dissolving the monasteries and sentencing to death all men of the Fitzgerald family, he indicated the start of a strongarm rule and the introduction of Protestantism to Ireland.

The reign of Elizabeth I witnessed the development of the island into a British colony, with plantations set up throughout Ireland. In 1592, on the site of a dissolved monastery near Dublin, she founded Trinity College as a seat of Protestant learning: a status it retained well into the 20th century.

Henry VIII with Bishop Sherbourne by Lambert Barnard (1519)

TIMELINE

1200	1250	1300	1350	1400	1450

1166 Dermot MacMurrough, King of Leinster, flees overseas

1172 Pope affirms King Henry II of England's lordship over Ireland

1297 First Irish Parliament meets in Dublin

1366 Statutes of Kilkenny forbid marriage between Anglo-Normans and Irish

1471 8th Earl of Kildare made Lord Deputy of Ireland

1169 Strongbow's Anglo-Normans arrive at invitation of exiled King of Leinster, Dermot MacMurrough

A section of Strongbow's tomb

1348 The Black Death: one third of population dies within three years

1394 King Richard II lands with army to reassert control; returns five years later but with inconclusive results

1487 Kildare crowns Lambert Simnel, Edward VI in Dublin

London's grip over Ireland intensified in 1649, when Oliver Cromwell arrived in Dublin. His infamous campaigns left several thousand dead or deported and he forced the Irish from their fertile lands in the east to the barren western province of Connaught.

The Rotunda Hospital in 1795, Dublin's first maternity hospital

THE PENAL LAWS

In 1690, the Catholic ex-king of England, James II, was defeated by the Dutch Protestant William Prince of Orange (King William III) at the Battle of the Boyne. In the years following, religious persecution was formalized into a Penal Code. Catholics were prohibited from voting, trading, buying land, holding elected or state office, or entering professions.

THE PROTESTANT ASCENDANCY

While William III's Penal Laws were spelling hard times for the Catholic population in the rest of Ireland, Dublin's middle classes and aristocrats (many of them absentee landlords who came to Ireland during the entertaining season) enjoyed a very comfortable existence.

William of Orange at the Battle of the Boyne

Throughout the 18th century they commissioned ostentatious homes such as Leinster House and Powerscourt House. The owners of the grand town houses employed master craftsmen from around the world, such as the German-English architect Richard Castle and the Swiss-Italian stuccodores Paolo and Filippo Francini.

Among the desirable addresses at the time were St Stephen's Green, Marlborough Street to the north of the Liffey and Ely Place on the southside. If they were ill, the Royal Hospital at Kilmainham attended their needs. Dublin also boasted the Rotunda Lying-In Hospital, the first maternity hospital in the British Isles. Much of the funding for this venture came from the adjacent and ornate Rotunda Gardens (no longer in existence), where members of high society frequently met and attended concerts. In Georgian times the privileged Protestants were able to patronize the arts: Handel premiered the *Messiah* in the city in 1742. Eleven years earlier, the still extant Royal Dublin Society was founded to promote the arts, science and agriculture. Many great academics and novelists also emerged from Trinity College, including the philosopher Edmund Burke, and Jonathan Swift, author of *Gulliver's Travels* and the Dean of St Patrick's Cathedral *(see p61)* from 1713 to 1745.

1500	1550	1600	1650	1700	1750

Trinity College (1592)

1592 Trinity College *(see pp38–9)* founded

1690 William of Orange defeats James II at Battle of the Boyne

1695 Penal Code severely reduces rights of Roman Catholics

1713 Jonathan Swift appointed Dean of St Patrick's Cathedral

1541 Henry VIII declared King of Ireland by the Irish Parliament

1585 Ireland is mapped and divided into 32 counties

1649 Cromwell lands in Dublin; razes Drogheda and Wexford; Catholic landowners transplanted to far west

Plasterwork from Newman House, built in 1765

1742 First performance of Handel's *Messiah* in Dublin

1731 Royal Dublin Society founded to encourage agriculture, arts and crafts

PUBLIC WORKS IN THE 18TH CENTURY

Many of the most impressive sights in Dublin today were built during the Protestant Ascendancy, in the Georgian era.

Among the most splendid structures of this period are Castletown House (1722–32), the Custom House (1791) and the Four Courts (1786–1802). The two latter buildings were both designed by James Gandon. Dublin was also one of the first cities in the world to enjoy planned development with the inauguration of the Wide Streets Commission in 1751. Further improvements came with the National Botanic Gardens in 1789.

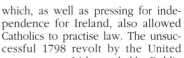

Lacquer cabinet, Castletown House

Commerce also helped shape the city. In the 1760s the Grand Canal was built and Ireland's most famous company began in 1759 when Arthur Guinness opened his brewery.

CATHOLIC EMANCIPATION AND RESISTANCE

Despite lengthy protests by pamphleteers and orators, the first real hint of relaxation of the penal laws came in 1782 when the Irish Parliament, led by Henry Grattan, passed a Declaration of Rights which, as well as pressing for independence for Ireland, also allowed Catholics to practise law. The unsuccessful 1798 revolt by the United Irishmen, led by Dublin Protestant Wolfe Tone, may have been instrumental in convincing the Westminster government to impose the 1800 Act of Union. This dissolved the Irish Parliament and saw the introduction of direct rule from England.

The first 19th-century revolt against British rule was led by Robert Emmet in 1803, who attempted to seize Dublin Castle. The most effective protest of the early part of the century was led by Daniel O'Connell, a Catholic lawyer, who later became known as "The Liberator" as a result of his efforts on behalf of the people who shared his religious beliefs. He supported mass peaceful protests and was elected an MP in 1828 but, as a Catholic, was unable to take his seat. In response to O'Connell's mass rallies and protests, the Emancipation Act of 1829 was passed. O'Connell was the first Catholic to be elected Mayor of Dublin in 1841 but, when he later called for a repeal of the Act of Union, he was jailed.

James Gandon's impressive Custom House, on the north bank of the Liffey

TIMELINE

1750	1775	1800	1825
1751 The Rotunda Lying-In Hospital *(see p72)* is first maternity hospital in the British Isles	**1791** James Gandon's Custom House *(see p70)* is built **1800** Act of Union: Ireland legally becomes part of Britain	**1817** The Royal Canal *(see p85)* is completed	**1838** Father Mathew founds temperance crusade – whiskey production is reduced by half
1759 Arthur Guinness buys the St James' Gate Brewery *(see pp82–3)*	 *Guinness Brewery Gate*	**1828** After a five-year campaign by Daniel O'Connell, Catholic Emancipation Act is passed, giving a limited number of Catholics the right to vote	**1845** Start of Great Famine, which lasts for four years

THE GREAT FAMINE AND FURTHER REBELLIONS

The history of 19th-century Ireland is dominated by the Great Famine of 1845–8, which was caused by the total failure of the potato crop. Although Irish grain was still being exported to England, around one million people died from hunger or disease. By 1900, the pre-famine population of eight million had fallen by half. Many of the poor

O'Connell Street shortly after the Easter Rising

moved into Dublin and the middle-class Dubliners moved out to the suburbs. Rural hardship fuelled a campaign for tenants' rights that evolved into demands for independence from Britain. Great strides towards "Home Rule" were made in Parliament by the charismatic politician, Charles Stewart Parnell.

Ration card from Famine period

SUPPORT FOR HOME RULE GROWS

In 1902 Arthur Griffith founded the Sinn Féin newspaper; its name, meaning "We, Ourselves", expressed their central policy thrust and it soon gave rise to a political party of the same name. In 1913 the Irish Volunteers (the forerunners of the Irish Republican Army) were formed. Political freedom was increasingly important at this time of stark poverty and violent clashes between workers and employers. One of the leaders of the workers' side, James Connolly, would soon broaden his political agenda to Republicanism.

Daniel O'Connell, "The Liberator"

WORLD WAR I AND THE EASTER RISING

Although the Home Rule Bill made its final passage through the British parliament, its implementation was suspended due to the outbreak of war. A small contingent felt that the best time to launch an attack on British rule was when Britain was at its weakest. Hence, on Easter Monday 1916, Patrick Pearse and other members of a provisional government proclaimed the Declaration of Independence from the General Post Office *(see p71)* in O'Connell Street. The band of rebels occupied several buildings in the capital.

The Easter Rising was put down within a few days but only after 300 citizens were killed and much of the city centre razed to the ground. The British forces lost patience with the Irish cause and the rebel leaders were shot for treason at Kilmainham Gaol. This overreaction made those executed into martyrs and renewed resentment towards Britain.

| 1853 Dublin Exhibition is opened by Queen Victoria | 1877 Charles Stewart Parnell becomes leader of the new Home Rule Party | 1907 JM Synge's *Playboy of the Western World* opens | *Despatch bag carried by rebel leader Constance Markievicz during the Easter Rising* |

1850 — **1875** — **1900** — **1925**

Main entrance to Kilmainham Gaol (see p81)

1881 Parnell is jailed in Kilmainham Gaol

1884 Founding of Gaelic Athletic Association, first group to promote Irish traditions

1916 The historic but unsuccessful Easter Rising is quashed by the British

1913 Irish Volunteers founded

View of O'Donovan Bridge which links the north and south sides of modern Dublin

INDEPENDENCE AND CIVIL WAR

The years after World War I were some of the busiest and bloodiest in Dublin's history. The resentment over the treatment of the Rising leaders, and a plan to bring in conscription in Ireland, helped the cause of the Sinn Féin party, which won three-quarters of Irish seats in the 1918 election. These new MPs refused to take up their seats and instead met at a newly formed Dáil Éireann (Parliament of Ireland) at the Mansion House *(see p41)*. The Dáil's Minister of Finance was Michael Collins, who was also head of the Irish Volunteers' campaign of urban guerrilla warfare. On the morning of 21 November 1920, Collins ordered the assassination of 14 undercover British officers in Dublin. That afternoon British forces retaliated in what soon became known as Bloody Sunday, when they shot 12 spectators at a big Gaelic football game at Croke Park stadium. Other small skirmishes continued throughout

the city, including the burning of the Custom House *(see p70)* in May 1921. Soon after this the British government instigated a truce and both sides signed the Anglo-Irish Treaty.

The treaty gave limited independence to what was to be called the Irish Free State, but six Ulster counties were to be excluded and members of the Free State parliament (the Dáil) would have to swear allegiance to the British monarch. A faction of the Dáil led by Eamon De Valera opposed the treaty and in June 1922 Civil War broke out. Anti-treaty forces occupied the Four Courts building *(see p76)* but this was bombed (as was much of O'Connell Street) by the army under Collins. The Free State government proved ruthless in its imprisonment and later execution of anti-treaty rebels, but Collins himself finally became a victim when the was ambushed and shot. In May 1923 De Valera ordered an end

Eamon De Valera, a major figure in modern Irish politics

TIMELINE

The Irish flag

1920	1930	1940	1950	1960

1918 Sinn Féin sweeps election; Countess Constance Markievicz elected first woman MP

1920 First "Bloody Sunday" at Croke Park

1921 Anglo-Irish treaty signed; leads to Civil War

1922 Michael Collins killed

Michael Collins, the leader of the Irish Volunteers

1941 German air raid on Dublin

1947 A statue of Queen Victoria is removed from the front courtyard of the Irish parliament buildings

1954 Brendan Behan's *The Quare Fellow* is published

1963 John F Kennedy, the first US President of Irish descent, visits Dublin

to the fighting by anti-treaty rebels and left the Sinn Féin party.

RECENT HISTORY

Within three years De Valera had formed a new party called Fianna Fáil (meaning "Warriors of Ireland"). By 1932, his party had acquired power. With only two short periods of time out of office, De Valera held the post of Taoiseach (prime minister) until 1959, when he became president for a further 14 years. His policies were largely insular and mirrored the Catholic Church on social issues. During World War II, De Valera kept Ireland neutral, so Dublin only experienced one Luftwaffe bombing.

European City of Culture doorway

After the war, Fianna Fáil were beaten in the election by Fine Gael. Though they were the descendants of the pro-treaty side, it was Fine Gael who oversaw the creation of the Republic of Ireland in 1949, which severed all ties with Britain by leaving the Commonwealth.

Dublin remained relatively immune to the political situation in Northern Ireland, as it does today, though in 1966 the IRA bombed the huge Nelson Pillar. Then in 1972, the British Embassy in Dublin was petrol-bombed, in retaliation for the shooting of 13 civilians on a protest march in Derry, in Northern Ireland, on what became

Young Irish dancers

known thereafter as Ireland's second Bloody Sunday. In May 1974 a series of car bombs in Dublin and Monaghan killed 33 people. The Ulster Volunteer Force claimed responsibility.

DUBLIN INTO THE MILLENNIUM

In 1991 Dublin was named European City of Culture, and this spurred the rejuvenation of Temple Bar (see pp58–9) into a world-class cultural quarter. The majority of new development was in the wealthier areas south of the river, though the divide between north and south has narrowed since the late 1990s and the economic boom. Dublin is now a lively, modern and cosmopolitan city.

In 2007, Unionists and Nationalists agreed to share power in a new Northern Ireland government. Dublin-born Taoiseach Bertie Ahern, and British counterpart Tony Blair were instrumental in the breakthrough deal.

Grafton Street in modernized southwest Dublin

1972 Ireland joins European Community	1988 Dublin celebrates its millennium; most historians, however, trace its founding to an even earlier date	President Mary Robinson (1990–97)	1998 Peace talks between the British and Irish governments, and parties in Northern Ireland, result in the Good Friday Agreement		
1970	**1980**	**1990**	**2000**	**2010**	**2020**
1976 British ambassador assassinated in Dublin	1979 Pope John Paul II celebrates mass in front of more than one million people	1996 Investigative journalist Veronica Guerin murdered 1990 Mary Robinson is the first woman elected as President of Ireland		2007 Unionists and Nationalists agree to share power in a new Northern Ireland government	

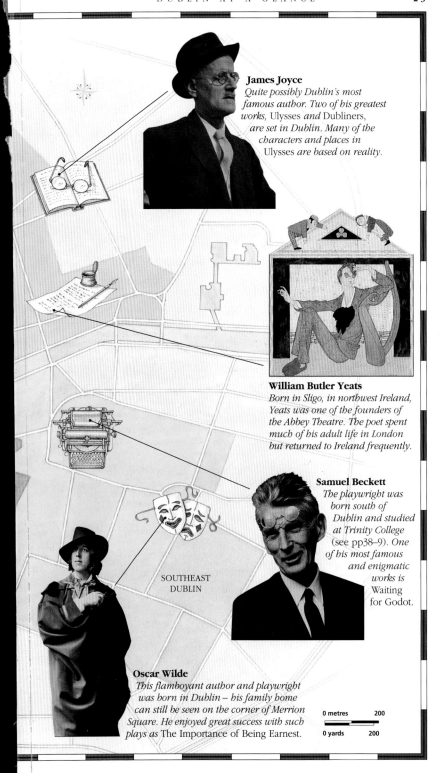

James Joyce
Quite possibly Dublin's most
famous author. Two of his greatest
works, Ulysses and Dubliners,
are set in Dublin. Many of the
characters and places in
Ulysses are based on reality.

William Butler Yeats
Born in Sligo, in northwest Ireland,
Yeats was one of the founders of
the Abbey Theatre. The poet spent
much of his adult life in London
but returned to Ireland frequently.

Samuel Beckett
The playwright was
born south of
Dublin and studied
at Trinity College
(see pp38–9). One
of his most famous
and enigmatic
works is
Waiting
for Godot.

SOUTHEAST
DUBLIN

Oscar Wilde
This flamboyant author and playwright
was born in Dublin – his family home
can still be seen on the corner of Merrion
Square. He enjoyed great success with such
plays as The Importance of Being Earnest.

0 metres   200

0 yards   200

Dublin's Best: Pubs

Everyone knows that Dublin is famous for its vast number of drinking establishments but, on arrival in the city, the choice can seem overwhelming. All the pubs are different – they range from vibrant, trendy bars to traditional pubs. Whatever your choice of environment and beverage, you can be guaranteed to find it in Dublin. These pages offer just a taster of the most popular pubs in the city and what they are famous for, but for a more complete listing, turn to pages 146–7.

Slattery's
Once a popular music pub just north of the Liffey, Slattery's has recently been totally modernized and is just as much of a success in its reincarnation as a trendy bar.

NORTH OF THE LIFFEY

The Stag's Head
This gorgeous Victorian pub has a long mahogany bar and has retained its original mirrors and stained glass. Located down an alley off Dame Street, this atmospheric pub is well worth seeking out.

SOUTHWEST DUBLIN

The Brazen Head
Reputedly the oldest pub in Dublin. The present building, still with its courtyard for coach and horses, dates back to 1750. The interior is full of dark wood panelling and old photographs of Dublin.

Hogan's
A café bar rather than a pub, Hogan's is a stylish establishment serving excellent drinks, and is popular with a young, trendy crowd. It is centrally situated on George's Street.

Oliver St John Gogarty
This famous old pub in the heart of Temple Bar is renowned for its live music throughout the day, and good food. It is named after the poet and friend of James Joyce. The atmosphere is relaxed and it is popular with visitors keen to sample a part of traditional Dublin.

O'Neill's
Just round the corner from Grafton Street, O'Neill's is one of the best places in the city for pub food. Its cosy atmosphere and location close to Trinity College make it a favourite with Dublin's student population.

LIFFEY

SOUTHEAST
DUBLIN

0 metres   200
0 yards   200

McDaid's
Playwright Brendan Behan downed many a pint in this pub, which dates from 1779. Though on the tourist trail, McDaid's retains a bohemian charm, and bars upstairs and downstairs provide space for a leisurely drink.

O'Donoghue's
A good mix of locals and tourists, young and old, frequent this pub in the heart of Georgian Dublin which has been a city favourite for years. Famous as the pub where the Dubliners folk group began in the 1960s, it is known today for its live traditional music.

DUBLIN THROUGH THE YEAR

Revellers at the
St Patrick's Day parade

The city is at its busiest in July and August, which are the most popular months for visiting Dublin. June and September can be pleasant but don't count on the weather, since Ireland's lush beauty is the product of a wet climate. Most Dublin sights are open all year round but, in the low season (generally November to March), some of them have limited opening hours or close completely. In summer, events are held in honour of anything from gardens to James Joyce, but a common thread is music, and few festivals are complete without it. Dublin is at its best when celebrating and is thus a treat at Christmas or New Year. Look out for the word *fleadh* (festival) in the city, but remember, too, that the Irish are a spontaneous people: festivities can spring from the air, or from a tune on a fiddle.

Trinity College rowers competing on the Liffey (March)

SPRING

After the quiet winter, spring sees a flurry of festivals and events. St Patrick's Day is often said to mark the beginning of the tourist season. This national holiday is celebrated with music and carnival-style abandon throughout the city. Accommodation is often in short supply around this time so do book in advance.

Annual parade through the streets of Dublin
to celebrate St Patrick's Day (March)

MARCH

St Patrick's Day Festival *(around 17 Mar)*. Numerous street theatre acts fill the city during colourful celebrations that centre on a parade on St Patrick's Day itself (17 March).
St Patrick's Day Celtic Winners Show *(mid-Mar)*, Cloghran. Popular annual championship dog show.
Colours Boat Race *(late Mar)*. A rowing race along the Liffey between University College Dublin and Trinity College.

APRIL

Howth Music Festival *(Easter weekend)*. This pretty fishing village on the outskirts of the city *(see p90)* plays host to three days of popular music.

Feis Ceoil *(Mar/Apr)*, various venues around Dublin play host to one of Europe's oldest and most prestigious classical music festivals.
Poetry Now Festival *(early Apr)*. Held in Dun Laoghaire, events include readings, masterclasses, workshops and children's activities.

MAY

May Day Parade *(first Mon in May)*. Celebrations and colourful parades through the city streets.

May Day Parade in central Dublin

Bloom in the Park *(late May or early Jun)*. Phoenix Park. Ireland's largest gardening event features gardening designs, floral displays and a food pavilion.
Laytown Beach Races *(late May or early Jun)*. Horse races on a beach north of Dublin.
Tour of Ireland Cycle Challenge *(second week)*. A five-day cycle race which starts in Dublin and ends in Lisburn.

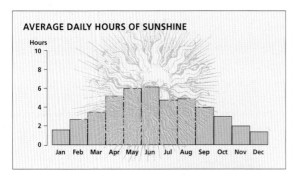

AVERAGE DAILY HOURS OF SUNSHINE

Sunshine Chart
Hours of sunshine in rainy Dublin are few and far between for most of the year. In summer, however, the days are often long, hot and very sunny. As in the rest of the country, the weather is notoriously unpredictable, so skies can cloud over in minutes.

SUMMER

Summer represents the height of the festive calendar for the visitor and the Dubliner alike and is the city's busiest time of year. There is a succession of outdoor music, arts and community festivals of all kinds, culminating in the city's top social event, the annual Dublin Horse Show.

JUNE

Temple Bar Cultural Trust Summer Programme *(May–Aug, see p159).)* Free, family-friendly events which include open-air cinema, weekly markets and a chocolate festival.
Dublin Writer's Festival *(first week).* An international literary festival celebrating Dublin's literary heritage and the very best of Irish and international writing.
Docklands Maritime Festival *(first week).* A community festival that centres on

Blues performance at one of Dublin's many summer festivals

Pearse Street and City Quay, with shows and activities for all ages.
Summer in Dublin Festival *(Jun–Aug).* Free music and family activities in the city's parks and public spaces.
County Wicklow Gardens Festival *(all month).* Held at private and public gardens south of Dublin, including Powerscourt *(see pp114–15).*
Bloomsday *(16 Jun).* Walks, lectures and pub talks to celebrate James Joyce's *Ulysses.*

Scurlogstown Olympiad Celtic Festival *(mid-Jun),* Trim *(see p122).* Traditional Irish music, dance, fair and selection of a festival queen.
Music in Great Irish Houses *(second and third weeks).* Classical music recitals in grand settings at various venues.
Darklight Film Festival *(end Jun).* Festival for filmmakers, animators and artists which explores the convergence of art, film and technology and also features games and workshops.

The Dublin Horse Show (August)

JULY

Oxygen *(mid-Jul).* Rock 'n' roll festival held over three days in Punchestown, outside Dublin.
Temple Bar Circus Festival *(mid-Jul).* Temple Bar's streets and public spaces are transformed into a circus arena for four days of performances.

AUGUST

Dublin Horse Show *(second week),* RDS Ballsbridge *(see p85).* Dublin's premier sporting and social event includes showjumping and dressage.
Festival of World Cultures *(late Aug).* Dun Laoghaire *(see p90).* A celebration of multiculturalism, with arts, crafts, music and more.

Powerscourt Gardens, part of the County Wicklow Gardens Festival (June)

AVERAGE MONTHLY RAINFALL

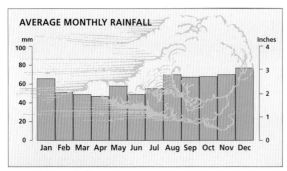

Rainfall Chart
Ireland is one of the wettest countries in Europe, with rainfall distributed evenly throughout the year. Fortunately, Dublin is situated in the drier eastern half of the country, but visitors should still be prepared for rain at any time of year.

Revellers on Hallowe'en (October)

AUTUMN

Autumn kicks off with the Liffey Swim, a race along Dublin's river attempted only by the strong hearted. Later the traditional sports of Gaelic football and hurling, the latter a kind of aerial hockey, hold their popular national finals in the city. The theatre festival held in October is world class.

SEPTEMBER

The Liffey Swim *(first Sat).* Swimmers brave the Liffey's murky waters from Watling Street Bridge to the Custom House *(see p70).*
Anna Livia International Opera Festival *(first week).* Opera performances around the city.
Dublin Fringe Festival *(mid two weeks).* Shows held at various venues in the city.
All-Ireland Hurling Final *(second Sun),* Croke Park.
All-Ireland Football Final *(fourth Sun),* Croke Park. Popular Gaelic football final.

Carpets at the annual Irish Antique Dealers' Fair (September)

Irish Antique Dealers' Fair *(last week),* RDS Ballsbridge *(see p85).* The country's most important antiques fair.

OCTOBER

Dublin Theatre Festival *(first two weeks).* Features new works by Irish playwrights, plus many foreign productions.
Dublin City Marathon *(last Mon).* Starting and finishing on O'Connell Street, the route takes in many Dublin land-marks, including Phoenix Park and Trinity College. Every year several thousands participate.
Hallowe'en (Samhain) *(31 Oct).* On the night when spirits rise, children wear fancy dress and celebrations include a parade and fireworks.

NOVEMBER

Opera Ireland *(a week in Nov).* Autumn run at the Gaiety Theatre. Another short season is put on in April.
Dublin Toy and Train Fair *(mid-Nov),* Clontarf Castle Hotel, Clontarf. Model cars, dolls, comics and teddy bears. Other fairs in February, May and September.

Large field of runners competing in the Dublin City Marathon (October)

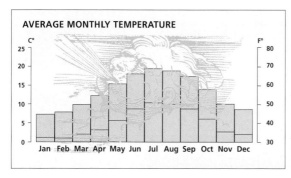

AVERAGE MONTHLY TEMPERATURE

Temperature Chart
This chart gives the average minimum and maximum temperatures for the city. Extremes of temperature are rare: the winter is mild, with the mercury seldom falling below zero. In summer, however, the occasional day can be very warm.

WINTER

Although winter is a quiet time for festivals, there is a range of entertainment on offer, including sporting and theatrical events. Christmas is the busiest social period and there are plenty of informal celebrations. There is also a wide choice of National Hunt (steeplechase) race meetings, especially at Leopardstown, south of the city centre.

Christmas scene at Mansion House

DECEMBER

Pantomime Season *(Dec–Jan).* Traditional pantomime performed at theatres in Dublin and throughout Ireland.
St Stephen's Day
(26 Dec). On the day after Christmas, Catholic boys dress up as Wren boys (chimney sweeps with blackened faces) and sing hymns to raise money for charitable causes.
Leopardstown Races
(26–29 Dec). This four-day meeting is the biggest in the country at

Glendalough *(see p110)* in the snow

this traditional time for horse racing.
New Year's Eve *(31 Dec).* Celebrations around the city to welcome in the New Year.

JANUARY

Salmon and Sea Trout Season
(1 Jan–Sep). Start of the season for one of the most popular pastimes in Ireland.
Irish Champion Hurdle
(late Jan). Major horse race at Leopardstown *(see p105).*
Temple Bar Tradfest *(Jan/Feb).* Five-day festival of Irish music and culture.

Hurdlers at Leopardstown (January)

FEBRUARY

Six Nations Rugby Tournament *(on various weekends Feb–Apr).* Ireland, England, Wales, Italy, Scotland and France compete; two/three matches in Dublin.
Malahide Food and Drink Affair *(late Feb, see p89).* A festival of Irish food and drink, plus cultural activities.

PUBLIC HOLIDAYS

New Year's Day (1 Jan)
St Patrick's Day (17 Mar)
Good Friday
Easter Monday
May Day (1 May)
June Bank Holiday (first Mon in Jun)
August Bank Holiday (first Mon in Aug)
October Bank Holiday (last Mon in Oct)
Christmas Day (25 Dec)
St Stephen's Day (26 Dec)

Façade of Trinity College, Southeast Dublin ▷

DUBLIN AREA BY AREA

SOUTHEAST DUBLIN 32–51

SOUTHWEST DUBLIN 52–65

NORTH OF THE LIFFEY 66–77

FURTHER AFIELD 78–91

THREE GUIDED WALKS 92–97

SOUTHEAST DUBLIN

This part of Dublin was virtually undeveloped until the founding of Trinity College in 1592. Even then, it was almost a hundred years before the land to the south was enclosed to create St Stephen's Green.

The mid-18th century saw the beginning of a construction boom in the area. During this time, public buildings such as the Old Library at Trinity College and

Window in the Government buildings

Leinster House were built. Many of the buildings in Merrion Square still have their original features.

Today, visitors are attracted to Southeast Dublin by the shops on Grafton Street and by the museums in the area, among them the excellent National Gallery and the National Museum (Archaeology) with its displays of Irish Bronze Age gold treasures and Iron Age bog bodies.

SIGHTS AT A GLANCE

Museums, Libraries and Galleries
Heraldic Museum **5**
National Gallery pp48–51 **18**
National Library **17**
National Museum (Archaeology) pp44–5 **14**
Natural History Museum (currently closed for refurbishment) **15**
Royal Hibernian Academy **20**
Science Gallery **22**

Historic Buildings
Bank of Ireland **1**
Government buildings **13**
Iveagh House **11**
Leinster House **16**
Mansion House **7**
Newman House **10**
Number 29 **21**
Royal College of Surgeons **8**
Trinity College pp38–9 **2**

Historic Streets
Ely Place **12**
Grafton Street **4**
Merrion Square **19**

Churches
St Ann's Church **6**
St Teresa's Church **3**

Parks and Gardens
St Stephen's Green **9**

KEY
▦ Street-by-Street map
See pp34–5
🚇 Railway station
🚉 DART station
🚊 Luas stop
ℹ Tourist information

GETTING THERE
Buses 4, 4A, 5, 7, 8, 10, 13, 14A, 15A, 45 and 46A go along Nassau Street which is in walking distance of most of the sights in this area. If you are coming from further afield, both the Luas and the DART serve the area.

0 metres   250
0 yards   250

◁ The lush gardens of Merrion Square

Street-by-Street: Southeast Dublin

The area around College Green, dominated by the façades of the Bank of Ireland and Trinity College, is very much the heart of Dublin. The alleys and malls cutting across busy pedestrianized Grafton Street boast many of Dublin's better shops, hotels and restaurants. Just off Kildare Street are the Irish Parliament, the National Library and the National Museum (Archaeology). To escape the city bustle many head for sanctuary in St Stephen's Green, which is overlooked by fine Georgian buildings.

← Dublin Castle

Bank of Ireland
This grand Georgian building was originally built as the Irish Parliament ❶

Statue of Molly Malone (1988)

Grafton Street
Brown Thomas department store is one of the main attractions on this pedestrianized street, alive with buskers and pavement artists ❹

St Ann's Church
The striking façade of the 18th-century church was added in 1868. The interior features lovely stained-glass windows ❻

Mansion House
This has been the official residence of Dublin's Lord Mayor since 1715 ❼

Fusiliers' Arch (1907)

★ St Stephen's Green
The relaxing city park is surrounded by many grand buildings. In summer, lunchtime concerts attract tourists and workers alike ❾

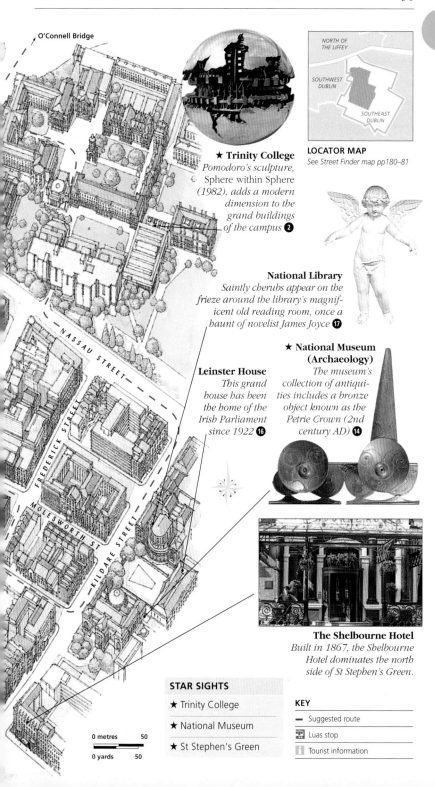

O'Connell Bridge

LOCATOR MAP
See Street Finder map pp180–81

NORTH OF
THE LIFFEY

SOUTHWEST
DUBLIN

SOUTHEAST
DUBLIN

★ **Trinity College**
Pomodoro's sculpture,
Sphere within Sphere
*(1982), adds a modern
dimension to the
grand buildings
of the campus* ❷

National Library
*Saintly cherubs appear on the
frieze around the library's magnificent old reading room, once a
haunt of novelist James Joyce* ⓱

★ **National Museum
(Archaeology)**
*The museum's
collection of antiqui-
ties includes a bronze
object known as the
Petrie Crown (2nd
century AD)* ⓮

Leinster House
*This grand
house has been
the home of the
Irish Parliament
since 1922* ⓰

NASSAU STREET
FREDERICK S STREET
MOLESWORTH ST
KILDARE STREET

The Shelbourne Hotel
*Built in 1867, the Shelbourne
Hotel dominates the north
side of St Stephen's Green.*

STAR SIGHTS

★ Trinity College

★ National Museum

★ St Stephen's Green

0 metres   50
0 yards   50

KEY

— Suggested route

🚊 Luas stop

ℹ Tourist information

Original Chamber of the Irish House of Lords at the Bank of Ireland

Bank of Ireland ❶

2 College Green. **Map** D3.
Tel 677 6801. ☐ 10am–4pm Mon–Fri (from 10:30am Wed, to 5pm Thu). 🌑 public hols. **House of Lords** 📷 10:30am, 11:30am & 1:45pm Tue.

The prestigious offices of the Bank of Ireland began life as the first purpose-built parliament house in Europe. The original central section was started by Irish architect Edward Lovett Pearce and completed in 1739 after his death. Sadly, Pearce's masterpiece, the great octagonal chamber of the House of Commons, was removed by order of the British government in 1802. The House of Lords, however, remains intact. Attendants lead tours that point out the coffered ceiling and oak panelling. There are also huge tapestries of the *Battle of the Boyne* and the *Siege of Londonderry*, and a 1,233-piece crystal chandelier that dates from 1788.

James Gandon added the east portico in 1785. Further additions were made around 1797. After the dissolution of the Irish Parliament in 1800, the Bank of Ireland bought the building. The present structure was completed in

1808 with the transformation of the former lobby of the House of Commons into a cash office and the addition of a curving screen wall and the Foster Place annexe. A statue by John Foley of Henry Grattan *(see p16)*, the most formidable leader of the old parliament, stands on College Green.

Trinity College ❷

See pp38–9.

St Teresa's Church ❸

Clarendon St or Johnson Court. **Map** D4. **Tel** 671 8466. ☐ 6:45am–6:30pm Mon–Fri, 6:45am–7:30pm Sat, 8:15am–7pm Sun. 📷 9:30am–5pm Mon–Sat.
www.clarendonstreet.com

The foundation stone of St Teresa's was laid in 1793, making it the first post-Penal Law church to be legally planned and built in the city after the passing of the Catholic Relief Act the same year *(see p16)*. The land was leased by a brewer named John Sweetman and was given to the Discalced Carmelite Fathers. The church did not in fact

Statue of the Virgin and child in St Teresa's Church

open until May 1797. The eastern transept was added in 1863 and the western transept was completed in 1876, at which stage it reached the form it remains in today.

Located in the middle of Dublin, St Teresa's is a relatively busy place of worship. Its T-shaped interior means that if you enter through the main door on Clarendon Street and walk through the church, you will arrive in the tight alleyway of Johnson Court, yards from Grafton Street. There are seven stained-glass windows in the church by Phyllis Burke, made in the 1990s, and a fine sculpture of Christ by John Hogan beneath the altar.

Street musicians outside Brown Thomas on Grafton Street

Grafton Street ❹

Map D4.

The spine of Dublin's most popular and stylish shopping district runs south from Trinity College to the glass-covered St Stephen's Green Shopping Centre. At the north end, at the junction with Nassau Street, is a bronze statue by Jean Rynhart of *Molly Malone* (1988), the celebrated "cockles and mussels" street trader from the traditional Irish folk song.

This busy pedestrianized strip, characterized by numerous energetic buskers and talented street theatre artists, boasts many shops, including many British chain stores. Next, River Island, HMV and Monsoon all contribute toward making it Dublin's fashion centre. Its most exclusive store, however, is Brown Thomas, one of

Monkeys playing billiards outside the Heraldic Museum

Dublin's most elegant department stores *(see p150)*, selling designer clothes, exclusive perfumes and fabulous shoes by designers such as Patrick Cox. Dublin's largest and most exclusive jewellers, Weir's, is also here.

The shops here attract Dublin's most beautiful people, and Grafton Street itself can seem like one long fashion catwalk. But it's not all about shopping, indeed No. 78 stands on the site of Samuel Whyte's school, whose illustrious roll included Robert Emmet *(see p16)*, leader of the 1803 Rebellion, and the Duke of Wellington. At this time, Grafton Street was actually paved with pinewood blocks to deaden the area from the harsh sound of horses' hooves and carriage wheels.

On many of the sidestreets off Grafton Street there are numerous pubs providing welcome refreshment for the exhausted shopper, among them the famous Davy Byrne's *(see p146)*, for years frequented by Dublin's literati.

Heraldic Museum and Genealogical Office ❺

2 Kildare St. **Map** E4. *Tel 603 0200.*
National Library Reading Room
◯ *9:30am–9pm Mon–Wed;*
9:30am–5pm Thu, Fri; 9:30am–1pm
Sat. **Heraldic Museum** ◯ *9:30am–*
8pm Mon–Wed; 10am–4:30pm Thu,
Fri; 10am–12:30pm Sat. **www**.nli.ie

The Genealogical Office is part of the National Library and offers free advice to anyone wishing to trace their Irish ancestry. Professional genealogists and library staff offer expert assistance together with access to reference material and finding aids.

The Heraldic Museum has a small but interesting collection of seals, regimental colours, coins, paintings, family crests and county shields. The museum is housed in a red-brick building in the Venetian style, which is unusual for Dublin. The exterior features some fanciful decorative aspects such as three monkeys playing billiards and bears playing violins just to the right of the entrance.

Window depicting Faith, Hope and Charity in St Ann's Church

St Ann's Church ❻

Dawson St. **Map** D2. *Tel 676 7727.*
◯ *10am–4pm Mon–Fri.* ✝
12:45pm Mon–Fri; 10:45am, 6:30pm
Sun. **www**.stannschurch.ie

Founded in 1707, St Ann's striking Romanesque façade was added by the architects Deane and Woodward in 1868. The best view of the façade is from Grafton Street, looking down Anne Street South. Inside the church are many colourful stained-glass windows that date back to the mid-19th century. St Ann's has a long tradition of charity work: in 1723 Lord Newton left a bequest specifically to buy bread for the poor. The original shelf used for the bread still stands adjacent to the altar.

Famous past parishioners of St Ann's include the Irish patriot Wolfe Tone *(see p16)*, who was married here in 1785, Douglas Hyde, the first president of Ireland, and Bram Stoker (1847–1912), the author of *Dracula (see p22).*

The milling crowds filling the pedestrianized Grafton Street

Trinity College ❷

Trinity College coat of arms

Trinity College was founded in 1592 by Queen Elizabeth I on the site of an Augustinian monastery. It was originally a Protestant college, and it was not until the 1970s that Catholics started entering the university. Among the many famous students to attend the college were playwrights Oliver Goldsmith and Samuel Beckett, and political writer Edmund Burke. Trinity's lawns and cobbled quads provide a pleasant haven in the heart of the city. The major attractions are the Old Library and the *Book of Kells*, housed in the Treasury.

★ Campanile
The 30-m (98-ft) bell tower was built in 1853 by Sir Charles Lanyon, architect of Queen's University, Belfast, in Northern Ireland.

Reclining Connected Forms (1969) by Henry Moore

Dining Hall (1761)

Chapel *(1798)*
This is the only chapel in the Republic to be shared by all denominations. The painted window above the altar dates from 1867.

Parliament Square

Statue of Edmund Burke (1868) by John Foley

Main entrance

Statue of Oliver Goldsmith (1864) by John Foley

SAMUEL BECKETT (1906–89)

Nobel prizewinner Samuel Beckett was born at Foxrock, south of Dublin. In 1923 he entered Trinity, where he was placed first in his modern literature class. He was also a keen member of the college cricket team. Forsaking Ireland, Beckett moved to France in the early 1930s. Many of his works such as *Waiting for Godot* (1951) were written first in French, and then later translated, by Beckett, into English.

Provost's House (c. 1760)

Examination Hall
Completed in 1791 to a design by Sir William Chambers, the hall features a gilded oak chandelier and ornate ceilings by Michael Stapleton.

Library Square
The red-brick building (known as the Rubrics) on the east of Library Square was built around 1700 and is the oldest surviving part of the college.

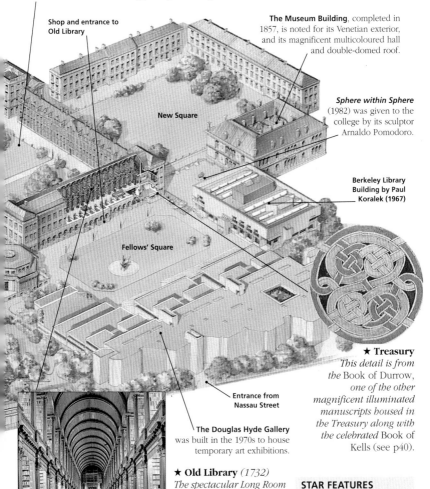

Shop and entrance to Old Library

The Museum Building, completed in 1857, is noted for its Venetian exterior, and its magnificent multicoloured hall and double-domed roof.

New Square

Sphere within Sphere (1982) was given to the college by its sculptor Arnaldo Pomodoro.

Berkeley Library Building by Paul Koralek (1967)

Fellows' Square

★ **Treasury**
This detail is from the Book of Durrow, *one of the other magnificent illuminated manuscripts housed in the Treasury along with the celebrated* Book of Kells *(see p40).*

Entrance from Nassau Street

The Douglas Hyde Gallery was built in the 1970s to house temporary art exhibitions.

★ **Old Library** *(1732)*
The spectacular Long Room measures 64 m (210 ft) from end to end. It houses 200,000 antiquarian texts, marble busts of scholars and the oldest surviving harp in Ireland.

STAR FEATURES

★ Old Library

★ Treasury

★ Campanile

The Book of Kells

The most richly decorated of Ireland's illuminated manuscripts, the *Book of Kells*, may have been the work of monks from Iona, who fled to Kells, near Newgrange *(see pp120–21)*, in AD 806 after a Viking raid. The book, which was moved to Trinity College *(see pp38–9)* in the 17th century, contains the four Gospels in Latin. The scribes who copied the texts embellished their calligraphy with intricate spirals as well as human figures and animals. Some of the dyes used were imported from as far as the Middle East.

Pair of moths

Stylized angel

The Greek letter "X"

The letter that looks like a "P" is a Greek "R".

The letter "I"

Interlacing motifs

Cat watching rats

The symbols *of the four evangelists are used as decoration throughout the book. The figure of the man symbolizes St Matthew.*

A full-page portrait *of St Matthew, shown standing barefoot in front of a throne, precedes the opening words of his Gospel.*

MONOGRAM PAGE
This, the most elaborate page of the book, contains the first three words of St Matthew's account of the birth of Christ. The first word "XRI" is an abbreviation of "Christi".

Rats eating bread could be a reference to sinners taking Holy Communion. The symbolism of the animals and people decorating the manuscript is often hard to interpret.

The text *is in a beautifully rounded Celtic script with brightly ornamented initial letters. Animal and human forms are often used to decorate the end of a line.*

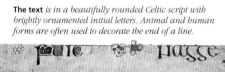

Mansion House ❼

Dawson St. **Map** E4. ◉ *to the public.* 🍴 www.mansionhouse.ie

Set back from Dawson Street, the Mansion House is an attractive Queen Anne-style building. It was built in 1710 for the aristocrat Joshua Dawson, after whom the street is named. The Dublin Corporation bought it in 1715 as the official residence of the city's Lord Mayor. A grey stucco façade was added in Victorian times.

The Dáil Éireann *(see p46)*, which adopted the Declaration of Independence, first met here on 21 January 1919. The Fire Restaurant in the old supper room is in period style and is open to the public.

Royal College of Surgeons ❽

123 St Stephen's Green. **Map** E4. **Tel** *402 2100.*

The west side of St Stephen's Green is home to one of the most striking buildings in the square, namely the squat granite-faced Royal College of Surgeons. The college opened in 1810 and 15 years later its façade was extended from three to seven bays when a central pediment was added. On top of this are three statues which from left to right are Hygieia, goddess of health, Asclepius, god of medicine and son of Apollo,

Royal College of Surgeons, which overlooks St Stephen's Green

and Athena, the goddess of wisdom and patron of the arts. Today, the main entrance is through the modern extension on York Street. The academy has almost 1,000 students.

The building itself played an important part in Irish history. During the 1916 Easter Rising *(see p17)*, a section of the Irish Citizen Army under Michael Mallin and Countess Constance Markievicz were in control of the college. They were the last detachment of rebels to surrender and, although Mallin was executed, Markievicz escaped sentence because of her gender and public status. She was later to become the first woman to be elected as an MP at Westminster in London, though she refused to take her seat in parliament. The front columns of the building still feature the old bullet holes, an ever-present reminder of its colourful past.

St Stephen's Green ❾

Map D5. ☐ *daylight hours.*

Originally one of three ancient commons in the old city, St Stephen's Green was enclosed in 1664. The 9-ha (22-acre) green was laid out in its present form in 1880, using a grant given by Lord Ardilaun, a member of the Guinness family. Landscaped with flowerbeds, trees, a fountain and a lake, the green is dotted with memorials to eminent Dubliners, including Ardilaun himself. There is a bust of James Joyce *(see p23)*, and a memorial by Henry Moore (1967) dedicated to W B Yeats *(see p23)*. At the Merrion Row corner stands a massive monument (1967) by Edward Delaney to 18th-century nationalist leader Wolfe Tone – it is known locally as "Tonehenge". The 1887 bandstand still has free daytime concerts in summer.

The busiest side of the Green is the north, known during the 19th century as the Beaux' Walk and still home to several gentlemen's clubs. The most prominent building is the venerable Shelbourne Hotel *(see p130)*. Dating back to 1867, its entrance is adorned by statues of Nubian princesses and attendant slaves. It is well worth popping in for a look at the chandeliered foyer and for afternoon tea in the Lord Mayor's Lounge.

Dubliners relaxing by the lake in St Stephen's Green

Stucco work in the Apollo room of No. 85 in Newman House

Newman House ⑩

85 & 86 St Stephen's Green. **Map** D5. **Tel** 716 7422. ☐ Jun–Aug: noon–4pm Tue–Fri; Sep–May: by appt only for groups. ♿ www.ucd.ie

Numbers 85 and 86 on the south side of St Stephen's Green are collectively known as Newman House, named for John Henry Newman, later Cardinal Newman and the first rector of the Catholic University of Ireland.

Founded as an alternative to the Protestant Trinity College, it became part of University College Dublin in 1907 and is still owned by that institution.

During the 1990s it has seen one of the most painstaking and diligent restorations ever undertaken in the city. It is the much smaller No. 85, designed by Richard Castle in 1738, that contains the most beautiful rooms with plaster-work by the Franchini brothers. Of particular interest are the Apollo Room, with a figure of the god above the mantle, and the upstairs Saloon. In the late 1800s the Jesuits covered the naked plaster bodies on the ceiling of the Saloon with rudimentary plaster casts to conceal what they thought to be shameful nudity. One of the figures is still covered today. A class-room, decorated as it would have been in the days when James Joyce was a student here, is open to the public, as

is the studio residence of the poet Gerard Manley Hopkins, who was a professor here in the late 19th century. Other famous past pupils include the writer Flann O'Brien and former president Eamon De Valera.

Iveagh House and Iveagh Gardens ⑪

80 & 81 St Stephen's Green. **Map** D5. ● to the public. **Gardens** ☐ daily.

Iveagh House, on the south side of St Stephen's Green, was originally two freestanding townhouses. No. 80 was de-signed in the 1730s by Richard Castle – his first commission in the city. The houses were combined in the 1860s when Sir Benjamin Guinness bought them. None of the original façade remains as Guinness linked the houses under a Portland stone façade and had the family arms engraved on the pedi-ment. The Guinness family also carried out much interior reconstruction, including the

Enjoying the secluded peace of Iveagh Gardens

addition of a large new ball-room, with a domed ceiling and liberal amounts of marble and onyx, to the rear of the house. Iveagh House was given to the state by Rupert Guinness, the second Earl of Iveagh, in 1939. It is now used by the Department of Foreign Affairs, both as the office of the minister and as a venue for state receptions. The rear

of Iveagh House faces on to Iveagh Gardens, an almost secret park that offers a quiet alternative to St Stephen's Green. It owes its tranquillity partly to the fact that its three entrances are discreet: one is behind the National Concert Hall on Earlsfort Terrace, another is off Clonmel Street and a new one, with disabled access, is off Hatch Street.

Ely Place ⑫

Map E5.

A cul-de-sac with several well-preserved Georgian houses, Ely Place is at the end of Merrion Street Upper. Most of the houses along the street were built in the 1770s and Ely Place soon became one of the most desirable addresses in the city at this time. Behind its red brick façade, 8 Ely Place, known as Ely House, has elegant plasterwork by the stuccodore Michael Staple-ton and an or-nate staircase covered with engravings of characters from the tales of the Labours of Hercules below the banister rail.

Modern buildings seal the end of the street. The Royal Hibernian Academy Gallagher Gallery *(see p47)* was built in 1973 and may look somewhat out of place on this otherwise rather grand stretch, but it offers one of the best gallery spaces in the city, exhibiting mostly 20th-century Irish art.

Detail of stucco from Ely House, featuring the mythical dog Cerberus

The elegant, Neo-Classical façade of the Government buildings

Government buildings ⑬

Upper Merrion St. **Map** E4. **Tel** 662 4888. ☐ Sat 10:30am–12:30pm, 1:30–3:30pm (call to check). Tickets available from National Gallery. ☑ hourly from 10:30am–1:30pm. **www**.gov.ie/taoiseach

Alongside the Natural History Museum and the National Gallery on Upper Merrion Street, facing the attractive Georgian town houses, stand the imposing Government buildings, built in a Neo-Georgian style.

The complex was opened in 1911 as the Royal College of Science (RCS) and it has the distinction of being the last major project planned by the British in Dublin. In 1922 the Irish government took over the north wing as offices and the RCS became part of University College Dublin. Academic pursuits continued here until 1989, when the government moved into the rest of the buildings and ordered a massive restoration of the façade. The city grime on the Portland stone was blasted away to restore it to its original near-white appearance.

The elegant domed buildings are set apart from the street by a cobbled courtyard and a large colonnade with columns that are strongly reminiscent of Gandon's Custom House (see p70). The tour takes in the office of the Taoiseach (pronounced Tee-Shuck) and the cabinet office. The interior is decorated with examples of works by contemporary Irish artists, most notably a huge stained-glass window, situated above the grand staircase, called *My Four Green Fields* by Dublin artist Evie Hone, which depicts the island's four provinces. This was designed for the 1939 World's Fair in New York. It was displayed in the Irish Pavilion there and afterwards returned to Dublin. For a number of years it lay packed away, until the 1960s, when it was put on display for a while in the Dublin Bus offices in O'Connell Street. It was finally moved to its present home in the Government buildings in 1991.

National Museum (Archaeology) ⑭

Natural History Museum ⑮

Merrion St. **Map** E4. **Tel** 677 7444. ◙ currently closed for refurbishment. ☑ limited. **www**.museum.ie

Known affectionately as the "Dead Zoo" by locals, this museum is crammed with antique glass cabinets housing stuffed animals from around the world. The museum was opened to the public in 1857 with an inaugural lecture by Dr David Livingstone. It remains virtually unchanged from Victorian times.

On the ground floor, the Irish room holds exhibits on local wildlife. Inside the front door are three skeletons of the extinct giant deer known as the "Irish elk". Also on this floor are shelves with jars of octopuses, leeches and worms, preserved in embalming fluid.

The upper gallery is home to the noted Blaschka Collection of glass models of marine life, and a display of buffalo and deer trophies. Hanging from the ceiling are the skeletons of a fin whale and a humpback whale, both found stranded on the Irish coast.

The advances made in taxidermy over the years are emphasized by a stuffed rhinoceros and an Indian elephant, both so heavily lacquered that they seem to be covered in tar.

Lawn and front entrance of the Natural History Museum on Merrion Street Upper

National Museum (Archaeology) ⑭

The National Museum of Ireland (Archaeology) was built in the 1880s to the design of Sir Thomas Deane. Its splendid domed rotunda features marble pillars and a zodiac mosaic floor. The Treasury houses items such as the Broighter gold boat, while an exhibition on Ireland's Bronze Age gold contains some beautiful jewellery. The museum shows life in prehistoric Ireland and at the time of the Vikings.

Egyptian Mummy
This mummy of the lady Tentdinebu is thought to date back to c.945–716 BC. Covered in brilliant colours, it is part of the stunning Egyptian collection.

★ **Ór – Ireland's Gold**
This is one of the most extensive collections of Bronze Age gold in Western Europe. This gold lunula (c.1800 BC), found in Athlone, is one of many pieces of ancient jewellery in this exhibition.

KEY TO FLOORPLAN

- ☐ Kingship and Sacrifice
- ☐ Ór – Ireland's Gold
- ☐ The Treasury
- ☐ Prehistoric Ireland
- ☐ Medieval Ireland
- ☐ Viking Ireland
- ☐ Ancient Egypt
- ☐ Rites of Passage at Tara
- ☐ Temporary exhibition space
- ☐ Non-exhibition space
- ☐ Ceramics and Glass from Ancient Cyprus
- ☐ Life and Death in the Roman World

★ **Bog Bodies**
This preserved hand (c.600 BC) is one of the pieces in a fascinating exhibition of Iron Age bodies discovered in 2003.

Main entrance

GALLERY GUIDE

The ground floor holds The Treasury, Ór – Ireland's Gold exhibition, Kingship and Sacrifice and the Prehistoric Ireland display. On the first floor is the Medieval Ireland exhibition, which illustrates many aspects of life in later medieval Ireland. Also on the first floor are artifacts from Ancient Egypt and from the Viking settlement of Dublin.

The domed rotunda, based on the design of the Altes Museum in Berlin, makes an impressive entrance hall.

The Treasury houses masterpieces of Irish crafts including the Ardagh Chalice.

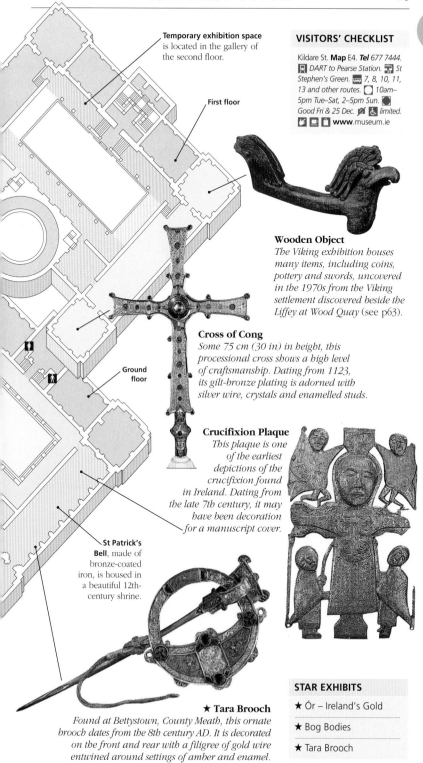

Temporary exhibition space
is located in the gallery of
the second floor.

First floor

VISITORS' CHECKLIST

Kildare St. **Map** E4. **Tel** 677 7444.
DART to Pearse Station. St
Stephen's Green. 7, 8, 10, 11,
13 and other routes. 10am–
5pm Tue–Sat, 2–5pm Sun.
Good Fri & 25 Dec. limited.
www.museum.ie

Wooden Object
*The Viking exhibition houses
many items, including coins,
pottery and swords, uncovered
in the 1970s from the Viking
settlement discovered beside the
Liffey at Wood Quay (see p63).*

Cross of Cong
*Some 75 cm (30 in) in height, this
processional cross shows a high level
of craftsmanship. Dating from 1123,
its gilt-bronze plating is adorned with
silver wire, crystals and enamelled studs.*

Ground
floor

Crucifixion Plaque
*This plaque is one
of the earliest
depictions of the
crucifixion found
in Ireland. Dating from
the late 7th century, it may
have been decoration
for a manuscript cover.*

**St Patrick's
Bell**, made of
bronze-coated
iron, is housed in
a beautiful 12th-
century shrine.

★ Tara Brooch
*Found at Bettystown, County Meath, this ornate
brooch dates from the 8th century AD. It is decorated
on the front and rear with a filigree of gold wire
entwined around settings of amber and enamel.*

STAR EXHIBITS

★ Ór – Ireland's Gold

★ Bog Bodies

★ Tara Brooch

Domed reading room on the first floor of the National Library

Leinster House 🔟

Kildare St. **Map** E4. **Tel** 618 3000.
◯ groups by appointment only
(foreign tourists must book through
their own embassy). 🔲 phone for
details. **www**.oireachtas.ie

This stately mansion houses
the Dáil and the Seanad – the
two chambers of the Irish
Parliament. It was originally
built for the Duke of Leinster
in 1745. Designed by Richard
Castle, the Kildare Street
façade resembles that of a
large town house. The rear,
which looks out on to Merrion
Square, has the air of a country
estate. The Royal Dublin
Society bought the building in
1815. The government bought
the entire building in 1924.
    Visitors can arrange to tour
the main rooms, including the
Seanad chamber.

National Library 🔟

Kildare St. **Map** E4. **Tel** 603 0200.
◯ 9:30am–9pm Mon–Wed,
9:30am–5pm Thu & Fri, 9:30am–
1pm Sat. ● public hols. **www**.nli.ie

Designed by Sir Thomas
Deane, the National Library
was opened in 1890. It was
built to house the collection
of the Royal Dublin Society
(see p85). The Library
contains first editions of every
major Irish writer and a copy
of almost every book ever
published in Ireland. There is

a huge collection of old maps,
papers, and a number of significant manuscripts. The first-
floor reading room has green-
shaded lamps and well-worn
desks. To go in, ask an attendant for a visitor's pass. A new
exhibition space, bookshop
and coffee shop are open to
both readers and non-readers.

National Gallery 🔟

See pp48–51.

Merrion Square 🔟

Map F4.

Merrion Square, a large and
grand Georgian square,
covers about 5 ha (12 acres)
and was laid out by John
Ensor around 1762.
    On the west
side are the
impressive
façades of
the National

Statue of Oscar Wilde by Danny
Osbourne in Merrion Square

THE IRISH PARLIAMENT

The Irish Free State, the
forerunner of the Republic
of Ireland, was first
inaugurated in 1922 (see
p18), although an unofficial
Irish parliament, the Dáil,
had already been in existence since 1919. Today,
the Irish parliament is
made up of two houses:
the Dáil (House of Repre-
sentatives) and Seanad
Éireann (Senate). The
prime minister is the
Taoiseach and the deputy,
the Tánaiste. The Dáil's
166 representatives –
Teachta Dála, commonly
known as TDs – are
elected by proportional
representation every five
years. The 60-strong
Seanad is appointed by
various individuals and
authorities, including the
Taoiseach and the
University of Dublin.

The first parliament of the Irish
Free State in 1922

History Museum, the National
Gallery and the front garden
of Leinster House. However,
they do not compare with
the attractive Georgian townhouses on the other three
sides. Many have brightly
painted doors with original
features such as wrought-iron
balconies and ornate door-
knockers. The oldest and finest
houses are on the north side.
    Many are now offices, with
plaques detailing the rich and
famous who once lived in
them. These include Catholic
emancipation leader Daniel
O'Connell (see p16), who lived
at No. 58 and poet W B Yeats
(see p23), who lived at No.
82. Oscar Wilde (see p23)

spent his childhood at No. 1. The attractive central park served as an emergency soup kitchen during the Great Famine of the 1840s *(see p17)*. On the northwest side stands the restored Rutland Fountain, originally erected in 1791 for the sole use of Dublin's poor.

Just off the square, at No. 24 Merrion Street Upper, is the birthplace of the Duke of Wellington.

Royal Hibernian Academy ❷⓪

15 Ely Place. **Map** E5. *Tel* 661 2558. ☐ *11am–7pm Mon–Sat, 2–5pm Sun.* ● *public hols and between exhibitions.* 🅰 **www**.royalhibernianacademy.com

The academy is one of the largest exhibition spaces in the city. It puts on exhibitions of Irish and international artists showing both traditional and innovative forms of visual art. This modern brick-and-plate-glass building does, however, look out of place at the end of Ely Place, an attractive Georgian cul-de-sac.

Number 29 ❷❶

29 Fitzwilliam St Lower. **Map** F5. *Tel* 702 6165. ☐ *10am–5pm Tue–Sat, noon–5pm Sun.* ● *two weeks prior to Christmas.* 📷 ✒ **www**.esb.ie/numbertwentynine

The recreated Georgian kitchen of Number 29, Fitzwilliam Street Lower

Number 29 is a corner townhouse, built in 1794 for a Mrs Olivia Beattie whose late husband was a wine and paper merchant. This museum gives visitors a behind-the-scenes look at how middle-class Georgians lived. Tours work their way through the building from the cellar upwards. Along the way are mahogany tables, chandeliers, Turkish carpets and landscape paintings, but of most interest are some of the quirkier items. Guides point out rudimentary hostess trolleys, water filters and even a Georgian baby walker, as well as an early exercise machine, used to tone up the muscles for horse riding. A tea caddy takes pride of place in one of the reception rooms: at today's prices a kilo of tea would have cost €800.

Science Gallery ❷❷

Trinity College, Pearse Street. **Map** E3. *Tel* 896 4091. ☐ *varies.* ● *Mon.* **www**.sciencegallery.com

The Science Gallery is a venture aiming to make science and technology accessible to all, especially young people. The focus on how it affects our lives now and in the future is explored through installations, festivals, performances and workshops promoting interaction and discussion. Past exhibitions at the state-of-the-art premises have featured light and sound installations and technological innovations in fashion, such as spray-on dresses and shirts that hug. The gallery was also once transformed into a neuroscience research lab.

The elegant gardens in Merrion Square, a quiet backwater in the centre of Dublin

National Gallery ⑱

This purpose-built gallery was opened to the public in 1864. It houses many excellent exhibits, largely due to generous bequests, such as the Milltown collection of works of art from Russborough House *(see p108)*. Playwright George Bernard Shaw was also a benefactor, leaving a third of his estate to the gallery. A new wing has been added to the gallery, which today has more than 500 works on display.

The Houseless Wanderer by John Foley

Although the emphasis is on Irish art, the major schools of European painting are well represented.

GALLERY GUIDE

The main entrance to the gallery is through the lofty Millennium Wing on Clare Street. Irish and British collections are housed on level 1, as is the National Portrait Gallery. The Italian and Spanish schools are located on level 2, with changing special exhibitions installed in the Millennium Wing.

★ Pierrot
This Cubist-style work, by Spanish-born artist Juan Gris, is one of many variations he painted on the theme of Pierrot and Harlequin. This particular one dates from 1921.

National Portrait Gallery

Mezzanine level

★ For the Road
The Yeats Museum houses works by Jack B Yeats (1871–1957). This mysterious painting reflects the artist's obsession with the Sligo countryside.

Shaw Room

Merrion Square entrance

STAR PAINTINGS

★ The Taking of Christ

★ Pierrot

★ For the Road

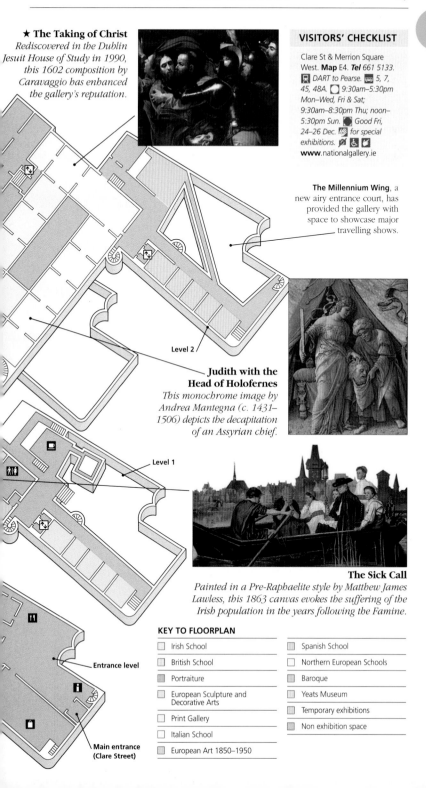

★ The Taking of Christ
Rediscovered in the Dublin Jesuit House of Study in 1990, this 1602 composition by Caravaggio has enhanced the gallery's reputation.

VISITORS' CHECKLIST

Clare St & Merrion Square West. **Map** E4. *Tel* 661 5133. DART to Pearse. 5, 7, 45, 48A. 9:30am–5:30pm Mon–Wed, Fri & Sat; 9:30am–8:30pm Thu; noon–5:30pm Sun. Good Fri, 24–26 Dec. for special exhibitions. www.nationalgallery.ie

The Millennium Wing, a new airy entrance court, has provided the gallery with space to showcase major travelling shows.

Level 2

Judith with the Head of Holofernes
This monochrome image by Andrea Mantegna (c. 1431–1506) depicts the decapitation of an Assyrian chief.

Level 1

The Sick Call
Painted in a Pre-Raphaelite style by Matthew James Lawless, this 1863 canvas evokes the suffering of the Irish population in the years following the Famine.

Entrance level

Main entrance (Clare Street)

KEY TO FLOORPLAN

- ☐ Irish School
- ☐ British School
- ☐ Portraiture
- ☐ European Sculpture and Decorative Arts
- ☐ Print Gallery
- ☐ Italian School
- ☐ European Art 1850–1950
- ☐ Spanish School
- ☐ Northern European Schools
- ☐ Baroque
- ☐ Yeats Museum
- ☐ Temporary exhibitions
- ☐ Non exhibition space

Exploring the National Gallery

Exhibitions throughout the gallery are laid out in an easy-to-follow manner. In addition to rooms dedicated to major Irish and European schools, there are displays illustrating such themes as art in the Dutch provinces, Caravaggio and his followers and Italian influences in the Northern countries. Major temporary exhibitions are held in the Millennium Wing, which also has a floor dedicated to the Irish schools of the 20th century.

IRISH SCHOOL

This is the largest collection on display and the richest part of the gallery. Stretching back to the late 17th century, works range from landscapes such as *A View of Powerscourt Waterfall* by George Barret to paintings by Nathaniel Hone the Elder, including *The Conjuror*. Portraiture includes work by James Barry and Hugh Douglas Hamilton.

The Romantic movement made a strong impression on artists in the early 19th century; Francis Danby's *The Opening of the Sixth Seal*, an apocalyptic interpretation from the Book of Revelations, is the best example of this genre. Other examples are the Irish landscapes of James Arthur O'Connor.

In the late 19th century many Irish artists lived in Breton colonies, absorbing Impressionist influences. Roderic O'Conor's *Farm at Lezaven, Finistère* and William Leech's *Convent Garden, Brittany*, with its

Convent Garden, Brittany, **by William Leech (1881–1968)**

refreshing tones of green and white, are two of the best examples from this period.

Jack B Yeats is regarded as Ireland's first internationally known modern artist and the Yeats Museum is dedicated to him and his talented family. It includes works by Anne Yeats and his father John B Yeats, a famous portrait artist. Jack B Yeats' paintings portray life in the west of Ireland in the early 20th century. His later paintings, such as *Men of Destiny* and *Above the Fair*, are also national treasures.

BRITISH SCHOOL

Works dating from the 18th century dominate in those rooms that are devoted to British artists. In particular, William Hogarth, Thomas Gainsborough and Joshua Reynolds are well represented. Reynolds was one of the great portrait painters of his time, but the gallery also showcases other portraits, by artists such as Philip Reinagle, Francis Wheatley and Henry Raeburn, that perfectly capture the family, military and aristocratic life of that period.

BAROQUE GALLERY

This large room accommodates 17th-century paintings, many by lesser-known artists. It also holds enormous canvases by more famous names such as Lanfranco, Jordaens and Castiglione, which are too big to fit into the spaces occupied by their respective schools. *The Annunciation* and *Peter Finding the Tribute Money* by Rubens are among the gallery's most eye-catching paintings.

FRENCH SCHOOL

The paintings in the galleries devoted to the French School are separated into the 17th and 18th centuries and the Barbizon, Impressionist, post-Impressionist and Cubist collections.

Among the earlier works are *The Annunciation*, a fine 15th-century panel by Jacques Yverni, and the *Lamentation over the Dead Christ* by Nicolas Poussin (1594–1665), one of the founders of European classicism.

The early 19th century saw the French colonization of North Africa. Many works were inspired by the colonization, including *Guards at the Door of a Tomb*, a painting by Jean-Léon Gérôme. Another fine 19th-century work is the painting known as *A Group of Cavalry in the Snow* by Jan Chelminski.

A View of Powerscourt Waterfall **by George Barret the Elder (c.1728–84)**

A Group of Cavalry in the Snow by Jan Chelminski (1851–1925)

The Impressionist paintings are among the most popular in the gallery and include Monet's *A River Scene, Autumn* from 1874. Works by Pissarro and Sisley are also displayed in this set of rooms.

Guards at the Door of a Tomb by Jean-Léon Gérôme (1824–1904)

SPANISH SCHOOL

Works from the Spanish school are rich and varied. One of the early pieces of note is El Greco's *St Francis Receiving the Stigmata*, a particularly dramatic work, dating from around 1595. Other notable acquisitions from this period are by Zurbarán, Velázquez and Murillo. There are four works on display by the controversial court painter Francisco de Goya (1746–1828) including a portrait of the actress Doña Antonia Zárata. Pablo Picasso's *Still Life With A Mandolin* and *Pierrot* by Juan Gris represent 20th-century Spanish art.

ITALIAN SCHOOL

As a result of a successful purchasing strategy at the time of the gallery's inauguration and various bequests, there is a strong collection of Italian art in the gallery.

Works of the Italian School spread over seven rooms. Andrea Mantegna's *Judith with the Head of Holofernes* is done in *grisaille*, a technique that creates a stone-like effect. Famous pieces by Uccello, Titian, Moroni and Fontana hang in this section, but it is Caravaggio's *The Taking of Christ* (1602) which is the most important item. It was discovered by chance in a Dublin Jesuit house where it had hung in obscurity for many years. It was first hung in the National Gallery in 1993.

Constantinople School icon

NORTHERN EUROPEAN SCHOOLS

The early Netherlandish School is comprised largely of paintings with a religious theme. One exception is Brueghel the Younger's lively *Peasant Wedding* (1620). In the Dutch collection there are many 17th-century works, including some by Rembrandt. Other highlights include *A Wooded Landscape* by Hobbema and *Lady Writing a Letter With Her Maid* by Vermeer. Rubens and van Dyck are two more famous names here, but there are also fine works by less well-known artists, such as van Uden's *Peasants Merry-making*. Portraits by artists such as Faber and Pencz from the 15th and 16th centuries dominate the German collection, though Emil Nolde's colourful *Two Women in the Garden* dates from 1915.

PORTRAITURE

The impressive Shaw Room is lined with full-length historical portraits including one of Charles Coote, the first Earl of Bellamont, dressed in flamboyant pink ceremonial robes. In the National Portrait Gallery, portraits of those who have made a contribution to Ireland from the 16th century to the present are displayed.

Peasant Wedding by Pieter Brueghel the Younger (1564–1637)

SOUTHWEST DUBLIN

The area around Dublin Castle was first settled in prehistoric times, and it was from here that the city grew. Dublin gets its name from the dark pool (*Dubb Linn*) which formed at the confluence of the Liffey and the Poddle, a river that originally ran through the site of Dublin Castle. It is now channelled underground. Archaeological excavations behind Wood Quay, on the banks of the river Liffey, reveal that the Vikings had a settlement here as early as AD 841.

Following Strongbow's invasion of 1170, a medieval city began to emerge; the Anglo-Normans built strong defensive walls around the castle.

A small reconstructed section of these old city walls can be seen at St Audoen's Church. More conspicuous reminders of the Anglo-Normans appear in the medieval Christ Church Cathedral and St Patrick's Cathedral. When the city expanded during the Georgian era, the narrow cobbled streets of Temple Bar became a quarter inhabited by skilled craftsmen and merchants. Today this area is a haven for culture and entertainment, and is home to a variety of alternative shops and cafés. The Powerscourt Townhouse is an elegant 18th-century mansion that has been converted into one of the city's best shopping centres.

Vibrant artwork typical of shops and galleries in Temple Bar

SIGHTS AT A GLANCE

Museums and Libraries
Chester Beatty Library ❷
Dublinia ⓭
Marsh's Library ❽

Historic Buildings
City Hall ❸
Dublin Castle pp56–7 ❶
Olympia Theatre ❺
Powerscourt Townhouse ❻
Tailors' Hall ⓫

Historic Areas
Temple Bar pp58–9 ❹

Churches
Christ Church Cathedral pp64–5 ⓮
St Audoen's Church ⓬
St Patrick's Cathedral ❾
St Werburgh's Church ❿
Whitefriar Street Carmelite Church ❼

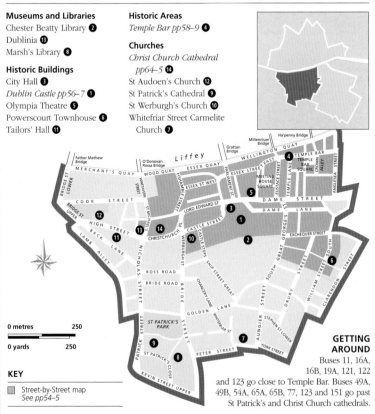

KEY

▢ Street-by-Street map
See pp54–5

0 metres 250
0 yards 250

GETTING AROUND
Buses 11, 16A, 16B, 19A, 121, 122 and 123 go close to Temple Bar. Buses 49A, 49B, 54A, 65A, 65B, 77, 123 and 151 go past St Patrick's and Christ Church cathedrals.

◁ **Colourful street in bustling Temple Bar**

Street-by-Street: Southwest Dublin

Despite its wealth of ancient buildings, such as Dublin Castle and Christ Church Cathedral, this part of Dublin lacks the sleek appeal of the neighbouring streets around Grafton Street. In recent years, however, redevelopment has rejuvenated the area, especially around Temple Bar, where the attractive cobbled streets are lined with shops, futuristic arts centres, galleries, bars and cafés.

Sunlight Chambers
Built in 1900, the delightful terracotta decoration on the façade advertises Lever's soap manufacturing business.

Wood Quay is where the Vikings established their first permanent settlement in Ireland around 841.

Dublin Viking Adventure

★ **Christ Church Cathedral**
Huge family monuments, including that of the 19th Earl of Kildare, can be found in Ireland's oldest cathedral, which also has a fascinating crypt 🄬

St Werburgh's Church
An ornate interior hides behind the somewhat drab exterior of this 18th-century church 🄺

City Hall
Originally built as the Royal Exchange in 1779, the city's municipal headquarters is fronted by a huge Corinthian portico ❸

★ **Dublin Castle**
The Drawing Room, with its Waterford crystal chandelier, is part of a suite of luxurious rooms built in the 18th century for the Viceroys of Ireland ❶

Dublinia
Medieval Dublin is the subject of this interactive museum, located in the former Synod Hall of the Church of Ireland. It is linked to Christ Church by a bridge 🄭

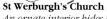

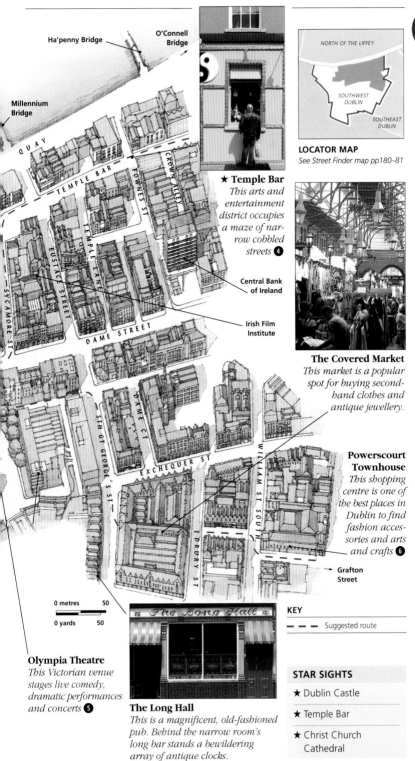

Ha'penny Bridge

O'Connell Bridge

Millennium Bridge

QUAY

TEMPLE BAR

FOWNES ST

CROWN ALLEY

EUSTACE STREET

TEMPLE LANE

SYCAMORE ST

DAME STREET

DAME CT

STH GT GEORGE'S ST

EXCHEQUER ST

DRURY ST

WILLIAM ST SOUTH

NORTH OF THE LIFFEY

SOUTHWEST DUBLIN

SOUTHEAST DUBLIN

LOCATOR MAP
See Street Finder map pp180–81

★ **Temple Bar**
This arts and entertainment district occupies a maze of narrow cobbled streets ④

Central Bank of Ireland

Irish Film Institute

The Covered Market
This market is a popular spot for buying second-hand clothes and antique jewellery.

Powerscourt Townhouse
This shopping centre is one of the best places in Dublin to find fashion accessories and arts and crafts ⑥

Grafton Street

0 metres 50
0 yards 50

KEY

‒ ‒ ‒ Suggested route

Olympia Theatre
This Victorian venue stages live comedy, dramatic performances and concerts ⑤

The Long Hall
This is a magnificent, old-fashioned pub. Behind the narrow room's long bar stands a bewildering array of antique clocks.

STAR SIGHTS

★ Dublin Castle

★ Temple Bar

★ Christ Church Cathedral

Dublin Castle **0**

Dublin gets its name from the ancient black pool harbour, or *Dubh Linn*, that occupied the site of the present castle gardens. Part of the town's 10th-century defence bank is visible at the undercroft. The upper castle yard corresponds closely to the castle established by King John in 1204, which became the most important fortification in Ireland and was the seat of colonial rule and the centre of military, political and social affairs. On the castle's southern side, the magnificent state apartments include St Patrick's Hall and the drawing and throne rooms. They were built as the residential quarters of the viceregal court and now host important state functions.

St Patrick by Edward Smyth

Figure of Justice
Facing the Upper Yard above the main entrance from Cork Hill, this statue aroused much cynicism among Dubliners, who felt she was turning her back on the city.

★ **Throne Room**
The throne in this room was built in 1821 for King George IV's visit to Ireland.

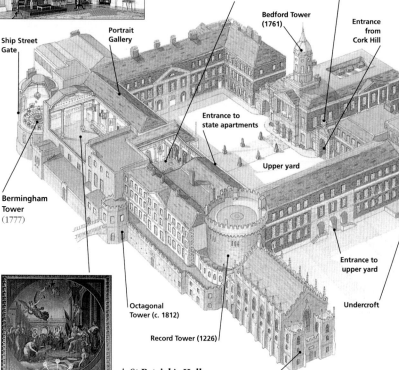

Ship Street Gate

Portrait Gallery

Bedford Tower (1761)

Entrance from Cork Hill

Entrance to state apartments

Upper yard

Bermingham Tower (1777)

Entrance to upper yard

Octagonal Tower (c. 1812)

Record Tower (1226)

Undercroft

★ **St Patrick's Hall**
This hall, with its banners of the now defunct Knights of St Patrick, has ceiling paintings by Vincenzo Valdré (1778), symbolizing the relationship between Britain and Ireland.

The Chapel Royal was completed in 1814 by Francis Johnston. The 100 heads on the exterior of this Neo-Gothic church were carved by Edward Smyth.

VISITORS' CHECKLIST

Off Dame St. **Map** C3. *Tel 677
7129.* 49, 56A, 77, 77A and
123. **State Apartments:**
*10am–5pm Mon–Fri, 2–5pm
Sat, Sun, public hols.* 1 Jan,
Good Fri, 24–26 Dec, during
state visits. obligatory.
www.dublincastle.ie

ROBERT EMMET

Robert Emmet (1778–1803),
son of the state physician
to the viceroy, led a failed
attack on Dublin Castle
in 1803. He was arrested
and interrogated in the
Record Tower. His final
defiant and patriotic speech
proved an inspiration to
future generations of Irish
freedom fighters. Publicly
hung, drawn and quartered,
the heroic Emmet became
known as "the father of
Irish Republicanism".

Treasury
building

Lower yard

Dame Street
and Palace
Street Gate

STAR FEATURES

★ St Patrick's Hall

★ Throne Room

**Manuscript (1874) from the Holy Koran written by calligrapher Ahmad
Shaikh in Kashmir, Chester Beatty Library**

Chester Beatty
Library ❷

Clock Tower Building, Dubh Linn
Gardens, Dublin Castle. **Map** C4.
Tel 407 0750. May–Sep: 10am–
5pm Mon– Fri; Oct–Apr: 10am–5pm
Tue–Fri; 11am–5pm Sat, 1pm–5pm
Sun all year. public hols.
www.cbl.ie

This world-renowned
collection of Oriental manuscripts and art was named
European Museum of the Year
in 2002. It was bequeathed to
Ireland by American mining
magnate Sir Alfred Chester
Beatty, who died in 1968.
This generous act no doubt
led to his selection as Ireland's
first honorary citizen in 1957.
    During his lifetime Beatty
accumulated almost 300 copies
of the Koran, representing the
works of master calligraphers
from Iran, Turkey and the
Arab world. Other exhibits
include some 6,000-year-old
Babylonian stone tablets,
Greek papyri dating from the
2nd century AD and biblical
material written in Coptic, the
original language of Egypt.
    In the Far Eastern collection
is a display of Chinese jade
books – each leaf is made from
thinly cut jade. Burmese and
Siamese art is represented in
the fine collection of 18th-
and 19th-century Parabaiks,
books of illustrated folk tales.
The Japanese collection also
includes many books as well
as paintings from the 16th to
the 18th centuries.

Turkish and Persian
miniatures, striking Buddhist
paintings and Chinese dragon
robes are among many other
fascinating exhibits in this
unusual museum.

City Hall ❸

Cork Hill, Dame St. **Map** C3. *Tel 222
2204.* 10am–5:15pm Mon–Sat,
2–5pm Sun, public hols. Good
Fri, 24–26 Dec.
    www.dublincity.ie/cityhall

Designed by Thomas Cooley,
this imposing building was
built between 1769 and 1779
as the Royal Exchange. It was
taken over by Dublin
Corporation in 1852 as a meeting place for the city council,
a role it keeps to this day.
    Tours are available of the
building, recently restored to
its original condition. *Dublin
City Hall – The Story of the
Capital*, is a permanent
exhibition housed in the
lower ground floor covering
1,000 years of history.

Façade of City Hall

Temple Bar ❹

The cobbled streets between Dame Street and the Liffey are named after Sir William Temple who acquired the land in the early 1600s. The term "bar" meant a riverside path. In the 1800s it was home to small businesses but over the years went into decline. In the early 1960s the land was bought up with plans to build a new bus station. Artists and retailers took short-term leases but stayed on when the redevelopment plans were scrapped. Temple Bar prospered

Palm tree seat

and today it is an exciting place, with bars, restaurants, shops and galleries. Stylish and eco-friendly architectural development is contributing further to the area's appeal.

Modern, floor-lit entrance hall of the Irish Film Institute

Exploring Temple Bar
The most dramatic way to enter Temple Bar is through the **Merchants' Arch** opposite Ha'penny Bridge *(see p77)*. Underneath the arch is a short, dark alley lined with bazaar-like retail outlets. The alley opens out into the modern airy space of **Temple Bar Square**, a popular lunchtime hangout, where there is a small but eclectic **book market** at weekends. Along the east side is **Crown Alley** with its brightly painted shops and cafés.

Galleries and gallery shops abound. In the northwest corner of the square is the **Temple Bar Gallery and Studios**, a renovated factory that combines exhibition and studio spaces. The **Original Print Gallery** on Temple Bar street and the **Graphic Studio Gallery** off Cope Street sell handmade prints.

The **Contemporary Music Centre**, on Fishamble Street, is Ireland's national archive

and resource centre for new music, supporting the work of composers throughout Ireland. The **Temple Bar Information Centre**, on East Essex Street, provides details of arts, culture and entertainment in the area.

Near Christ Church Cathedral in the Old City district, is **Cow's Lane**, a new pedestrian street complete with designer shops and its own fashion and design market every Saturday (except in winter).

In the evening, there are a huge number of restaurants, bars and pubs to choose from, many with live jazz, rock, and traditional Irish music. **Button Factory** offers an exciting mix of mainly homegrown talent, from alternative to hip-hop and electro. For international names, try the **Olympia Theatre**, where the world's biggest bands

The Temple Bar logo

have played. This Victorian theatre also stages comedy, musicals and, occasionally, drama.

Meeting House Square
Named after a Quaker place of worship which once stood here, this outdoor performance space is a wonderful asset to the city. It is one of the main venues for the Temple Bar Summer Programme *(see p159)* which features lunchtime and evening concerts, and open-air theatre. Screenings of films and numerous family events also take place in the square. Every Saturday, an excellent gourmet food market is held here.

Project Arts Centre
39 East Essex Street. **Tel** 881 9613/14. ◯ 11am–7pm Mon–Sat; shows nightly. &. 🍸 www.project.ie
Project Arts Centre, which started in 1966, has an international reputation for its exciting year round programme of avant garde theatre, dance, music, film and visual art. The centre has launched the careers of actors Gabriel Byrne and Liam Neeson, and even U2 cut their teeth here. Two performance spaces showcase productions from some of Ireland's most successful festivals and companies, alongside the work of new and emerging artists. The gallery presents a series of free exhibitions throughout the year.

Shoppers in the streets of Temple Bar

Gallery of Photography
Meeting House Square. *Tel 671 4654.*
○ *11am–6pm Mon–Sat, 1–6pm Sun.*
▣ **www**.galleryofphotography.ie
This bright, contemporary
space runs exhibitions of high
quality Irish and international
photography, some of which
feature talks by the artist
exhibiting. The shop has an
extensive selection of photos,
postcards and specialist titles.

National Photographic Archive
Meeting House Square. *Tel 603
0374.* ○ *10am–5pm Mon–Fri,
10am–2pm Sat.* **www**.nli.ie
The National Library's
collection of around 300,000
photographs is housed here.
   The Archive has rolling
exhibitions, mainly featuring
items from the collections.
Subject matter ranges from
social and political history to
early tourist postcards and
dramatic landscape shots,
offering a window into a time
when Ireland really was a
land of thatched cottages
and donkey carts.

Irish Film Institute
6 Eustace Street. *Tel 679 5744.*
○ *daily.* ▣ ▣ **www**.irishfilm.ie
Opened in November 1992,
in the wake of international
hits such as *The Commitments*
(1991), this was the first major

Cheese stall at the weekly gourmet market in Meeting House Square

cultural project completed in
Temple Bar. A neon sign indicates the main entrance, which
runs through a floor-lit corridor
before opening into an airy
atrium where visitors can
browse in the bookshop or
have a snack, meal or drink in
the bar and restaurant. The
IFI's two screens focus on
cult, arthouse and independent
films as well as showing
archive screenings and docu-
mentaries. There are also
seminars, workshops, seasons
on various themes, nations or
directors, and the Jameson
International Film Festival
each year. A small temporary
membership fee is payable
on top of the ticket price.

Cultivate Sustainable Living Centre
15–19 Essex Street West. *Tel 674 5773.*
○ *10am–5:30pm Mon–Sat.* ●
public hols. ▣ **www**.cultivate.ie
Learn about the green development of Temple Bar at this
ecological centre with exhibitions, screenings of cutting-
edge films and a demonstration
garden. Interactive maps
show sites of environmental
interest, from bicycle routes
to eco-cultural tourist sites.
   Once a year, in spring,
Cultivate hosts the four-day
Convergence Festival, high-
lighting key ecological issues
through drama, film, live
music, art, workshops and
presentations.

TEMPLE BAR
Button Factory ④
Contemporary Music Centre ⑫
Cultivate ⑪
Gallery of Photography ⑧
Graphic Studio Gallery ③
Irish Film Institute ⑨
National Photographic Archive ⑤
Olympia Theatre ⑩
Original Print Gallery ①
Project ⑦
Temple Bar Gallery ②
Temple Bar Information Centre ⑥

0 metres 400
0 yards 400

The light and airy interior of Powerscourt Townhouse shopping centre

Olympia Theatre **⑤**

73 Dame St. **Map** C3. **Tel** 679 3323.
☐ *10:30am–8:30pm Mon–Sat (box office). See also **Theatre in Dublin** pp158–9.*

Dublin's oldest theatre is a former Victorian music hall. The large auditorium is now used as both a theatre and a venue for live bands.

The theatre was originally built in 1879 by Dan Lowrey as the Star of Erin Music Hall and was eventually demolished and rebuilt as the Olympia Theatre in 1897. Its 19th-century Victorian canopy was accidentally destroyed in 2004 but there are plans to rebuild it.

Façade of Olympia Theatre

Powerscourt Townhouse **⑥**

South William St. **Map** D4. **Tel** 671 7000. ☐ *10am–6pm Mon–Fri (8pm Thu), 9am–6pm Sat, noon–6pm Sun. See also **Shopping in Dublin** pp148–51.* **www**.powerscourtcentre.com

Completed in 1774 by Robert Mack, this grand mansion was originally built as the city home of Viscount Powerscourt, who also had a country estate at Enniskerry, just south of Dublin. Granite from the Powerscourt estate was used in the construction of this mansion.

Today the building houses one of Dublin's best shopping centres. Inside it still features the original grand mahogany staircase, and finely detailed plasterwork by stuccodore Michael Stapleton. In 1807, Powerscourt Townhouse was sold to the government, and the architect Francis Johnston was appointed to add three groups of buildings around the courtyard for use as a stamp office, and to erect the clock tower and bell on Clarendon Street.

The building became a drapery warehouse in the 1830s, and major restoration in the late 1970s turned it into a centre of galleries, antique shops, jewellery stalls and other shop units. The central courtyard café, topped by a glass dome, is a popular meeting place with many Dubliners. Another entrance is via the Johnson Court alley, just off Grafton Street.

Whitefriar Street Carmelite Church **⑦**

56 Aungier St. **Map** C4. **Tel** 475 8821. ☐ *8am–6:30pm Mon & Wed–Fri, 8am–9pm Tue, 8am–7pm Sat, 8am–7:30pm Sun, 9.30am–1pm public hols.* **www**.carmelites.ie

Designed by George Papworth, this Catholic church was built in 1827. It stands alongside the site of a medieval Carmelite foundation.

In contrast to the two Church of Ireland cathedrals, St Patrick's and Christ Church, which are usually full of tourists, this church is frequented by worshippers from all over Dublin. Every day they come to light candles to various saints, including St Valentine – the patron saint of lovers. His remains, previously buried in the cemetery of St Hippolytus in Rome, were offered to the church as a gift from Pope Gregory XVI in 1836. Today they rest beneath the commemorative statue to the saint, which stands in the northeast corner of the church beside the high altar.

Nearby is the figure of Our Lady of Dublin, a Flemish oak statue dating from the late 15th or early 16th century. It may have belonged to St Mary's Abbey *(see p76)* and is thought to be the only wooden statue of its kind to have escaped destruction when Ireland's monasteries were sacked during the time of the Reformation *(see p14)*.

Statue of Our Lady of Dublin in Whitefriar Street Carmelite Church

The entrance to Marsh's Library, adjacent to St Patrick's Cathedral

Marsh's Library ⑧

St Patrick's Close. **Map** B4.
Tel *454 3511.* ⬜ *9:30am–1pm, 2–5pm Mon, Wed–Fri, 10am–1pm Sat.* ⬤ *24 Dec–2 Jan, public hols.* 🖼 **www**.marshlibrary.ie

Built in 1701 for Archbishop Narcissus Marsh, this is the oldest public library in Ireland. It was designed by Sir William Robinson, architect of the Royal Hospital Kilmainham *(see p84)*.
To the rear of the library, at the bottom of the second gallery, wired cages can be found where readers were once locked in with rare books. The vast collection of over 25,000 books spans from the 16th to the 18th centuries.

St Patrick's Cathedral ⑨

St Patrick's Close. **Map** B4. ***Tel*** *475 4817.* ⬜ *9am–5pm Mon–Fri (to 6pm Sat), 10–11am, 12:30–2pm, 4:30–5:30pm Sun. Tours are not admitted during services.* 🖼 ♿
www.stpatrickscathedral.ie

Ireland's largest church was founded beside a sacred well where St Patrick is said to have baptized converts around AD 450. The original building was just a wooden chapel and remained so until 1192, when Archbishop John Comyn rebuilt it in stone.
In the mid-17th century, Huguenot refugees from France arrived in Dublin, and were given the Lady Chapel by the Dean and Chapter as

their place of worship. The chapel was separated from the rest of the cathedral and used by the Huguenots until the late 18th century. Today St Patrick's is the Protestant Church of Ireland's national cathedral.
Much of the present building dates back to work completed between 1254 and 1270. The cathedral suffered over the centuries from desecration, fire and neglect but, thanks to Sir Benjamin Guinness, it underwent extensive restoration in the 1860s. The building is 91 m (300 ft) long; at the western end is a 43-m (141-ft) tower, restored by Archbishop Minot in 1370 and now known as Minot's Tower. The spire was added in the 18th century.

The interior is dotted with memorial busts, brasses and monuments. A leaflet available at the front desk helps identify and locate them. Famous citizens remembered in the church include the harpist Turlough O'Carolan (1670–1738), Douglas Hyde (1860–1949), the first President of Ireland and of course Jonathan Swift and his beloved Stella.
At the west end of the nave is an old door with a hole in it – a relic from a feud between the Lords Kildare and Ormonde in 1492. The latter took refuge in the Chapter House, but a truce was soon made and a hole was cut in the door by Lord Kildare so that the two could shake hands in friendship.

St Patrick's Cathedral with Minot's Tower and spire

Nave of St Werburgh's Church, showing gallery and organ case

St Werburgh's Church ⓪

Entrance through 7–8 Castle St. **Map** C4. **Tel** 478 3710. ☐ 10am–4pm Mon–Fri, ring bell if doors locked.

Built on late 12th-century foundations, St Werburgh's was designed by Thomas Burgh in 1715, after an act of parliament which appointed commissioners to build a new church. Around 85 people made donations. By 1719 the church was complete but had an unfinished tower. Then in 1728 James Southwell bequeathed money for a clock and bells for the church on condition that the tower was completed within three years of his death. It was finally finished in 1732. After a fire in 1754 it was rebuilt with the financial help of George II. It served as the parish church of Dublin Castle, hosting many state ceremonies, including the swearing-in of viceroys. However, this role was later taken over by the Church of the Most Holy Trinity within the castle walls.

Beyond the shabby pallor of its exterior walls lies some fine decorative work. There are massive memorials to members of the Guinness family, and a finely carved Gothic pulpit by Richard Stewart. Also worth seeing are the 1767 organ case and the beautiful stuccowork in the chancel.

Beneath the church lie 27 vaults including that of Lord Edward Fitzgerald, who died during the 1798 Rebellion *(see p16)*, and also Sir James Ware. The body of Fitzgerald's captor, Major Henry Sirr, is in the graveyard. John Field, the creator of the nocturne, was baptized here in 1782.

Tailors' Hall ⓫

Back Lane. **Map** B4. **Tel** 454 1786. ● to the public. **www**.antaisce.org

Dublin's only surviving guild-hall preserves a delightful corner of old Dublin in an otherwise busy redevelopment zone. Built in 1706, it stands behind a limestone arch in a quiet cobbled yard. The building is the oldest guildhall in Ireland and was used by various trade groups including hosiers, saddlers and barber-surgeons as well as tailors. It was regarded as the most fashionable venue in Dublin for social occasions such as balls and concerts for many years until the New Music Hall in Fishamble Street opened and the social scene transferred to there. It also hosted many political meetings – the Protestant leader of the United Irishmen, Wolfe Tone, famously made a speech at the convention of the Catholic Committee on 2nd December 1792 before the 1798 rebellion *(see p16)*.

The building closed in the early 1960s due to neglect, but an appeal by Desmond Guinness saw the hall totally refurbished. Since 1985 is has been the home of An Taisce (the Irish National Trust).

Façade of Tailors' Hall, today the home of the Irish National Trust

St Audoen's Church ⓬

High St, Cornmarket. **Map** B3. **Tel** 677 0088 ☐ May–Oct: 9:30am–5:30pm, last adm 4:45pm. 🏷 🛈 **www**.heritageireland.ie

Sited in the heart of the walled Medieval City, and designated a National Monument, St Audoen's Church is Dublin's earliest surviving medieval church. It is dedicated to Saint Ouen, the 7th century Bishop of

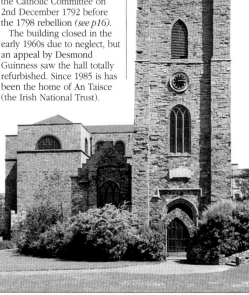

The 12th-century tower of St Audoen's Church, the oldest in Ireland

Rouen and Patron Saint of Normandy. The 15th-century nave remains intact and the three bells date from 1423. The Guild Chapel of St Anne houses an exhibition on the importance of this church in the life of the medieval city. To the rear, steps lead down to St Audoen's Arch, the last remaining gateway of the old city. Flanking the gate are restored sections of the 13th-century city walls.

Next door stands St Audoen's Roman Catholic Church, which was begun in 1841 and completed in 1847. It was built by Patrick Byrne, of Talbot Street, who studied at the Dublin Society School. The parish priest, Patrick Mooney, completed the plasterwork and also installed the organ. In 1884 the dome of the church collapsed and was replaced with a plaster circle. The portico was added to the building in 1899. The Great Bell, dedicated on All Saints Day in 1848 and known as The Liberator after Daniel O'Connell, rang to announce his release from prison and also tolled on the day of his funeral. The two Pacific clam shells by the front of the church hold holy water.

Dublinia ⓮

St Michael's Hill. **Map** B3. *Tel* 679 4611. 🔲 *Apr–Sep: 10am–5pm daily; Oct–Mar: 10am–5pm Mon–Fri (last adm 4:15pm), 10am–4pm Sat, Sun & public hols (last adm: 3:15pm).* 🔲 *17 Mar, 23–26 Dec.* 📷 *minimum charge to enter Christ Church Cathedral via bridge.* 🔲 **www.**dublinia.ie

Managed by the non-profit-making Medieval Trust, the Dublinia exhibition covers the formative period of Dublin's history from the arrival of the Anglo-Normans in 1170 to the closure of the monasteries in the 1540s. The exhibition is housed in the Neo-Gothic Synod Hall, which, up until 1983, was home to the ruling body of the Church of Ireland. The building and the bridge linking it to Christ Church Cathedral date from the 1870s.

Former Synod Hall, now home to the Dublinia Exhibition

Before Dublinia was established in 1993, the Synod Hall was briefly used as a nightclub.

The exhibition is entered via the basement where visitors walk through life-sized reconstructions of the Medieval City complete with realistic sounds and smells. These depict major events in Dublin's history, such as the Black Death and the rebellion of Silken Thomas *(see p14).* The ground floor houses a large-scale model of Dublin as it was around 1500, and reconstructions including the inside of a late medieval merchant's kitchen. There is also a display of artifacts from the Wood Quay excavation. This was the site of the first Viking settlement in Ireland. Excavations in the 1970s revealed remains of Norse and Norman villages, and artifacts including

Medieval key in the Dublinia exhibition

pottery, swords, coins and leatherwork. Many of these finds are also on display at the National Museum *(see pp44–5).* However, the city chose not to develop the Wood Quay site, but instead built two large civic offices there. If you go to Wood Quay today all you will find is a plaque and an unusual picnic site by the Liffey in the shape of a Viking longboat. A fascinating exhibition depicts the world of archaeology. It is interactive, and enables visitors to become investigators of Dublin's Viking and Medieval past.

Mid 13th-century jug in Dublinia

Also in the exhibition are information panels on the themes of trade, merchants and religion. On the first floor is the wood-panelled Great Hall, one of the finest examples of Victorian Gothic style in Dublin. The building's 60m-high (190-ft) St Michael's Tower offers one of the best vantage points for views of the city.

Reconstruction of a Viking street in Dublinia

Christ Church Cathedral ⑭

Christ Church Cathedral was established by the Hiberno-Norse king of Dublin, Sitric "Silkbeard", and the first bishop of Dublin, Dunan. It was rebuilt by the Anglo-Norman archbishop, John Cumin from 1186. It is the cathedral for the Church of Ireland (Anglican) diocese of Dublin and Glendalough. By the 19th century it was in a bad state of repair, but was completely remodelled by architect George Street in the 1870s. The vast 12th-century crypt was restored in 2000.

Arms on Lord Mayor's pew

★ **Medieval Lectern**
This beautiful brass lectern was hand-made during the Middle Ages. It stands on the north side of the nave, in front of the pulpit. The matching lectern on the south side is Victorian.

Medieval stone carvings are on display in the North Transept. Dating from about 1200, these exquisite Romanesque capitals include a troupe of musicians and two human faces enveloped by legendary griffons.

Nave
The 25-m (68-ft) high nave has some fine early Gothic arches. On the north side, the 13th-century wall leans out by as much as 50 cm (18 in) due to the weight of the original roof.

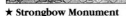

Entrance

The bridge to the Synod Hall was added when the cathedral was being rebuilt in the 1870s.

★ **Strongbow Monument**
The large effigy in chain armour is probably not Strongbow (see p14). However, his remains are buried in the cathedral and the curious half-figure may be part of his original tomb.

STAR FEATURES

★ Strongbow Monument

★ Crypt

★ Medieval Lectern

Chapel of St Laud
The casket on the wall contains the heart of St Laurence O'Toole. The chapel features original medieval floor tiles.

VISITORS' CHECKLIST

Christchurch Place. **Map** B3. **Tel** 677 8099. 50, 66, 77 & many other routes. 9:45am–5pm daily (Jun–Aug: 9am–6pm daily). 26 & 27 Dec. 10am and 12:45pm Mon–Fri, 11am and 3:30pm Sun. limited. **www.cccdub.ie**

The Lady Chapel is used to celebrate the daily Eucharist.

★ **Crypt**
This decorated plate by Francis Garthorne is part of a collection presented to Christ Church Cathedral by King William III to mark his victory at the Battle of the Boyne in 1690.

Stairs to crypt

Crypt

The foundations of the original chapter house date back to the late 13th century.

Romanesque Doorway
Leading to the south transept, this ornately carved doorway is one of the finest examples of 12th-century Irish stonework.

TIMELINE

1000	1200	1400	1600	1800
c.1030 Construction of original Viking cathedral	**c.1240** Completion of stone cathedral	**1600** Shopkeepers rent crypt space	**1689** King James II of England worships in cathedral	**1983** Cathedral ceases using Synod Hall
		1541 King Henry VIII alters constitution of cathedral		
1186 The first Anglo-Norman archbishop, John Cumin, begins work on the new cathedral	*Meeting takes place between Lambert Simnel and the Earl of Kildare*	**1487** Coronation of 10-year-old Lambert Simnel as "King of England"	**1742** Choir participates in first performance of Handel's Messiah	**1871** Major rebuilding of the cathedral begins, including Synod Hall and bridge

NORTH OF THE LIFFEY

D ublin's north side was the last part of the city to be developed during the 18th century. The city authorities envisioned an elegant area of leafy avenues, but the reality of today's traffic has rather spoiled their original plans. Nonetheless, O'Connell Street is an impressive thoroughfare, lined with department stores, monuments and historic public buildings.
    There are many notable buildings in the area, such as James Gandon's glorious Custom House and majestic Four Courts, together with the famous General Post Office, or GPO *(see p71)*.
    The Rotunda Hospital, Europe's first purpose-built maternity hospital, is another fine building. Dublin's two most celebrated theatres, the Abbey and the Gate, act as cultural magnets, as do the Dublin Writers' Museum and the James Joyce Cultural Centre, two museums that are dedicated to writers who spent most of their lives in the city.

**Bookshop sign on
Ormond Quay Lower**

SIGHTS AT A GLANCE

Historic Buildings
Chief O'Neill's
    Viewing Tower ❾
Custom House ❶
Four Courts ⓬
King's Inns ❽
Tyrone House ❹

Historic Streets and Bridges
Ha'penny Bridge ⓰
O'Connell Street ❸
Parnell Square ❼
Smithfield ❿

Theatres
Abbey Theatre ❷

Churches
St Mary's Church ⓯
St Mary's Pro-Cathedral ❺
St Michan's Church ⓭

Museums and Galleries
Old Jameson Distillery ⓫
James Joyce Cultural Centre ❻
St Mary's Abbey Exhibition ⓮

GETTING AROUND
Numerous buses, including the 3, 4, 10, 11, 13, 16 and 16A, go along O'Connell Street and round Parnell Square. To get to Smithfield, take a 67A, 68, 69, 79 or 90. The Tallaght to Connolly Station Luas line runs through the area.

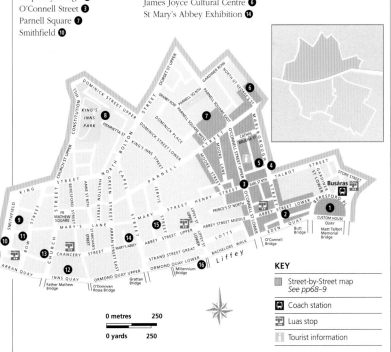

KEY

| | Street-by-Street map
See pp68–9 |
	Coach station
	Luas stop
	Tourist information

0 metres   250

0 yards   250

◁ **Portico of the Custom House, illuminated at night**

Street-by-Street: Around O'Connell Street

Throughout the Georgian era, O'Connell Street was the fashionable part of Dublin in which to live. However, the 1916 Easter Rising destroyed many of its fine buildings, including much of the General Post Office – only its original façade

Pavement mosaic, Moore Street

remains. Today, this main thoroughfare is lined with shops and businesses. Other nearby attractions include St Mary's Pro-Cathedral and James Gandon's Custom House, overlooking the Liffey.

James Joyce Cultural Centre
This well-restored Georgian town house contains a small Joyce museum **6**

Parnell Monument (1911)

The Gate Theatre was founded in 1928 and is renowned for its productions of contemporary drama.

The Rotunda Hospital
Housing a chapel built in the 1750s to the design of German architect Richard Castle, this hospital features lovely stained-glass windows, fluted columns, panelling and intricate iron balustrades.

Moore Street Market
Be prepared for the cries of the stall holders offering an enormous variety of fresh fruit, vegetables and cut flowers.

The Monument of Light, an elegant stainless steel spire, rises to 120 m (394 ft).

The General Post Office, the grandest building on O'Connell Street, was the centre of the 1916 Rising.

James Larkin Statue (1981)

KEY

━ Suggested route

🚊 Luas stop

ℹ Tourist information

0 metres   50

0 yards   50

STAR SIGHTS

★ Custom House

★ O'Connell Street

St Mary's Pro-Cathedral
*Built around 1825, this is
Dublin's main place of
worship for Catholics. The
plaster relief above the
altar in the sanctuary
depicts* The Ascension **5**

LOCATOR MAP
See Street Finder map pp180–81

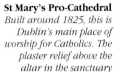

The statue of James Joyce (1990)
*This work by Marjorie Fitzgibbon
commemorates one of Ireland's most
famous novelists. Born in Dublin in
1882, Joyce catalogued the people and
streets of Dublin in his celebrated books.*

Abbey Theatre
*Ireland's national
theatre is known
throughout the world
for its productions by
Irish playwrights,
such as Sean O'Casey
and JM Synge* **2**

★ O'Connell Street
*This monument to Daniel
O'Connell by John Foley took
19 years to complete from the
laying of its foundation
stone in 1864* **3**

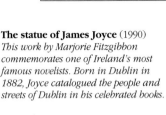

CUSTOM HOUSE QUAY

Butt Bridge

LIFFEY

**O'Connell
Bridge**

**Trinity
College**

★ Custom House
*This striking head, by
Edward Smyth, symbolizes
the River Liffey. It is one of
14 carved keystones that
adorn the building* **1**

Illuminated façade of the Custom House reflected in the Liffey

Custom House ❶

Custom House Quay. **Map** E2.
Tel *888 2538.* ⏲ *10am–12:30pm
Mon–Fri (Nov–Mar: Wed–Fri),
2–5pm Sat, Sun.* 📷 ♿ *weekdays.*

This majestic building was
designed as the Custom
House by the English architect
James Gandon. However, the
1800 Act of Union *(see p16)*
transferred the custom and
excise business to London,
rendering the building practi-
cally obsolete. In 1921, Sinn
Féin voters celebrated their
election victory by setting light
to what they saw as a symbol
of British imperialism. The fire
blazed for five days causing
extensive damage. Reconstruction took place in 1926, but the
building was not completely
restored until 1991, when it reopened as government offices.
    The main façade is made
up of pavilions at each end
with a Doric portico in its
centre. The arms of Ireland
crown the two pavilions, and
a series of 14 allegorical
heads by Dublin sculptor
Edward Smyth form the keystones of arches and
entrances. These

heads depict Ireland's main
rivers and the Atlantic Ocean.
A statue of Commerce tops
the central copper dome.
    The best view of the building
is from the south of the Liffey
beyond Matt Talbot Bridge.

Logo of the Abbey Theatre

Abbey Theatre ❷

26 Lower Abbey St. **Map** E2. ***Tel*** *878
7222 Box office.* ⏲ *for performances,
some tours. See also* **Entertainment**
pp154–9. **www**.abbeytheatre.ie

Founded in 1898 with WB
Yeats and Lady Gregory as
co-directors, the Abbey staged
its first play in 1904.
The early years of this
much lauded national
theatre saw works by
W B Yeats, J M Synge
and Sean O'Casey.
Many were controver-
sial: nationalist
sensitivities were
severely tested in 1926
at the premiere of
O'Casey's *The Plough
and the Stars,* when
the flag of the Irish
Free State appeared in
a scene featuring a
pub frequented by prostitutes.
    While presenting the
work of eminent foreign
authors from time to time,
the prime objective of the
Abbey, and the smaller
Peacock Theatre downstairs,
is to provide a performance
space for Irish dramatic
writing. Some of the most
acclaimed performances
have been Brian Friel's
Dancing At Lughnasa,
Patrick Kavanagh's *Tarry
Flynn, The Colleen Bawn* by
Dion Boucicault and Hugh
Leonard's *Love in the Title.*

O'Connell Street ❸

Map D1–D2.

O'Connell Street is very
different from the original
plans of Irish aristocrat Luke
Gardiner. When he bought
the land in the 18th century,
Gardiner envisioned a grand
residential parade with an
elegant mall running
along its centre.
Such plans were
short-lived. The

O'Connell Bridge spanning the Liffey, viewed from the Butt Bridge

construction of Carlisle (now O'Connell) Bridge in 1790 transformed the street into the city's main north-south route. Also, several buildings were destroyed during the 1916 Easter Rising and the Irish Civil War. Since the 1960s many of the old buildings have been replaced by the plate glass and neon of fast food joints and amusement arcades.

A few venerable buildings remain, such as the General Post Office (1818), Gresham Hotel (1817), Clery's department store (1822) and the Royal Dublin Hotel, part of which occupies the street's only original townhouse.

A walk down the central mall is the most enjoyable way to see the street's mix of architectural styles. At the south end stands a huge monument to Daniel O'Connell *(see p16)*, unveiled in 1882. The street, which throughout the 19th century had been called Sackville Street, was renamed for O'Connell in 1922. Higher up, almost facing the General Post Office, is an expressive statue of James Larkin (1867–1943),

Clock outside Clery's department store

leader of the Dublin general strike in 1913. The next statue is of Father Theobald Mathew (1790–1856), founder of the Pioneer Total Abstinence Movement. At the north end of the street is the obelisk-shaped monument to Charles Stewart Parnell (1846–91), who was leader of the Home Rule Party and known as the "uncrowned King of Ireland" *(see p17)*. A new addition to O'Connell Street is the Monument of Light, erected on the site where Nelson's column used to be. The monument is a stainless steel, conical spire which tapers from a three-metre diameter base to a 10-centimetre pointed tip of optical glass at a height of 120 metres.

Tyrone House ❹

Marlborough St. **Map** D2.
🌑 *to the public.*

Considered to be the most important Dublin building by German-born Richard Castle (also known as Cassels) after

Leinster House, this Palladian-style structure was completed around 1740 as a townhouse for Sir Marcus Beresford, later Earl of Tyrone. Its interior features elaborate plasterwork by the Swiss Francini brothers, as well as a grand mahogany staircase. The premises were bought by the government in the 1830s and today house a section of the Department of Education; the minister has one of the most ornate state offices in what used to be a reception room.

Austere Neo-Classical interior of St Mary's Pro-Cathedral

St Mary's Pro-Cathedral ❺

Marlborough St. **Map** D2. **Tel** 874 5441. 🕐 7:30am–6:45pm Mon–Sat, 9am–1:45pm & 5:30–7:30pm Sun. **www**.procathedral.ie

Dedicated in 1825 before Catholic emancipation *(see p16)*, St Mary's backstreet site was the best the city's Anglo-Irish leaders would allow a Catholic cathedral.

The façade is based on the Temple of Theseus in Athens. Its six Doric columns support a pediment with statues of St Laurence O'Toole, 12th-century Archbishop of Dublin and patron saint of the city, St Mary and St Patrick. The most striking feature of the interior is the intricately carved high altar.

St Mary's is home to the famous Palestrina Choir. In 1904 the great Irish tenor, John McCormack, began his career with the choir, which sings at the 11am Sunday service.

THE GENERAL POST OFFICE (GPO)

Built in 1818 halfway along O'Connell Street, the GPO became a symbol of the 1916 Irish Rising. Members of the Irish Volunteers and Irish Citizen Army seized the building on Easter Monday, and Patrick Pearse *(see p17)* read out the Proclamation of the Irish Republic from its steps. Shelling from the British finally forced the rebels out after a week. At first, many Irish people viewed the Rising unfavourably. However, as WB Yeats wrote, matters "changed utterly" and a "terrible beauty was born" when, during the

Irish Life magazine cover showing the 1916 Easter Rising

following weeks, 14 of the leaders were shot at Kilmainham Gaol *(see p81)*. Inside the GPO is a sculpture of the Irish mythical warrior Cúchulainn, dedicated to those who died.

James Joyce Cultural Centre ❻

35 North Great George's St. **Map** D1. **Tel** 878 8547. ☐ 9:30am–5pm Mon–Sat, 12:30–5pm Sun. ⬤ Good Fri, 23–27 Dec. 📷 🖥 www.jamesjoyce.ie

Although born in Dublin, Joyce spent most of his adult life in Europe. He used Dublin as the setting for his major works, including *Ulysses, A Portrait of the Artist as a Young Man and Dubliners.*

This centre is located in a 1784 townhouse which was built for the Earl of Kenmare. Michael Stapleton, one of the greatest stuccodores of his time, contributed to the plaster-work with noteworthy friezes.

The main literary display is an absorbing set of biographies of around 50 characters from *Ulysses,* who were based on real Dublin people. Professor Dennis J Maginni, a peripheral character in *Ulysses,* ran a dancing school from this town-house. Leopold and Molly Bloom, the central characters of *Ulysses,* lived a short walk away at No. 7 Eccles Street. The centre also organizes walking tours of Joyce's Dublin, so a visit is a must for all Joycean zealots.

At the top of the road, on Great Denmark Street, is the Jesuit-run Belvedere College attended by Joyce between 1893 and 1898. He recalls his unhappy schooldays there in *A Portrait of the Artist as a Young Man.* The college's interior contains some of Stapleton's best and most colourful plasterwork (1785).

Portrait of James Joyce (1882–1941) by Jacques Emile Blanche

Parnell Square ❼

Once as affluent as the now-restored squares to the south of the Liffey, Parnell Square is today sadly neglected. However, it still holds many points of interest, including the historic Gate Theatre and the peaceful Garden of Remembrance. There are hopes that this once-elegant part of the city will one day be renovated and restored to its original splendour.

Stained-glass window (c. 1863) in the Rotunda Hospital's chapel

Gate Theatre

1 Cavendish Row. **Map** D1. **Box Office Tel** 874 4045. ☐ 10am–7pm Mon–Sat, for performances at 8pm. See also **Entertainment in Dublin** pp140–45. www.gate-theatre.ie

Originally the grand supper room in the Rotunda, today the Gate Theatre is renowned for its staging of contemporary international drama in Dublin. It was founded in 1928 by Hilton Edwards and Mícheál Mac Liammóir. The latter is now best remembered for *The Importance of Being Oscar,* his long-running one-man show about the writer Oscar Wilde *(see p23).* An early success was Denis Johnston's *The Old Lady Says No,* so-called because of the margin notes made on one of his scripts by Lady Gregory, founding director of the Abbey Theatre *(see p70).* Although still noted for stag-ing productions of new plays, the Gate's current output often includes classic Irish plays including Sean O'Casey's *Juno and the Paycock.*

Entrance to the Gate Theatre

Many famous names in the acting world got their first break at the Gate Theatre, including James Mason and a teenage Orson Welles.

Rotunda Hospital

Parnell Square West. **Map** D1. **Tel** 873 0700.

Standing in the middle of Parnell Square is Europe's first purpose-built maternity hospital. Founded in 1745 by Dr Bartholomew Mosse, the design of the hospital is similar to that of Leinster House *(see p46).* The German-born architect Richard Castle designed both buildings. At the east end of the hospital is the Rotunda, after which the hospital is named. It was built in 1764 by John Ensor as Assembly Rooms to host fundraising functions and concerts. Franz Liszt gave a concert here in 1843.

On the first floor is a chapel featuring striking stained-glass windows and Rococo plaster-work and ceiling (1755) by the stuccodore Bartholomew

Cramillion. On the other side of the road from the hospital is Conway's Pub. Opened in 1745, it has been popular with expectant fathers for years.

Garden of Remembrance
Parnell Square. **Map** C1.
◯ dawn–dusk daily.

At the northern end of Parnell Square is a small, peaceful park, dedicated to the men and women who have died in the pursuit of Irish freedom. The Garden of Remembrance marks the spot where several leaders of the Easter Rising were held overnight before being taken to Kilmainham Gaol (see p81), and is also where the Irish Volunteers movement was formed in 1913.

Designed by Daithí Hanly, the garden was opened by President Eamon de Valera (see p18) in 1966, to mark the 50th anniversary of the Easter Rising. In the centre is a cruciform pool with a mosaic depicting broken swords, shields and spears, symbolizing peace. At one end of the garden is a large bronze sculpture by Oisín Kelly (1971) of the legendary *Children of Lir*, the children of King Lir who were changed into swans by their jealous stepmother.

Children of Lir in the Garden of Remembrance

Gallery of Writers at Dublin Writers' Museum

Dublin Writers' Museum
18 Parnell Square North. **Map** C1.
Tel 872 2077. ◯ Sep–May: 10am–5pm Mon–Sat (last adm 4:15pm), 11am–5pm Sun & public hols; Jun–Aug: 10am–6pm Mon–Fri (last adm 5:15pm). ● 25 & 26 Dec. 🖼
www.writersmuseum.com

Opened in 1991, the museum occupies an 18th-century townhouse. There are displays relating to Irish literature over the last thousand years, although there is little about writers in the latter part of the 20th century. The exhibits include paintings, manuscripts, letters, rare editions and mementos of Ireland's finest authors. There are many temporary exhibits and a lavishly decorated Gallery of Writers. The museum also hosts poetry readings and lectures. There is also a pleasant café and a specialist bookstore, which provides a useful out-of-print search service.

Hugh Lane Municipal Gallery of Modern Art
Charlemont House, Parnell Square North. **Map** C1. **Tel** 222 5550. ◯ 10am–6pm Tue–Thu, 10am–5pm Fri, Sat, 11am–5pm Sun. ● 24–26 Dec, public hols. 🖼 www.hughlane.ie

Noted art collector Sir Hugh Lane donated his valuable collection of Impressionist paintings to Dublin Corporation in 1905. However, the failure to find a suitable location for them prompted Lane to consider transferring his gift to the National Gallery in London. The Corporation then proposed Charlemont House, the townhouse of Lord Charlemont, who built Marino Casino (see p88) and Lane relented. However, in 1915, before Lane's revised will could be witnessed, he died on board the torpedoed liner *Lusitania*. This led to a 50-year dispute which has been resolved by Dublin Corporation and the National Gallery swapping the collection every five years. As well as the Lane bequest the gallery also has a sculpture hall with work by Rodin and others. There is also a collection of modern Irish paintings.

An exciting new addition is the contents of Francis Bacon's studio at 7 Reece Mews, London, donated by Bacon's sole heir, John Edwards, and reconstructed in the Gallery in its entirety.

A side extension, completed in 2006, has doubled the available exhibition space.

Sur la Plage (c. 1876) by Edgar Degas, Hugh Lane Municipal Gallery

The impressive façade of the King's Inns, on Constitution Hill

King's Inns ➑

Henrietta St/Constitution Hill.
Map B1. ◉ *to the public, except the gardens.*

This classically proportioned public building was founded in 1795 as a place of both residence and study for barristers in Dublin. The King's Inns was the name taken by the Irish lawyers' society upon Henry VIII declaring himself King of Ireland.

To build it, James Gandon, famous as the architect of the Custom House (*see p70*), chose to seal off the end of Henrietta Street, which was Dublin's first Georgian street and, at the time, one of the city's most fashionable addresses. In 1816, Francis Johnston added the graceful cupola, and the building was finally completed the following year.

Inside, there is a fine dining hall, and the Registry of Deeds (formerly the Preroga-tive Court). The west façade has two doorways flanked by elegant Classical caryatids (statues used in place of pillars) carved by sculptor Edward Smyth. The male figure, holding book and quill, is representa-tive of the law.

Statue at the
entrance to
King's Inns

Sadly, much of the area around Constitution Hill today is less attractive than it was in Georgian times. However, the King's Inns' gardens, which are open to the public, are still pleasant to stroll around.

Chief O'Neill's Viewing Tower ➒

Map A2. **Tel** 817 3838.
☐ *10am–5:30pm Mon–Sat, 11am–5:30pm Sun.* ◉

During the past few years, an ongoing programme of urban regeneration has transformed the look of the Smithfield neighbourhood, one of Dublin's oldest trading and residential areas. As part of this programme, the chimney of the Old Jameson Distillery (*see p75*) has been converted into a viewing tower. Now part of the Park Inn Hotel chain, the 56-m (185-ft) tall chimney comprises a glass-walled lift that takes visitors to a two-tiered glass-enclosed viewing platform. From here, vistors can enjoy unique 360-degree panoramic views over the city, as far as Dublin Bay.

Smithfield ➓

Map A2.

Laid out in the mid-17th century as a marketplace, Smithfield used to be one of Dublin's oldest trading and residential areas, playing host to people coming to the cattle- and horsefairs for which the area was famous. The traditional Horsefair still takes place here on the first Sunday of every month, even though the two-and-a-half-acre area has received a €3.5-million makeover and is subject to extensive property development.

The transformation of Smithfield Plaza, commonly known as Smithfield Square, beside the famous fruit and fish markets, is part of Dublin Council's Historical Area Regeneration Programme, a project set up in 1995 in response to the severe decline suffered by the area between 1940 and 1985. The remit of the programme was to make the inner city attractive again.

Children riding saddle-free through the cobbled streets of Smithfield market

The cobbled pedestrian plaza is atmospherically lit by 12 gas lighting masts, each 26 m (85 ft) high, and provides the city with its first dedicated venue for outdoor civic events.

The transformation of Smithfield also includes some riverside public housing, a hotel, several craft shops and a growing selection of bars and restaurants. The area is now said to be the largest purpose-built urban space in Europe, with an expanding legal and commercial district, too.

Horses tethered at the Sunday Horsefair

Old Jameson Distillery ⓫

Bow St. **Map** A2.
Tel 807 2355. ⬜ daily 9:30am–6pm (last tour at 5:30pm). ⬤ Good Fri, 25 & 26 Dec. 🅿 ♿ 🚻 🔲
www.jamesonwhiskey.com

Proof of significant investment in the emerging Smithfield area of Dublin's northside is evident in this large exhibition, set in a restored building that formed part of John Jameson's distillery. Whiskey was produced here from 1780 until 1971. While the place is run by Irish Distillers Limited, who are obviously keen to talk up their products (the four main names are Jameson, Paddy, Bushmills and John Power), it is an impressive, entertaining and educational experience. Visits start with a video, *Uisce Beatha* (the Water of Life; *uisce* meaning "water"

Sampling different whiskeys at the Old Jameson Distillery

and the origin of the word "whiskey"). Further whiskey-related facts are then explained to visitors in the 40-minute tour. This moves around displays set out as a working distillery with different rooms devoted to the various stages of whiskey production, from grain storage right through to bottling. The tour guides are keen to point how the barley drying process differs from that used in the production of Scotch whisky: in Ireland the grain is dried through clean dry air while in Scotland it is smoked over peat. They claim that this results in a smoother Irish tipple compared to its more smoky Scottish counterpart. At the end of the tour, visitors can test this claim in the nicely appointed bar.

IRISH WHISKEY

It is widely claimed that the Irish were the first to produce whiskey. This is quite possibly the case, since the monks spreading Christianity across Europe supposedly learnt the skills of distillation in the East where perfume was made. Some even believe that it was St Patrick who introduced the art. In the late 1800s and early 1900s Irish whiskey was superseded somewhat by the lighter blended Scotch. In addition, sales suffered in the United States as a result of the Prohibition. Today however, Irish whiskeys are enjoying a comeback and provide fierce competition for Scotch whiskies.

Old Bushmills *is a blended whiskey made from just one malt and a single grain. The end result is a pleasant blend of malty sweetness and aromatic dryness.*

Jameson 1780, *at 12 years old, has a classic smooth Jameson character. It is a hearty taste of Dublin's distilling heritage.*

Paddy *is the classic whiskey of Cork, Ireland's second city. It is firm-bodied, with the crisp finish typical of native Cork whiskeys.*

Power and Son's *Gold Label Irish, sometimes known as "Three Swallows", is a well-balanced and malty whiskey. Originally from Dublin, today it is very much a national brand.*

James Gandon's Four Courts overlooking the River Liffey

Four Courts ⓬

Inns Quay. **Map** B3. **Tel** 872 5555.
◯ 9:30am–12:30pm, 2–4:30pm
Mon–Fri (when courts in session).

Completed in 1796 by James Gandon, this majestic building was virtually gutted 120 years later during the Irish Civil War *(see p17)* when government forces bombarded anti-Treaty rebels into submission. The adjacent Public Records Office, with documents dating back to the 12th century, was destroyed by fire. In 1932, the main buildings were restored using Gandon's original design. A copper-covered lantern dome rises above the six-columned Corinthian portico, which is crowned with the figures of Moses, Justice, Mercy, Wisdom and Authority. This central section is flanked by two wings holding the four original courts: Common Pleas, Chancery,

Exchequer and King's Bench. It is possible to walk in to the central waiting hall under the grand dome. An information panel to the right of the entrance details the building's history and functions.

St Michan's Church ⓭

Church St. **Map** B3. **Tel** 872 4154.
◯ mid-Mar–Oct: 10am–12:45pm,
2–4:45pm Mon–Fri, 10am–12:45pm
Sat; Nov–mid-Mar: 12:30–3:30pm
Mon–Fri; 10am–12:45pm Sat. 🈂
🈂 🈂 🈂 limited.

Largely rebuilt in 1686 on the site of an 11th-century Hiberno-Viking church, the dull façade of St Michan's hides a more exciting interior. Deep in its vaults lie several bodies that have barely decomposed due to the dry atmosphere created by the church's magnesian limestone walls. Their

wooden caskets have cracked open, revealing the preserved bodies, complete with skin and hair. Among those thought to have been mummified in this way are the brothers John and Henry Sheares, leaders of the 1798 rebellion *(see p16)*, who were executed that year.

Other, less gory, attractions include the magnificent wood-carving of fruits and violins and other instruments above the choir. There is also an organ (1724) on which Handel is said to have played.

St Mary's Abbey Exhibition ⓮

Meetinghouse Lane. **Map** C2. **Tel**
833 1618. ◯ mid-Jun–mid-Sep:
10am–5pm Wed, Fri (last adm
4:30pm). 🈂 🈂 off season; 086 606
2729. **www**.heritageireland.ie

Founded by Benedictine monks in 1139, but then transferred to the Cistercian order eight years later, this was one of the largest and most important monasteries in medieval Ireland. When it was built, the surrounding land was peaceful countryside; to-day, what is left of this historically

Detail of woodcarving (c. 1724) at St Michan's Church

important abbey is hidden away in the sprawling back-streets that are found on the north side of the river Liffey.

As well as having control over extensive estates, including whole villages, mills and fisheries, the abbey acted as state treasury and meeting place for the Council of Ireland. It was during a council meeting in St Mary's that "Silken Thomas" Fitzgerald *(see p14)* renounced his allegiance to Henry VIII and marched out to raise the short-lived rebellion of 1534. The monastery was dissolved a few years later in 1539 and, during the 17th century, the site served as a quarry. Stone from St Mary's was pillaged and used in the construction of Essex Bridge (which was later replaced by Grattan Bridge in 1874), just to the south of the abbey.

Sadly, all that remains of the abbey today is the vaulted chamber of the old Chapter House. This houses a display on the history of the abbey and a model of how it would have looked 800 years ago.

The old vaulted Chapter House in St Mary's Abbey

St Mary's Church **⑮**

Mary St (at Wolfe Tone St). **Map** C2. **Tel** 828 0102. **www**.thechurch.ie

In among the produce stalls and family-run stores in the warren of streets to the west of O'Connell Street stands what was once one of the most important society churches in 18th- and 19th-century Dublin. Dating back to 1627, its design is usually credited to Sir William Robinson, the Surveyor General who also built the beautiful Royal Hospital Kilmainham *(see p84)*, and it is reckoned to be the first church in the city with a

Impressive organ in St Mary's Church

gallery. Famous past parishioners here include Arthur Guinness, who got married here in 1793, and Wolfe Tone, the leader of the United Irishmen, who was born within a stone's throw of the church and baptized here in the 1760s. The cross street and the small park to the rear of the church are named in his honour today. The playwright Sean O'Casey was also baptized at St Mary's in 1880. Church services finally ceased in the mid-1980s. The building now houses several bars, a café, restaurant and nightclub and is called The Church. All the listed features were restored by specialist craftsmen and a church-like feel has been preserved in the decor. Look out for the organ and impressive stained-glass windows.

Detail of carving in St Mary's Church

Ha'penny Bridge **⑯**

Map D3.

Linking Temple Bar and Liffey Street on the north bank of the river, this attractive high-arched footbridge is made of cast iron and is used by thousands of people every day to cross Dublin's river. It was built by John Windsor, an ironworker from Shropshire, England. One of Dublin's most popular and most photographed sights, it was originally named the Wellington Bridge, after the Duke of Wellington. Its official name today is in fact the Liffey Bridge, but it is also known simply as the Metal Bridge. Originally opened in 1816, the bridge got its better-known nickname from the halfpenny toll that was first levied on it. The toll was scrapped in 1919 but the nickname stuck and is still used with some fondness by Dubliners and visitors alike. A recent restoration job on the bridge, which included the installation of original period lanterns, has made it even more attractive. This is particularly true at night when it is lit up as people cross over it to go through Merchant's Arch and into the bustling nightlife of the Temple Bar area *(see pp58–9)* with all its pubs, clubs and restaurants.

The Ha'penny Bridge looking from Temple Bar to Liffey Street

FURTHER AFIELD

There are many interesting sights just outside Dublin. In the western suburbs is the Museum of Modern Art, housed in the splendid setting of the Royal Hospital Kilmainham. Phoenix Park, Europe's largest city park, offers the opportunity for a stroll in a leafy setting. Further north are the National Botanic Gardens, home to over 20,000 plant species from around the world. Nearby, Marino Casino is a fine example of Palladian architecture. The magnificent coastline is easily admired by taking the DART railway. The highlight of the riviera-like southern stretch is around Dalkey village, especially lovely Killiney Bay. One of the many Martello towers built as defences now houses a museum to James Joyce. To the northeast, slightly further from the centre, is Malahide Castle, once home of the Talbot family.

Michael Collins' gravestone

SIGHTS AT A GLANCE

Museums and Galleries
Collins Barracks **6**
Fry Model Railway Museum **14**
Guinness Storehouse **4**
James Joyce Tower **17**
Kilmainham Gaol **3**
Irish Museum of Modern Art/
    Royal Hospital Kilmainham **5**

Shaw's Birthplace **7**
Waterways Visitors' Centre **9**

Parks and Gardens
Dublin Zoo **2**
Glasnevin Cemetery **12**
National Botanic Gardens **11**
Phoenix Park **1**

Historic Buildings
Malahide Castle **13**
Marino Casino **10**

Towns and Villages
Ballsbridge **8**
Dalkey **18**
Dun Laoghaire **16**
Howth **15**
Killiney **19**

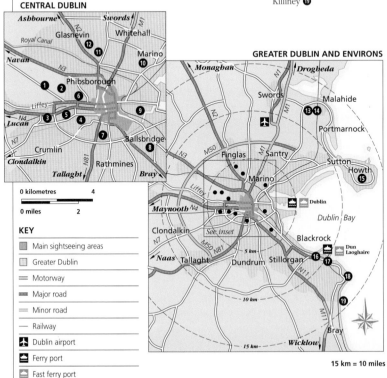

CENTRAL DUBLIN

GREATER DUBLIN AND ENVIRONS

0 kilometres   4
0 miles   2

KEY

▢ Main sightseeing areas
▢ Greater Dublin
═ Motorway
▬ Major road
═ Minor road
— Railway
✈ Dublin airport
⚓ Ferry port
⚓ Fast ferry port

15 km = 10 miles

◁ **Boat moored in Dun Laoghaire harbour at dusk**

Phoenix Park ❶

Park Gate, Conyngham Rd, Dublin
8. 🚌 *10, 37, 38, 39, 66, 67; plus
shuttle bus service from Heuston
(Park Gate St) through the park.* 🕐
7am–11pm daily. **Phoenix Park
Visitor Centre** *Tel 677 0095.* 🕐
*Nov–mid-Mar: 10am–5pm Wed–Sun;
mid- to end Mar & Oct: 10am–
5:30pm daily; Apr–Sep: 10am–6pm
daily (last adm: 45 mins before
closing).* 🍴 ♿ 🏠 **President's
House** 📷 *Oct– mid-Apr: 10:30am–
3:30pm Sat; mid-Apr–Sep: 10:30am–
4:30pm Sat.* **www.heritageireland.ie**

To the west of the city centre,
ringed by an 11-km (7-mile)
wall, is Europe's largest
enclosed city park. Phoenix
Park is over 700 ha (1,700
acres) in size. The name
"Phoenix" is said to be a
corruption of the Gaelic *Fionn
Uisce*, meaning "clear water".

The Phoenix Column topped by a
statue of the mythical bird

The **Phoenix Column** is crowned
by a statue of the mythical bird.
Phoenix Park originated in
1662, when the Duke of
Ormonde turned the land into
a deer park. Deer still roam in
the park today. In 1745 it was
landscaped and opened to the
public by Lord Chesterfield.

Near Park Gate is the lake-
side **People's Garden** – the only
part of the park which
has been cultivated. A
little further on is the
famous **Dublin Zoo**.

In addition to the
Phoenix Column, the
park has two other
striking monuments. The
Wellington Testimonial, a 63-
m (204-ft) obelisk, was begun
in 1817 and completed in
1861. It allegedly took so long
to be built because of the
Duke of Wellington's fall from
public favour. Its bronze
bas-reliefs were made from
captured French cannons.
The 27-m (90-ft) steel **Papal
Cross** marks the spot where
Pope John Paul II celebrated
Mass in front of more than
one million people in 1979.

Most Saturdays, the visitors'
centre issues tickets to the public for a free guided tour of
Áras an Uachtaráin, the Irish
President's official residence,
which was built within the
park in 1751. It was home to
various British viceroys before
becoming the residence of the
president in 1937. **Deerfield**,
also dating to the 18th century,
is the residence of the US
Ambassador and was once the
home of Lord Cavendish, the
British Chief Secretary for
Ireland who was murdered in
1882 by an Irish nationalist.
Ashtown Castle, a restored

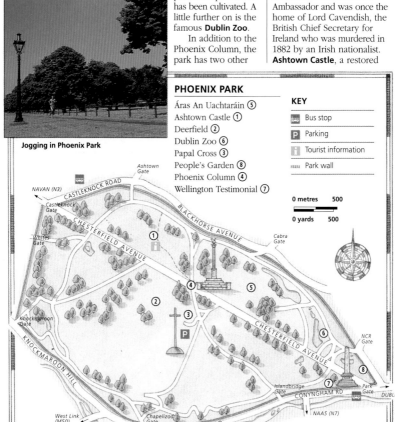

Jogging in Phoenix Park

PHOENIX PARK

Áras An Uachtaráin ⑤
Ashtown Castle ①
Deerfield ②
Dublin Zoo ⑥
Papal Cross ③
People's Garden ⑧
Phoenix Column ④
Wellington Testimonial ⑦

KEY

🚌 Bus stop

🅿 Parking

ℹ Tourist information

▨▨▨ Park wall

0 metres   500

0 yards   500

Orang-utan mother and baby at Dublin Zoo

17th-century tower house, is adjacent to the Phoenix Park Visitor Centre.

Five times the size of Hyde Park in London and over double the size of New York's Central Park, Phoenix Park can fit playing fields for Gaelic football, hurling and polo, plus running, cycling and horseriding trails.

Visitors watching giraffe at Dublin Zoo

Dublin Zoo ❷

Phoenix Park, Dublin 8. **Tel** *474 8900.* 🚌 *10, 10A, 25, 25A, 26, 66, 66A, 66B, 67, 67A, 68, 69, 90 (also Phoenix Park shuttle).* 🗓 *Mar–Sep: 9:30am–6pm daily (from 10:30am Sun); Oct–Feb: 9:30am– dusk daily (from 10:30am Sun).* 🖼 ♿ 🍴 🛗
www.dublinzoo.ie

Opened in 1830 with one wild boar and an admission price of 6d (2.5 pence), Dublin Zoo was one of the world's first zoos. In its long history, there have been many changes, and today's facility would be unrecognizable to its first

visitors. A recent development is the impressive African Plains sector. This 13-ha (32-acre) savannah, with a large lake and mature woodland, has doubled the size of the zoo and is home to giraffe, rhino, lion, zebra, hippo and cheetah.

Other sectors include the World of Primates, World of Cats, and Fringes of the Arctic, with highlights such as the orang-utan, Sumatran tiger, snow leopard and grey wolf.

Dublin Zoo has always prided itself on its breeding programme and cooperates with zoos worldwide in the conservation of endangered species. Lion breeding began in 1857, and 670 lions have been born here, including the lion that roars at the start of MGM movies.

Education is another aspect of the zoo's work: visitors will find skulls, skins, eggs and other objects at the Discovery Centre. Kids also enjoy the City Farm and the Nakuru Safari Train that runs daily in summer and at weekends in winter from the African Plains.

Kilmainham Gaol ❸

Inchicore Rd, Kilmainham, Dublin 8. **Tel** *453 5984.* 🚌 *51B, 78A, 79, 79A.* 🗓 *Apr–Sep: 9:30am–6pm daily; Oct–Mar: 9:30am–5pm Mon–Sat, 10am–6pm Sun (last adm 1hr before closing).* 🌐 *25 & 26 Dec.* 🖼 🎬 🏠 💻 **www**.heritageireland.ie

A long tree-lined avenue runs from the Royal Hospital Kilmainham to the grim, grey

bulk of Kilmainham Gaol. The building dates from 1796, but was restored in the 1960s. From the 1790s to the mid-19th century, Kilmainham was used as a transportation depot for prisoners bound for Australia.

During its 130 years as a prison, Kilmainham housed many of those involved in the fight for Irish independence, including Robert Emmet *(see p16)* and Charles Stewart Parnell *(p17)*. The last prisoner held during the Civil War was Eamon de Valera *(p18)*, the future President of Ireland, who was released on 16 July 1924, just prior to the gaol's closure.

The tour of the Gaol starts in the chapel, where Joseph Plunkett married Grace Gifford just a few hours before he faced the firing squad for his part in the 1916 Rising *(see p17)*. The tour ends in the prison yard where Plunkett's badly wounded colleague James Connolly, unable to stand up, was strapped into a chair before being shot. It also passes the dank cells of those involved in the 1798, 1803, 1848 and 1867 uprisings, as well as a hard-labour yard. Of the 16 executions that took place in the few days following the Easter Rising, 14 were carried out here. There is a video presentation, and in the exhibition space are pieces depicting various events which took place in the gaol until it finally closed in 1924. There are also personal mementos of some of the former inmates.

Doorway and gates of the historic Kilmainham Gaol

Tasting a pint of Guinness at a local pub

Guinness Storehouse ❹

St James's Gate, Dublin 8. *Tel 408 4800.* 🚌 *51B, 78A, 123.* ⏰ *9:30am–5pm daily (8pm Jul–Aug).* 🚫 *Good Fri, 24–26 Dec.* 📷 ♿ 🍴 🛍 📷 *www. guinness-storehouse.com*

The Guinness Storehouse is a new development based in St James's Gate Brewery, the original house of Guinness, now completely remodelled. This 1904 listed building covers nearly four acres of floor space over seven floors built around a huge pint glass atrium. The first impression the visitor has is of walking into a large glass pint with light spilling down from above and a copy of the original lease signed by Arthur Guinness enshrined on the floor. The Ingredients section is next where visitors can touch, smell and feel the ingredients through interactive displays. The tour continues into an authentic Georgian anteroom to 'meet' Arthur Guinness and see him at work. The Brewing Process is a noisy, steamy and 'hoppy' area giving the impression of brewing all around with full explanation of the process. The historical development of Guinness cooperage is accompanied by video footage of the craft. Models and displays tell the story of Guinness's transportation, the appeal of Guinness worldwide, and their popular advertising campaigns. The tour ends with a generous tasting of draught Guinness, either in the traditional Brewery Bar or the rooftop Gravity Bar with 360-degree views across Dublin.

The Brewing of Guinness

Label from a Guinness bottle

Guinness is a black beer, known as "stout", renowned for its distinctive malty flavour and smooth, creamy head. From its humble beginnings over 200 years ago, the Guinness brewery site at St James's Gate now covers 26 ha (65 acres) and has its own water and electricity supply. It is the largest brewery in Europe and exports beers to more than 120 countries. Other brands owned by Guinness include Harp Lager and Smithwick's Ale.

HOW GUINNESS IS MADE
The four main ingredients used to brew Guinness are barley, hops, yeast and water which, contrary to popular belief, comes from the Wicklow Mountains rather than the River Liffey.

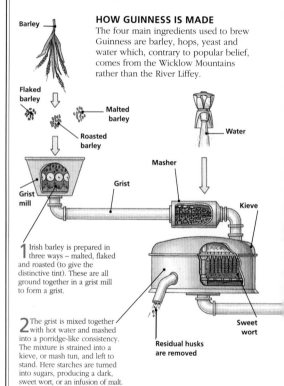

Barley

Flaked barley

Malted barley

Roasted barley

Grist mill

Grist

Water

Masher

Kieve

Sweet wort

Residual husks are removed

1 Irish barley is prepared in three ways – malted, flaked and roasted (to give the distinctive tint). These are all ground together in a grist mill to form a grist.

2 The grist is mixed together with hot water and mashed into a porridge-like consistency. The mixture is strained into a kieve, or mash tun, and left to stand. Here starches are turned into sugars, producing a dark, sweet wort, or an infusion of malt.

Guinness advertising *has become almost as famous as the product itself. Since 1929, when the first advertisement announced that "Guinness is Good for You", poster and television advertising campaigns have employed many amusing images of both animals and people.*

ARTHUR GUINNESS

Arthur Guinness

In December 1759, 34-year-old Arthur Guinness signed a 9,000-year lease at an annual rent of £45 to take over St James's Gate Brewery, which had lain vacant for almost ten years. At the time the brewing industry in Dublin was at a low ebb – the standard of ale was much criticized and in rural Ireland beer was virtually unknown, as whiskey, gin and poteen were the more favoured drinks. Furthermore, Irish beer was under threat from imports. Guinness started brewing ale, but was also aware of a black ale called porter, produced in London. This new beer was so called because of its popularity with porters at Billingsgate and Covent Garden markets. Guinness decided to stop making ales and develop his own recipe for porter (the word "stout" was not used until the 1920s). So successful was the switch that he made his first export shipment in 1769.

Engraving (c. 1794) of a satisfied customer

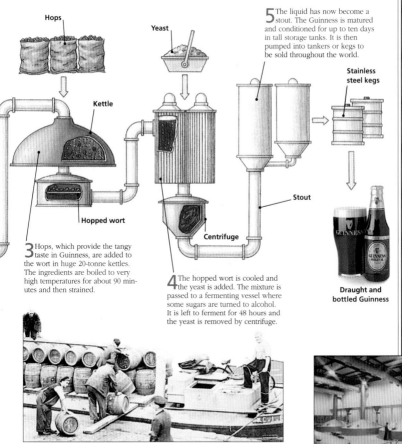

Hops

Yeast

5 The liquid has now become a stout. The Guinness is matured and conditioned for up to ten days in tall storage tanks. It is then pumped into tankers or kegs to be sold throughout the world.

Stainless steel kegs

Kettle

Hopped wort

Stout

Centrifuge

3 Hops, which provide the tangy taste in Guinness, are added to the wort in huge 20-tonne kettles. The ingredients are boiled to very high temperatures for about 90 minutes and then strained.

4 The hopped wort is cooled and the yeast is added. The mixture is passed to a fermenting vessel where some sugars are turned to alcohol. It is left to ferment for 48 hours and the yeast is removed by centrifuge.

Draught and bottled Guinness

The Guinness brewery *has relied heavily on water transport since its first export was shipped to England in 1769. The barges which, up until 1961, made the short trip with their cargo down the Liffey to Dublin Port, were a familiar sight on the river. Once at port, the stout would be loaded on to huge tanker ships for worldwide distribution.*

Steel kettles used in modern-day brewing

The elegant façade of the Royal Hospital Kilmainham

Irish Musem of Modern Art – Royal Hospital Kilmainham ❺

Kilmainham, Dublin 8. *Tel 612 9900.* Heuston Station. 26, 51, 51B, 78A, 79, 90, 123. **Irish Museum of Modern Art** 10am–5:30pm Tue, Thu–Sat; 10:30am–5:30pm Wed; noon–5:30pm Sun & public hols (last adm: 5:15pm). Good Fri, 24–26, 29 Dec. limited. **www**.modernart.ie

Ireland's finest surviving 17th-century building was laid out in 1680, and styled on Les Invalides in Paris. It was built by Sir William Robinson, who also built Marsh's Library *(see p61)*, as a home for 300 wounded soldiers, rather than as a hospital as its name suggests. It retained this role until 1927 and was the first such institution in the British Isles, erected even before the Chelsea Hospital in London. When it was completed, people were so impressed by its elegant Classical symmetry that it was suggested it would be better used as the main campus of Trinity College. The building's design is functional, but the Baroque chapel has fine wood carvings and intricate heraldic stained glass. The plaster ceiling is a replica of the original, which fell down in 1902.

In 1991, the hospital's former residential quarters were imaginatively converted

to house the **Irish Museum of Modern Art**. The collection includes a cross-section of Irish and international modern and contemporary art. Works are displayed on a rotating basis and include group and solo shows, retrospectives and special visiting exhibitions.

National Museum at Collins Barracks ❻

See pp86–7.

Shaw's Birthplace ❼

33 Synge St, Dublin 8. *Tel 475 0854.* 16, 16A, 19, 19A, 122. May–Sep: 10am– 1pm & 2–5pm Mon–Fri, 2–5pm Sat, Sun & public hols (groups by arrangement). Wed. **www**.visitdublin.com

Playwright and Nobel prize-winner George Bernard Shaw was born in this Victorian house on 26 July 1856. In 1876 he followed his mother to London. She had left four years

The recreated Victorian kitchen in Shaw's Birthplace

earlier with her daughters, fed up with her husband's drinking habits. In London, Shaw met his wife-to-be Charlotte Payne-Townsend. He never returned to Dublin, remaining in England until his death.

Inside the house, visitors can see the young Shaw's bedroom and the kitchen where the author drank "much tea out of brown delft left to 'draw' on the hob until it was pure tannin". Also on view are the nursery, the maid's room and the drawing room.

Although there is little in the museum on Shaw's productive years, the house does give an interesting insight into the lives of a typical middle-class Victorian family.

GEORGE BERNARD SHAW

Born in Dublin in 1856, Shaw moved to England at the age of 20 where he began his literary career somewhat unsuccessfully as a critic and novelist. It was not until his first play was produced in 1892 that his career finally took off. One of the most prolific writers of his time, Shaw's many works include *Heartbreak House, Man and Superman*, and, perhaps most famously, *Pygmalion*, which was later adapted into the successful musical *My Fair Lady*. He often attacked conventional thinking and was a supporter of many causes, including vegetarianism and feminism. He lived an abstemious life and died in 1950 at the age of 94.

Ballsbridge

Co Dublin. 🚌 *4, 4A, 7, 8, 18, 45.*

Laid out mostly between 1830 and 1860, the suburb of Ballsbridge is a very exclusive part of Dublin, attracting many wealthy residents. Many of the streets are named after military heroes. Running off Pembroke Road the elegant tree-lined streets such as Raglan Road and Wellington Road are lined with prestigious red-brick houses. The area is also home to several foreign embassies – look for the striking cylindrical US Embassy building at the junction of Northumberland and Eglin roads – as well as a number of upmarket hotels and guesthouses.

Close to Baggot Street Bridge is a statue of the poet Patrick Kavanagh, depicted reclining on a bench. This attractive stretch of the Grand Canal at Lower Baggot Street was one of the poet's favourite parts of Dublin.

The southeast sector of Ballsbridge, just across the River Dodder, is dominated by the Royal Dublin Society Showgrounds (often simply abbreviated to RDS). Founded in 1731 to promote science, the arts and agriculture, the Royal Dublin Society was an instrumental mover behind the creation of most of Ireland's national museums and

Late 18th-century engraving of a passenger ferry passing Harcourt Lock on the Grand Canal, taken from a painting by James Barralet

DUBLIN'S CANALS

The affluent Georgian era witnessed the building of the Grand and Royal canals linking Dublin with the River Shannon and the west coast. These two canals became the main arteries of trade and public transport in Ireland from the 1760s until the coming of the railways, which took much of the passenger business, almost a century later. However, the canals continued to carry freight until after World War II, finally closing to commercial traffic in 1960. Today the canals are well maintained and used mainly for pleasure-boating, cruising and fishing.

galleries. The two major events at the sprawling yet graceful showgrounds are the Spring Show in May and the Horse Show in August *(see p27)*. Throughout the rest of the year the showground plays host to various conventions, exhibitions and concerts.

The Lansdowne Road stadium, the home of the Irish national rugby and soccer teams, is another Ballsbridge landmark. It is undergoing redevelopment to become a 50,000-seat stadium, due for completion in 2010.

Stretch of the Grand Canal near the Waterways Visitors' Centre

Waterways Visitors' Centre  ❾

Grand Canal Quay, Dublin 2. *Tel* 677 7510. 🚇 *DART to Grand Canal Dock.* 🚌 *2, 3.* ⬤ *closed for refurbishment.* 📷 📹 *on request.* **www**.waterwaysireland.org

Fifteen minutes' walk from Trinity College along Pearse Street, the Waterways Visitors' Centre overlooks the Grand Canal Basin. Audiovisual displays and models illustrate the history of Ireland's inland waterways. One of the most interesting focuses on their construction: in the 1700s, canals were often called "navigations" and the men who built them were "navigators", a term that was shortened to "navvies". There are also exhibits on the wildlife found in the canals and surrounding marshlands.

The Royal Dublin Showground at Ballsbridge

The National Museum at Collins Barracks **6**

Silver coffee pot

Commissioned by William III in 1700, this was the largest barracks in his domain, with living accommodation for over 5,000 soldiers. Originally known as Dublin Barracks, it was renamed Collins Barracks after Michael Collins *(see p18)* following Irish independence. This decorative arts and history site of the National Museum *(see pp44–5)* displays the fine exhibits, from furniture to silver, by making full use of up-to-date technology including a multimedia catalogue and clever lighting. Currently occupying only two blocks, the museum is planned to extend eventually to fill all four wings.

Scientific Instruments
The fascinating display of surveying and navigation instruments includes this astrolabe (c.1580–90), which was made in Prague by Erasmus Habermel.

South block

Entrance

Ground floor

East block

Skinners Alley Chair
Dating back to c.1730, this impressive gilt chair is part of the museum's collection of Irish period furniture. It was made for the Protestant aldermen of the Corporation of Skinners Alley, who were removed from the Dublin Assembly by James II. The society was eventually incorporated into the Orange Order.

STAR EXHIBITS

★ William Smith O'Brien Gold Cup

★ Irish Silver

★ The Fonthill Vase

★ Irish Silver
This silver-gilt bowl by Thomas Bolton dates from 1703. Also known as a monteith, it was used for cooling wine glasses.

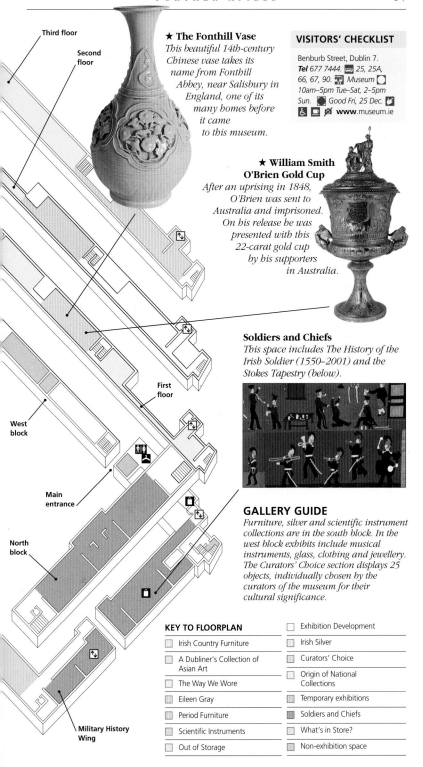

★ **The Fonthill Vase**
This beautiful 14th-century Chinese vase takes its name from Fonthill Abbey, near Salisbury in England, one of its many homes before it came to this museum.

VISITORS' CHECKLIST

Benburb Street, Dublin 7.
Tel 677 7444. 🚌 25, 25A,
66, 67, 90. 🚇 Museum ◯
10am–5pm Tue–Sat, 2–5pm
Sun. ◯ Good Fri, 25 Dec. ♿
♿ 🔲 📷 www.museum.ie

★ **William Smith O'Brien Gold Cup**
After an uprising in 1848, O'Brien was sent to Australia and imprisoned. On his release he was presented with this 22-carat gold cup by his supporters in Australia.

Soldiers and Chiefs
This space includes The History of the Irish Soldier (1550–2001) and the Stokes Tapestry (below).

Third floor

Second floor

First floor

West block

Main entrance

North block

Military History Wing

GALLERY GUIDE
Furniture, silver and scientific instrument collections are in the south block. In the west block exhibits include musical instruments, glass, clothing and jewellery. The Curators' Choice section displays 25 objects, individually chosen by the curators of the museum for their cultural significance.

KEY TO FLOORPLAN

- ☐ Irish Country Furniture
- ☐ A Dubliner's Collection of Asian Art
- ☐ The Way We Wore
- ☐ Eileen Gray
- ☐ Period Furniture
- ☐ Scientific Instruments
- ☐ Out of Storage
- ☐ Exhibition Development
- ☐ Irish Silver
- ☐ Curators' Choice
- ☐ Origin of National Collections
- ☐ Temporary exhibitions
- ▨ Soldiers and Chiefs
- ☐ What's in Store?
- ▨ Non-exhibition space

Marino Casino ⑩

Cherrymount Crescent, off Malahide Rd. *Tel* 833 1618. ☐ DART to Clontarf. ▥ 20A, 20B, 27A, 27B, 42, 42C, 123 IMP. ◯ Mar, Apr & Nov: noon–5pm Sat & Sun; May & Oct: 10am–5pm daily; Jun–Sep: 10am–6pm daily. For group bookings outside these times, call 086 606 2729. ▨ ▧ obligatory (last tour: 45 mins before closing). **www**.heritageireland.ie

This delightful little villa, designed by Sir William Chambers in the 1760s for Lord Charlemont, now sits next to a busy road. Originally built as a summer house for the Marino Estate, the villa survives today although the main house was pulled down in 1921. The Casino is one of the finest examples of Neo-Classical architecture in Ireland. Some innovative features were used in its construction, including chimneys disguised as urns and hollow columns that accommodate drains.

Outside, four fine carved stone lions stand guard at each of the corners. The building's squat, compact exterior conceals 16 rooms arranged on three floors around a central staircase. The ground floor comprises a spacious hall and a saloon, with beautiful silk hangings. On the first floor is the state bedroom.

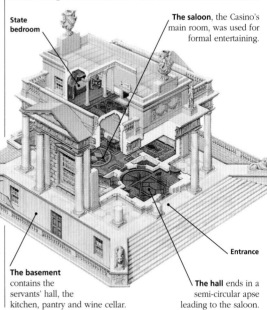

State bedroom

The saloon, the Casino's main room, was used for formal entertaining.

Entrance

The basement contains the servants' hall, the kitchen, pantry and wine cellar.

The hall ends in a semi-circular apse leading to the saloon.

Spectacular giant water lilies in the Lily House, National Botanic Gardens

National Botanic Gardens ⑪

Botanic Ave, Glasnevin, Dublin 9. *Tel* 857 0909. ▥ 13, 19, 19A, 83, 134. ◯ Apr–Oct: 9am–6pm daily; Nov–Mar: 9am–4:30pm daily. ⬤ 25 Dec. ▯ ♿ ▧ free Sun at 2:30pm. **www**.botanicgardens.ie

Opened in 1795, these gardens are home to Ireland's foremost centre of botany and horticulture. They still possess an old-world feel, thanks to the beautiful cast-iron Palm House and other curvilinear glasshouses. These were built between 1843 and 1869 by Richard Turner, who was also responsible for the Palm House at Kew Gardens, London, and the glasshouses in Belfast's Botanic Gardens. The 20-ha (48-acre) park contains over 16,000 different plant species. A particularly attractive feature is the colourful display of Victorian carpet bedding. Other highlights include a renowned rose garden and rich collections of cacti and orchids. Pampas grass and the giant lily were first grown in Europe here.

One path, known as Yew Walk, has trees that date back to the early 18th century and there is also a giant redwood that towers to 30 m (100 ft).

Glasnevin Cemetery ⑫

Finglas Rd, Glasnevin. *Tel* 830 1133. ▥ 40, 40A, 40B from Parnell St, 40C. ◯ 8am–4:30pm daily.

Originally known as Prospect Cemetery, this is Ireland's largest graveyard, with

Impressive gravestones in Glasnevin Cemetery

approximately 1.2 million people buried here. It was established by Daniel O'Connell in 1832 and was viewed as a great achievement on his part, since Catholics were previously unable to conduct graveside ceremonies because of the Penal Laws.

O'Connell's endeavours have been rewarded with the most conspicuous monument – a 51-m (167-ft) tall roundtower in the early Irish Christian style stands over his crypt.

While the maze of head-stones exhibits a tremendous variety of designs, none, apart from O'Connell's, has been allowed by the cemetery's committee to be too resplend-ent. However the graves conjure up a very Irish feel with high crosses and insignia such as shamrocks, harps and Irish wolfhounds.

The most interesting sector is the oldest part by Prospect Square, on the far right-hand side. Look for the two watch-towers built into the medieval-looking walls. These were erected as lookouts for the bodysnatchers hired by 19th-century surgeons. Before the Anatomy Act permitted corpses to be donated to science, this was the only way medical students could learn. Tours are available to visit the graves of people of interest, such as Charles Stewart Parnell and Eamon De Valera. A small Republican plot holds the remains of Countess Constance Markievicz and Maud Gonne MacBride, while the body of poet Gerard Manley Hopkins lies in the Jesuit Plot.

Glasnevin also reveals some interesting landscaping; the paths that run between the plots follow the same routes as the original woodland trails. Copses of mature sycamore and oak have been maintained while some of the more interesting imports among the thousand trees to be found here include a Califor-nian Giant Sequoia and a Cedar of Lebanon.

The oak-beamed Great Hall at Malahide Castle

Malahide Castle ⑬

Malahide, Co Dublin. 🚆 ⏹ *42.*
***Tel** 846 2184.* ⬜ *Apr–Sep: 10am–5pm Mon–Sat, 10am–6pm Sun, public hols; Oct–Mar: 10am– 5pm Mon–Sat, 11am–5pm Sun, public hols.* 📷 🛒 ♿ *last tours 4:30pm.* www.visitdublin.com

Near the seaside dormitory town of Malahide stands a huge castle set in 100 ha (250 acres) of grounds. The castle's core dates from the 14th century but later additions, such as its rounded towers, have given it a classic fairy-tale appearance. Originally a fortress, the building served as a stately home for the Talbot family until 1973. They were staunch supporters of James II: the story goes that, on the day of the Battle of the Boyne in 1690 *(see p15),* 14 members of the family breakfasted here; none came back for supper.

Guided tours take in the impressive oak-beamed Great Hall, the Oak Room with its carved panelling, and the castle's collection of 18th-century Irish furniture. Part of the Portrait Collection, on loan from the National Gallery *(see*

Candelabra at Malahide Castle

pp48–51), can be seen here. It includes portraits of the Talbot family, and other figures such as Wolfe Tone *(see p16).*

Fry Model Railway Museum ⑭

Malahide Castle grounds, Malahide, Co Dublin. ***Tel** 846 3779.* ⏹ *42 from Beresford Place, near Busáras.* 🚆 ⬜ *Apr–Sep: 10am–1pm, 2–5pm Thu–Sat, Mon, Tue; 2–6pm Sun, public hols.* ⬛ *Wed & Oct–Mar.* 📷 ♿ www.visitdublin.com

Set in the grounds of Mala-hide Castle, this collection of handmade models of Irish trains and trams was started by Cyril Fry, a railway engi-neer and draughtsman, in the 1920s. It is one of the largest such displays in the world. Running on a 32-mm wide (0-gauge) track, each detailed piece is made to scale and journeys through a landscape featuring the major Dublin landmarks, including the River Liffey complete with model barges. As well as his-toric trains, there are also models of the DART line, trains, buses and ferries.

A smaller room exhibits static displays of memorabilia and larger-scale models.

Howth ⓯

Co Dublin. 🚃 *DART.* **Howth Castle grounds** ⬜ *8am–sunset daily.*

The commercial fishing town of Howth marks the northern limit of Dublin Bay. Before Dun Laoghaire, or Kingstown as it was known then, took over, Howth was the main harbour for Dublin.

Howth Head, a huge rocky mass, has lovely views of the bay. A footpath runs around the tip of Howth Head, which is known locally as the "Nose". Nearby is Baily Lighthouse (1814). Sadly, much of this area – some of Ireland's prime real estate – has suffered from building development.

To the west of the town is Howth Castle, which dates back to Norman times. Its grounds are particularly beautiful in May and June when the rhododendrons and azaleas are in full bloom. The National Transport Museum in the grounds is worth a visit.

Ireland's Eye, an islet and bird sanctuary where puffins nest, can be reached by a short boat trip from Howth.

Yachts anchored in Dun Laoghaire harbour

Dun Laoghaire ⓰

Co Dublin. 🚃 *DART.* **National Maritime Museum** *Tel 280 0969.* **Comhaltas Ceoltóirí Éireann** *Tel 280 0295.* ⬜ *music Tue, Wed, Fri & Sat nights, céilís Fri.* 🗓 🍴 📷 **Lambert Puppet Theatre** *Tel 280 0974.* ⬜ *for performances Sat & Sun 3:30pm.* 🗓

Dublin's southern ferry port and yachting centre, with its bright villas, parks and palm trees, makes a surprising introduction to Ireland, usually known for its grey dampness. For a time Dun Laoghaire (pronounced Dunleary) was called Kingstown, after a visit by King George IV of England in 1821. Its original name was restored under the Free State in 1921, though the building of a rail line to Dublin in 1834 resulted in the demolition of the original *dún* or fort after which it is named.

Many visitors arriving on the ferry head straight for Dublin or the countryside. However, the town offers some magnificent walks around the harbour and to the lighthouse along the east pier. The pretty **People's Park** at the end of George's Street has a coffee shop and hosts a flower show on the second weekend in August and a farmer's market every Sunday. The outlying villages of Sandycove and Dalkey can be reached via "The Metals"; a footpath that runs alongside the railway line.

In the Mariners' Church is the **National Maritime Museum**, now under renovation. Exhibits include a longboat used by French officers during Wolfe Tone's unsuccessful invasion at Bantry in 1796.

Just up the road (or DART line) in Monkstown's Belgrave Square, is the **Comhaltas Ceoltóirí Éireann**, Ireland's main centre for traditional music and dancing, with regular music sessions and *ceilís* (dances). Nearby, the **Lambert Puppet Theatre** on Clifton Lane offers classic pantomime fun for kids by the creators of beloved children's TV show *Wanderly Wagon.*

Martello Tower at Howth Head just north of Dublin

James Joyce Tower ⓱

Sandycove, Co Dublin. **Tel** 280 9265.
🚇 DART to Sandycove. ⬜ Apr–Sep:
10am–5pm Mon–Sat, 2–6pm Sun,
public hols. ⬤ 1–2pm weekdays. 📷

Standing on a rocky promontory above the village of Sandycove is this Martello tower. It is one of 15 defensive towers which were erected between Dublin and Bray in 1804 to withstand a threatened invasion by Napoleon. They were named after a tower on Cape Mortella in Corsica. One hundred years later James Joyce (see p23) stayed in this tower for a week as the guest of Oliver St John Gogarty, poet and model for the Ulysses character Buck Mulligan. Gogarty rented the tower for a mere £8 per year. Today, inside the squat 12-m (40-ft) tower's granite walls is a small museum with some of Joyce's correspondence, personal belongings, such as his guitar, cigar case and walking stick, and his death mask. There are also photographs and several first editions of his works, including a deluxe edition (1935) of Ulysses illustrated by Henri Matisse. The roof, originally a gun platform but later used as a sunbathing deck by Gogarty, affords

Guitar at the museum, James Joyce Tower

marvellous views across Dublin Bay. Directly below the tower is the Forty Foot Pool, which was traditionally an all-male nude bathing spot, but is now open to both sexes.

Dalkey ⓲

Co Dublin. 🚇 DART.

Dalkey was once known as the "Town of Seven Castles", but only two of these fortified mansions, dating from the 15th and 16th centuries, now remain. They are both on the main street of this attractive village whose tight, winding roads and charming villas give it a Mediterranean feel.

A little way offshore is tiny Dalkey Island, a rocky bird sanctuary with a Martello tower and a medieval Benedictine church, both now in a poor state of repair. In summer the island can be reached by a boat ride from the town's Coliemore Harbour. The island was, at one time, held by Danish pirates. In the 18th century, a Dublin club used to gather on the island to crown a mock "King of Dalkey" and his officers of state. Originally done simply for fun, the ceremony was stopped in 1797 by Lord Clare when it became a political issue. It began again in the late 1970s.

Shopfronts lining the main street of Dalkey village

Killiney ⓳

Co Dublin. 🚇 DART to Dalkey or Killiney.

South of Dalkey, the coastal road climbs uphill before tumbling down into the winding leafy lanes around Killiney village. The route offers one of the most scenic vistas on this stretch of the east coast, with views that are often compared to those across the Bay of Naples in Italy. Howth Head is clearly visible to the north, with Bray Head (see p116) and the foothills of the Wicklow Mountains (see p113) to the south. There is another exhilarating view from the top of windswept Killiney Hill Park, off Victoria Road. It is well worth tackling the steep trail up from the village to see it. Down below is the popular pebbly beach, Killiney Strand.

View southwards from Killiney Hill over Killiney Bay towards the Wicklow Mountains

THREE GUIDED WALKS

The scale of the city and the lack of many hills make Dublin an ideal place for walking. Many of the tourist attractions and the loveliest Georgian squares are within short distances of each other. The weather can be changeable, but that is a good excuse to drop into a local pub for a drink until the rain clears up.

Draught and bottled Guinness

The following walks give you a sense of three very different faces of the city. You can discover remnants of the old Viking town around Christ Church Cathedral; follow in the footsteps of Dublin's best-known literary figures; or take a trip to the nearby medieval village of Dalkey. There, you can enjoy great views of Dublin Bay and the beautiful Wicklow Mountains, only a short distance away. In addition to these walks, each of the three areas in the *Area-by-Area* section of the book offers a short walk on its *Street-by-Street* map.

CHOOSING A WALK

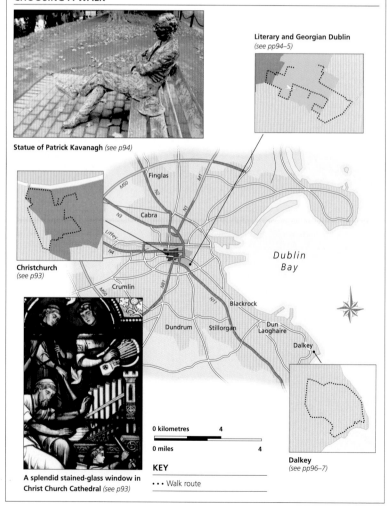

Statue of Patrick Kavanagh (see p94)

Literary and Georgian Dublin (see pp94–5)

Christchurch (see p93)

Dublin Bay

Finglas

Cabra

Crumlin

Dundrum   Stillorgan

Blackrock

Dun Laoghaire

Dalkey

Dalkey (see pp96–7)

A splendid stained-glass window in Christ Church Cathedral (see p93)

0 kilometres   4

0 miles   4

KEY

••• Walk route

A 45-Minute Walk Around Christchurch

Although every part of Dublin boasts a rich heritage, it is in Christchurch, at the heart of the original Viking town, that the layers of history lie thickest on the ground. Much evidence of the past has sadly been lost through development; however, a few precious hints remain, including sections of the city wall and street names that suggest past uses, stories and personalities.

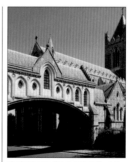

The bridge to the Synod Hall, part of Christ Church Cathedral (7)

Begin at the grand entrance to **City Hall** (1) *(see p55)* and head up Parliament Street towards the Liffey. You will pass an old sign for **Thomas Reade's Cutlers** (2), a 17th-century sword shop. Turn left into **Essex Gate** (3), one of the old entrances into the town. If you look through the ground-level bar grille of the corner building on Exchange Street, it is possible to see the base of **Isolde's Tower** (4), part of the 13th-century Anglo-Norman wall. Go down Essex Street West and stop for a coffee at **Cultivate** (5). Continue to Fishamble Street (6), named after the fish market that was located here in medieval times.

Cross over to John's Lane East, behind the spectacularly imposing **Christ Church Cathedral** (7) *(see pp64–5)*, Ireland's oldest cathedral. Viewing windows allow you to admire a section of the Hiberno-Norse town wall, located in the basement of the **Civic Offices** (8).

Head up Winetavern Street, on to Merchant's Quay and pause at **Father Matthew Bridge** (9), site of the original ford over the Liffey where the city was founded. Stop for a

drink at the **Brazen Head** (10) *(see p146)*, the city's oldest pub. Turn left onto Cook Street and cross the grounds of **St Audoen's Church** (11) *(see pp62–3)* via its famous arch, the last remaining gateway of the old city. Turn right and follow Thomas Street West

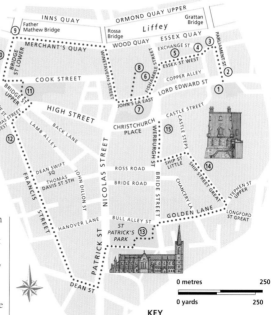

until the crossroads with St Augustine Street. This former Gaelic crossing point pre-dates the Vikings. Go down **Francis Street** (12), lined with a number of attractive antiques shops. Turn left towards **St Patrick's Cathedral** (13) *(see p61)*, Ireland's largest church. Cross the grounds to Golden Lane and turn left onto Ship Street Great, behind ancient **Dublin Castle** (14) *(see pp56–7)*. Follow Ship

Street Little to **St Werburgh's Church** (15) *(see p62)*, and back on to Christchurch Place where you can catch a bus to various points across the city.

The sign for Thomas Reade's Cutlers, a 17th-century sword shop (2)

TIPS FOR WALKERS

Starting point: *City Hall.*
Length: *2.5 km (1.5 miles).*
Getting there: *Buses 49X, 50, 50X, 51B, 77X, 78A, 123 and 206 to Christchurch Place. Stopping-off points: Cultivate for a Fairtrade coffee; the Brazen Head for a pint or Guinness stew; and Leo Burdock's (see p141) for the best fish 'n' chips in Dublin.*

KEY

• • • Walk route

A 90-Minute Walk Through Literary And Georgian Dublin

Dublin has an enviable literary heritage and, as a result, there are endless routes one could take to follow in the footsteps of world-famous poets, dramatists and novelists. The walk detailed below passes through some of the city's loveliest Georgian squares and parks and along an attractive section of the Grand Canal, finishing up where many Irish writers got their inspiration – their local pubs.

Trinity to the Grand Canal

Begin at **Trinity College** ① *(see pp38–40)*, alma mater to Jonathan Swift *(see p61)*, author of the world-famous *Gulliver's Travels*; JM Synge, a renowned Irish dramatist; and Nobel Prize-winning playwright Samuel Beckett *(see p23)*, best known for *Waiting for Godot*. Walk east from the Lincoln Place entrance, passing Westland Row, where the prolific literary genius Oscar Wilde *(see p23)* was born. At the corner of Lincoln Place is **Sweeny's Chemist** ②, where Leopold Bloom, the protagonist of James Joyce's masterpiece *Ulysses (see p23)*, would buy lemon soap. Head to Merrion Square. As a child, Wilde lived at **No. 1** ③, and it was on this corner that Joyce was stood up on a first date by his future wife, Nora Barnacle. Continue to the reclining **Wilde Statue** ④ and then to the plaques on the square's south side, commemorating the celebrated poet WB Yeats, who lived at **No. 82** ⑤; influential Irish writer AE

Russell worked at **No. 84** ⑥; and Joseph Le Fanu, a Gothic writer who impressed both Bram Stoker *(see p22)* and Joyce, lived at **No. 70** ⑦. On the corner of Mount Street Upper is **Number 29** ⑧ *(see p47)*, a re-creation of a Georgian house. Continue to **St Stephen's Church** ⑨. Pass Herbert Street, on your right, where the successful Irish dramatist Brendan Behan lived in the 1950s. The Grand Canal is ahead. Turn right, following the path by the water.

KEY

• • • Walk route

Grand Canal to the RHA

On Herbert Place is a plaque to novelist Elizabeth Bowen, born at **No. 15** ⑩ in 1899. As a boy, Flann O'Brien (aka Brian O'Nolan), author of *The Third Policeman*, lived at **No. 25** ⑪. Continue along the canal to the **Statue of Patrick Kavanagh** ⑫. This immensely popular poet often referred to the canal and nearby streets in his works. Turn up Cumberland Road to **Fitzwilliam Square** ⑬. In the 1930s, WB Yeats lived at No. 42. Exit the square, returning to Fitzwilliam Street, and continue to Baggot Street Lower. At No. 3 is the

Pretty Georgian terrace houses lining Fitzwilliam Square ⑬

United Arts Club ⑭, founded in 1907 by WB Yeats and AE Russell among others to promote writing, visual art and music. Continue down Baggot Street to **Toner's Pub** ⑮, the only Dublin bar Yeats ever had a drink in. At the next crossroads, you come to **Ely Place** ⑯ *(see p42)*. Oscar Wilde proposed to Constance Lloyd at No. 1, while surgeon and writer Oliver St John Gogarty lived at what is now the Royal Hibernian Academy *(see p47)*.

Plaque for Bram Stoker

St Stephen's Green to the Carmelite Church

Continue on Merrion Row to St Stephen's Green, past the 17th-century **Huguenot Cemetery** ⑰ (closed to visitors) and the **Shelbourne Hotel** ⑱ *(see p130)*. Among the writers who lived on or around **St Stephen's Green** ⑲ *(see p41)* are the 19th-century poet James Clarence Mangan; 19th-century Gothic writer Charles Maturin; and James Stephens, poet and writer of fairy tales. Gothic master Bram Stoker was born at No. 30 Kildare Street, just off the green to the right. Cross the green to emerge at **Newman House** ⑳ *(see p42)* to the south. Poet Gerard Manley Hopkins lived and taught here. You can see his room and the classroom of James Joyce, who studied here when it was part of University College Dublin. Continue round the green, taking a left at York Street. Walk to the **Whitefriar Street Carmelite Church** ㉑ *(see p60)*.

The façade of the grand Shelbourne Hotel on St Stephen's Green ⑱

Ghosts, pubs and old books

Also on Aungier Street is the birthplace of poet Thomas Moore at No. 12, now a pub. Joseph Le Fanu based some ghost stories around here, too.

Take a right on to Stephen Street Lower for Chatham Street, and visit **McDaid's** ㉒, Brendan Behan's local pub; he and Patrick Kavanagh were never allowed in at the same time to avoid fisticuffs. Turn left into Grafton Street and right to Duke Street. More refreshment awaits in three famous pubs: **Davy Byrne's** ㉓, the setting for a famous scene in *Ulysses*, and **The Duke** ㉔ and **The Bailey** ㉕, both frequented by Brendan Behan, Patrick Kavanagh, Flann O'Brien, James Joyce among others. Finally, go into **Cathach Books** ㉖ to browse through rare editions of old favourites. Catch a bus from Nassau Street.

TIPS FOR WALKERS

Starting point: *Lincoln Gate, Trinity College.*
Length: *2.5 km (1.5 miles).*
Getting there: *DART to Pearse Street; a huge number of buses serve the area around Trinity. Stopping along Nassau Street are 4, 4A, 5, 7, 7A/B/C/D, 8, 10, 11, 11A/B, 14, 14A, 45, 46A/B/C/D/E, 63, 74, 92, 116, 117, 118, 145.*
Stopping-off points: *There are several pleasant eateries near Baggot Street Bridge, or you can have lunch on La Peniche barge restaurant (see p139), near the Kavanagh statue, on the Grand Canal. Ely Winebar (see p139) is on Ely Place, and there are many pubs along the route for drinks.*

Pearse Street

MERRION SQ N

MERRION SQUARE

MERRION SQ SOUTH

MERRION SQ E

FITZWILLIAM LANE

MOUNT ST UPPER

JAMES'S STREET EAST

FITZWILLIAM ST LOWER

FITZWILLIAM ST UPPER

BAGGOT STREET LOWER

HERBERT STREET

HERBERT LANE

HERBERT PLACE

PERCY PLACE

LAD LANE

WILTON PLACE

WILTON TERRACE

CUMBERLAND RD

MESPIL ROAD

0 metres 300

0 yards 300

The tranquil surroundings of the Grand Canal

A 90-Minute Walk Around Dalkey

The picturesque village of Dalkey (see p91) has a fascinating history and stunning coastal views. In medieval times, it was Dublin's main deep-water port, and it thrived on maritime trade until the 1600s, when Dublin itself became a safe port for shipping. Dalkey then declined into a sleepy fishing village. Its fortunes turned once again in the 19th century, with the decision to build a protective pier at nearby Dún Laoghaire. Granite for the pier was quarried in Dalkey, bringing the town into the limelight once more. This walk goes along winding streets and past homely cottages snuggling up to grand mansions, now home to the rich and famous.

Roseate tern from a colony breeding off Dalkey Island

Castle Street to Coliemore Harbour and Dillon's Park

Start at the **Tramyard** ① on Castle Street, a short stroll from the Dart station. This is where trams from Dublin used to be parked for the night and the horses stabled. The last tram ran from Dublin to Dalkey in 1949.

The former site of most of Dalkey's seven medieval castles, **Castle Street** ② now boasts the only two surviving fortified mansions. Walk to the crossroads, turn left down Convent Road and take the first right into Coliemore Road. From here, you will catch tantalizing glimpses of the sea and Dalkey Island in-between colourful gardens, quirky cottages and grand mansions. Pass the fairy-tale **Cliff Castle** ③, a famous hotel in the 1920s and now the Moroccan embassy. Further along is **Inniscorrig** ④, a mansion once owned by Dominic Corrigan, a physician who brought running water to Dalkey. If the gate is open, you will see his face carved above the doorway.

At **Coliemore Harbour** ⑤, home to lobster fishermen, you will get a better view of Dalkey Island. Named after its shape (its Gaelic name, _Deilg Inis_, means "Thorn Island"), the island has been inhabited since 4,500 BC; these days only goats live there. On the island are the ruins of a 9th-century church and a Martello tower, one of 26 built between Dublin and Bray as defence posts against a Napoleonic invasion that never came. Note the outlying rocks, Lamb Island and Maiden Rock, which was named after some local girls who drowned while collecting shellfish. These are now a

Pretty Coliemore Harbour ④, with a clear view of Dalkey Island

TIPS FOR WALKERS

Starting point: _Castle Street._
Length: _2.5 km (1.5 miles)._
Getting there: _30 minutes by DART south from the city centre; buses number 8 (very infrequent) and 59 from Dún Laoghaire._
Stopping-off points: _There are high-quality restaurants and cafés all along Castle Street. On Coliemore Road is Nosh (see p144)._

0 metres   250

0 yards   250

breeding ground for a rare species of roseate tern.

Continue to **Dillon's Park** ⑥. A Mrs Dillon operated tea rooms here in Victorian times. Take a rest, and enjoy the clear view of Dalkey Island.

Famous residents

Walk a little further and take the steps on the right up to **Sorrento Park** ⑦. Follow the path past a rock face with a mosaic of John Dowland, an Elizabethan poet said to have been born in Dalkey, who was a friend of William

Goats roaming on Dalkey Island

to the ultra-wealthy. Further up the road, opposite a house called Strawberry Hill, the high wall on your right will break for zigzagging steps. Known as the **Cat's Ladder** ⑩, this is the hardest climb of the walk, but there are low walls for rest stops en route. At the top, turn right into Torca Road. A short way up on the left is **Torca Cottage** ⑪, the childhood home of renowned author/ playwright George Bernard Shaw. The road eventually turns into Ardbrugh Road. On your left is **Dalkey Quarry** ⑫, which supplied the granite used for the piers of nearby Dún Laoghaire Harbour. Just

before the road forks, a grassy slope down a steep hill appears on your right, separated from the road by bollards. This was the route of the funicular railway that serviced the quarry, and is marked by flagstones. Head down this hill and turn right onto Dalkey Avenue, then stop at the corner of Old Quarry and Summerfield House. Within the grounds of Summerfield House was **Clifton School** ⑬, which features in James Joyce's masterpiece *Ulysses*. At the end of Dalkey Avenue turn right, back into Castle Street.

Castles and Queens

On your right is **Archbold's Castle** ⑭, one of the street's two extant medieval mansions. Beside it is the **Church of the Assumption** ⑮. Cardinal Newman, first rector of the Catholic University of Ireland, spent time here while he lived in Dalkey.

Almost opposite is **Dalkey Castle & Heritage Centre** ⑯, in the 14th-century Goats Castle. The centre provides entertaining, in-depth historical and literary walking tours of the area, plus a tour of the castle led by characters in full period dress. Entrance includes access to the 10th-century St Begnet's Church and a Rathdown Slab, one of 28 unique to the area, believed to be a 10th-century Viking burial marker.

End your walk with a drink at **The Queens** ⑰ *(see p145)*, a landmark pub that's been here since 1745. Turn right at the end of Castle Street to return to the DART station.

KEY

• • • Walk route

🚉 Dart station

Shakespeare. As the path splits, veer left to reach **Sorrento Point** ⑧. Pause here to enjoy stunning views of Dalkey Island, Killiney Bay and Hill, and the Wicklow Mountains. This panoramic vista is often compared to the views across the Bay of Naples in Italy.

Exit the park and turn right to reach **Vico Road** ⑨, home

The exterior of the 14th-century Goat Castle

Herb garden, Ardgillan Castle ▷

BEYOND DUBLIN

ROBERTSTOWN
BOG OF ALLEN NATURE CENTRE
MONASTEREVIN • KILDARE 104–105

CASTLETOWN HOUSE 106–107

RUSSBOROUGH HOUSE
BROWNE'S HILL DOLMEN
AVONDALE HOUSE 108–109

GLENDALOUGH
MOUNT USHER GARDENS 110–111

A TOUR OF THE MILITARY ROAD
WICKLOW MOUNTAINS
KILRUDDERY HOUSE 112–113

POWERSCOURT 114–115

BRAY • NEWBRIDGE • ARDGILLAN
DROGHEDA • MONASTERBOICE 116–117

CARLINGFORD • DUNDALK
MELLIFONT ABBEY
THE BOYNE VALLEY 118–119

NEWGRANGE 120–121

SLANE • HILL OF TARA • TRIM
MULLINGAR • KILBEGGAN 122–123

BEYOND DUBLIN

A short way out of central Dublin, the beautiful Irish countryside offers a wealth of pretty villages, dramatic mountains and elegant stately homes to visit. South of Dublin, the coastline down to Dun Laoghaire and beyond, with its dramatic backdrop of the Wicklow Mountains, is stunning. To the north can be found traces of some of the earliest residents in the area – the Celts.

North of Dublin, the fertile Boyne Valley in County Meath was settled during the Stone Age. The remains of ancient sites from this early civilization fill the area and include New-grange, the finest Neolithic tomb in Ireland. In Celtic times, the focus shifted south to the Hill of Tara, the seat of the High Kings of Ireland and the Celts' spiritual and political capital. Tara's heyday was in the 3rd century AD, but it retained its importance until the Norman invasion in the 1100s.

Coracle from the Millmount Museum in Drogheda

Norman castles, such as the immense fortress at Trim in County Meath, attest to the shifting frontiers around the region of English influence known as the Pale *(see p108)*. By the end of the 16th century, this area incorporated nearly all the counties in the Midlands. The Boyne Valley returned to prominence in 1690, when the Battle of the Boyne ended in a land-mark Protestant victory over the Catholics *(see p15)*.

The area to the south of Dublin had the strongest English influence in all of Ireland. From the 18th century onwards, wealthy Anglo-Irish families were drawn to what they saw as a stable zone, and felt confident enough to build fine mansions like the Palladian masterpieces of Russ-borough, Newbridge and Castletown.

For a refreshing breath of fresh air, stroll along the cliffs at Bray Head, or follow one of the invigorating walking routes in the Wicklow Mountains.

Traditional kitchen in Newbridge House

◁ View towards the sea beyond Ardgillan Castle

Exploring Beyond Dublin

The countryside around Dublin is stunning and offers everything from stately homes to ancient burial sites and dramatic mountains to seaside villages. The Wicklow Mountains have excellent walking territory and are also home to some of the best sights, such as the elegant gardens of Powerscourt House and the monastic complex at Glendalough. The coastal stretch to the south of Dublin towards Bray is particularly scenic.

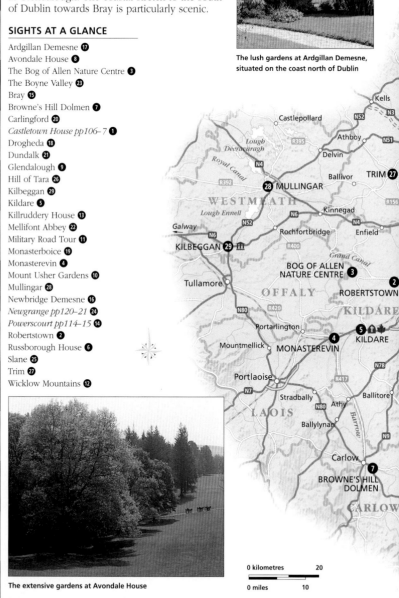

The lush gardens at Ardgillan Demesne, situated on the coast north of Dublin

SIGHTS AT A GLANCE

Ardgillan Demesne 🅐
Avondale House 🅗
The Bog of Allen Nature Centre 🅑
The Boyne Valley 🅓
Bray 🅕
Browne's Hill Dolmen 🅖
Carlingford 🅙
Castletown House pp106–7 🅐
Drogheda 🅘
Dundalk 🅑
Glendalough 🅖
Hill of Tara 🅒
Kilbeggan 🅙
Kildare 🅔
Killruddery House 🅓
Mellifont Abbey 🅒
Military Road Tour 🅗
Monasterboice 🅙
Monasterevin 🅓
Mount Usher Gardens 🅐
Mullingar 🅑
Newbridge Demesne 🅖
Newgrange pp120–21 🅓
Powerscourt pp114–15 🅒
Robertstown 🅑
Russborough House 🅕
Slane 🅔
Trim 🅒
Wicklow Mountains 🅑

The extensive gardens at Avondale House

0 kilometres 20
0 miles 10

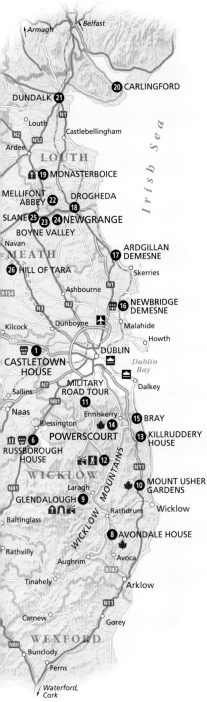

Elegant stuccoed hall and staircase in Castletown House

Map labels:

- Armagh
- Belfast
- 20 CARLINGFORD
- DUNDALK 21
- Louth
- N1
- Castlebellingham
- N2 N52
- Ardee
- *LOUTH*
- 19 MONASTERBOICE
- MELLIFONT ABBEY 22
- DROGHEDA
- SLANE 25 23 24 NEWGRANGE
- BOYNE VALLEY
- 18
- *Irish Sea*
- Navan
- *MEATH*
- ARDGILLAN DEMESNE 17
- 26 HILL OF TARA
- Skerries
- R154
- Ashbourne
- N1
- N3 N2
- Dunboyne
- NEWBRIDGE DEMESNE 16
- Kilcock
- Malahide
- M4
- DUBLIN
- Howth
- CASTLETOWN HOUSE 1
- *Dublin Bay*
- Sallins
- N7
- MILITARY ROAD TOUR
- Dalkey
- Naas
- N81
- 11
- Blessington
- Enniskerry
- 15 BRAY
- POWERSCOURT 14
- RUSSBOROUGH HOUSE 6
- KILLRUDDERY HOUSE 13
- *WICKLOW*
- 12
- N81
- Laragh
- N11
- GLENDALOUGH 9
- MOUNT USHER GARDENS 10
- Baltinglass
- Rathdrum
- Wicklow
- *WICKLOW MOUNTAINS*
- Rathvilly
- 8 AVONDALE HOUSE
- Aughrim
- Avoca
- Tinahely
- R747
- Arklow
- Carnew
- N11
- Gorey
- *WEXFORD*
- N80
- Bunclody
- Ferns
- Waterford, Cork

KEY

═══	Motorway
═ ═	Under construction
═══	Secondary road
───	Minor road
⋯⋯	Scenic route
───	Main railway
───	Minor railway
───	International border
▬▬▬	County border

SEE ALSO

- *Where to Stay* pp128–33
- *Where to Eat* pp138–45

GETTING AROUND

Several motorways and main roads fan out from Dublin. The M1 goes north to Dundalk, the N11 south, following the scenic coastline. Regular train services operate around the country from Heuston and Connolly stations. Coach services also run all around the country from Dublin. The DART railway line runs north and south from the city along the coast and has several stops in central Dublin.

Castletown House ❶

See pp106–7.

Robertstown ❷

Co Kildare. 🚶 *240.* 💻 *www. robertstownholidayvillage.com*

Ten locks west along the Grand Canal from Dublin, Robertstown is a characteristic 19th-century canalside village, with warehouses and cottages flanking the waterfront. Freight barges plied the route until about 1960, but pleasure boats have since replaced them. Barge cruises leave from the quay and the old Grand Canal Company's Hotel, built in 1801 for canal passengers, is now used for banquets.

Near Sallins, about 8 km (5 miles) east, the canal is carried over the River Liffey along the **Leinster Aqueduct**, an impressive structure built in 1783.

Bog of Allen Nature Centre ❸

Lullymore, Co Kildare. **Tel** *045 860133.* 🚌 *to Newbridge & Kildare.* 🚌 *to Allenwood.* 🕐 *all year: 10am–4pm Mon–Fri.* ♿ *limited.* **www.ipcc.ie**

Anyone interested in the natural history of Irish bogs should visit the Nature Centre, an exhibition housed in an old farm at Lullymore, 9 km (6 miles) northeast of Rathangan. It lies at the heart of the Bog of Allen, a vast expanse of raised bog that extends across the counties of Offaly, Laois and Kildare.

Japanese Gardens at Tully near Kildare

The exhibition explains the history and ecology of the bog, and features displays of flora and fauna as well as archaeological finds from the surrounding area. Guided walks are also organized to introduce visitors to the bog's delicate ecosystem and the careful conservation work that is being done.

Stacking peat for use as fuel

Monasterevin ❹

Co Kildare. 🚶 *2,200.* 🚌

This Georgian market town lies west of Kildare, where the Grand Canal crosses the River Barrow. Waterborne trade brought prosperity to Monasterevin in the 18th century, but the locks now see little traffic. However, you can still admire the aqueduct, which is a superb example of canal engineering.

Moore Abbey, next to the church, was built in the 18th century on the site of a Cistercian monastery which was founded by St Evin, but the grand Gothic mansion owes a great deal to Victorian remodelling. Originally the ancestral seat of the earls of Drogheda, in the 1920s Moore Abbey became the home of the internationally celebrated Irish tenor, John McCormack. It is now a Sisters of Charity convent.

Kildare ❺

Co Kildare. 🚶 *4,200.* 🚌 🚌 ℹ️ *Market House, May–Sep: 045 521 240.* 🛍️ *Thu.*

The charming and tidy town of Kildare is dominated by **St Brigid's Cathedral**, which commemorates the saint who founded a religious community on this site in AD 480. Unusually, monks and nuns lived

The Grand Canal Company's Hotel in Robertstown

here under the same roof, but this was not the only unorthodox practice associated with the community. Curious pagan rituals, including the burning of a perpetual fire, continued until the 16th century. The fire pit is visible in the grounds today. So too is a round tower, which was probably built in the 12th century and has a Romanesque doorway. The cathedral was rebuilt in the Victorian era, but the restorers largely adhered to the original 13th-century design.

🔒 St Brigid's Cathedral
Market Square. ◯ *May–Sep: daily.* 🖼 *donation.* ♿

Environs
Kildare lies at the heart of racing country: the Curragh racecourse is nearby, stables are scattered all around and bloodstock sales take place at Kill, northeast of town.

The **National Stud** is a semi state-run bloodstock farm at Tully, just south of Kildare. It was founded in 1900 by an eccentric Anglo-Irish colonel, William Hall-Walker. He sold his foals on the basis of their astrological charts, and put skylights in the stables to allow the horses to be "touched" by sunlight or moonbeams. Hall-Walker received the title Lord Wavertree in reward for bequeathing the farm to the British Crown in 1915.

Visitors can explore the 400-ha (1,000-acre) grounds and watch the horses being exercised. Mares and stallions are generally kept in separate paddocks. The breeding stallions are expected to cover more than 100

HORSE RACING IN IRELAND

Ireland has a strong racing culture and, thanks to its non-elitist image, the sport is enjoyed by all. Much of the thoroughbred industry centres around the Curragh, a grassy plain in County Kildare stretching unfenced for more than 2,000 ha (5,000 acres). This area is home to many of the country's studs and training yards, and every morning horses are put through their paces on the gallops. Most of the major flat races, including the Irish Derby, take place at the Curragh racecourse just east of Kildare. Other popular fixtures are held at nearby Punchestown – most famously the steeplechase festival in April – and at Leopardstown, which also hosts major National Hunt races (see p29).

Finishing straight at the Curragh racecourse

mares per season. There is a foaling unit where the mare and foal can rest for a few days after the birth.

The farm has its own forge and saddlery, and also a Horse Museum. Housed in old stable block, this illustrates the importance of horses in Irish life. Exhibits include the frail skeleton of Arkle, the champion steeplechaser who raced to fame in the 1960s.

Sharing the same estate as the National Stud are the **Japanese Gardens**, created by Lord Wavertree at the height of the Edwardian penchant for Orientalism. The gardens were laid out in 1906–10 by a Japanese landscape gardener called Tassa Eida, with the help of his son Minoru and 40 assistants. The impres-

sive array of trees and shrubs includes maples, mulberries, bonsai, magnolias, cherry trees and sacred bamboos.

The gardens take the form of an allegorical journey from the cradle to the grave, beginning with life emerging from the Gate of Oblivion (a cave) and leading to the Gateway of Eternity, a Zen rock garden.

St Fiachra's Garden was a millennium project completed in 1999. It was designed by Professor Martin Hallinan and commemorates St Fiachra, the Patron Saint of Gardeners.

🍁 National Stud, Japanese & St Fiachra Gardens
Tully. *Tel 045 521617.*
◯ *mid-Feb–Dec 23: 9:30am–5pm daily.*
🖼 ♿ 🅿 *Stud only.*
▢ ▢ **www**.irish-national-stud.ie

St Brigid's Cathedral and roofless round tower in Kildare town

Castletown House ❶

Built in 1722–32 for William Conolly, the Speaker of the Irish Parliament, the façade of Castletown was the work of Florentine architect Alessandro Galilei and gave Ireland its first taste of Palladianism. The magnificent interiors date from the second half of the 18th century. They were commissioned by Lady Louisa Lennox, wife of William Conolly's great-nephew, Tom, who lived here from 1759. Castletown remained in the family until 1965, when it was taken over by the Irish Georgian Society. The state now owns the house and it is open to the public.

Conolly crest on an armchair

★ **Long Gallery**
The heavy ceiling sections and friezes date from the 1720s and the walls were decorated in the Pompeian manner in the 1770s.

Green drawing room

Red drawing room
The red damask covering the walls of this room is probably French and dates from the 19th century. This exquisite mahogany bureau was made for Lady Louisa in the 1760s.

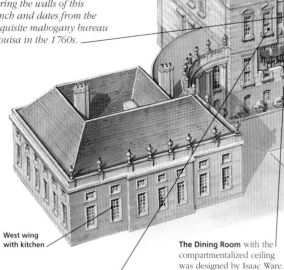

West wing with kitchen

The Dining Room with the compartmentalized ceiling was designed by Isaac Ware.

Boudoir wall paintings
The boudoir's decorative panels, moved here from the Long Gallery, were inspired by the Raphael Loggia in the Vatican.

★ Print room
*In this, the only intact 18th-century print room in Ireland,
Lady Louisa indulged her taste for Italian engravings. It was
fashionable at the time for ladies to paste prints directly on
to the wall and frame them with elaborate festoons.*

VISITORS' CHECKLIST

Celbridge, Co Kildare.
Tel 628 8252.
🚌 67, 67A from Dublin.
⏱ mid-Mar–end Oct: 10am–
6pm Tue–Sun, public hols. 🏷
♿ 🍴 🛒 📷 obligatory. First
tour 10:30am, last adm 4:45pm.
Summer concerts.
www.castletown.ie

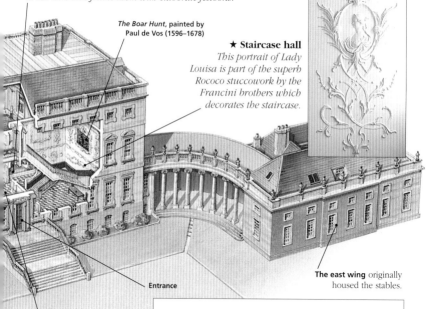

The Boar Hunt, painted by
Paul de Vos (1596–1678)

★ Staircase hall
*This portrait of Lady
Louisa is part of the superb
Rococo stuccowork by the
Francini brothers which
decorates the staircase.*

The east wing originally
housed the stables.

Entrance

The entrance hall is an
austere Neo-Classical room.
Its most decorative feature is
the delicate carving on the
pilasters of the upper gallery.

STAR FEATURES

★ Long Gallery

★ Print room

★ Staircase hall

CONOLLY'S FOLLY

This folly, which lies just
beyond the grounds of
Castletown House, provides
the focus of the view from
the Long Gallery. Speaker
Conolly's widow, Katherine,
commissioned it in 1740
as a memorial to her late
husband, and to provide
employment after a harsh
winter. The unusual structure
of superimposed arches
crowned by an obelisk was
designed by Richard Castle,
architect of Russborough
House *(see p108)*.

Saloon in Russborough House with original fireplace and stuccowork

Russborough House ⑥

Blessington, Co Wicklow. *Tel 045 865239.* 🚌 *65 from Dublin (check times).* ⏰ *May–Sep: 10am–6pm daily; Apr & Oct: 10am–6pm Sun & public hols only.* 📷 🎫 *obligatory.* 💻 🏠 *www.russborough.ie*

This Palladian mansion, built in the 1740s for Joseph Leeson, later Earl of Milltown, is one of Ireland's finest houses. Its architect, a German called Richard Castle, also designed Powerscourt House (see pp114–15) and is credited with introducing the Palladian style to Ireland. Unlike many grand estates in the Pale, Russborough has survived magnificently, both inside and out. The house claims the longest frontage in Ireland, with a façade adorned by heraldic lions and curved colonnades. The interior is even more impressive. Many rooms feature superb stucco decoration, which was done largely by the Italian Francini brothers, who also worked on Castletown House

Vernet seascape in the drawing room

(see pp106–7). The best examples are found in the music room, saloon and library, which are embellished with exuberant foliage and cherubs. Around the main staircase, a riot of Rococo plasterwork depicts a hunt, with hounds clasping garlands of flowers. The stucco mouldings in the drawing room were designed especially to enclose marine scenes by the French artist, Joseph Vernet (1714–89). The paintings were sold in 1926, but were tracked down more than 40 years afterwards and returned to the house.

Russborough House has many other treasures to be seen, including finely worked fireplaces made of Italian marble, imposing mahogany doorways and priceless collections of silver, porcelain and Gobelins tapestries.

Such riches aside, one of the principal reasons to visit Russborough is to see the **Beit Art Collection**, famous for its Flemish, Dutch and Spanish Old Master paintings. Sir Alfred Beit, who bought the house in 1952, inherited the pictures from his uncle – also named Alfred Beit. The family's wealth had come from gold mines and

An 18th-century family enjoying the privileged lifestyle that was typical within the Pale

THE HISTORY OF THE PALE

The term "Pale" refers to an area around Dublin which marked the limits of English influence from Norman to Tudor times. The frontier fluctuated but, at its largest, the Pale stretched from Dundalk in County Louth to Waterford town. Gaelic chieftains outside the area could keep their lands provided they agreed to raise their heirs within the Pale.

The Palesmen supported their rulers' interests and considered themselves the upholders of English values. This widened the gap between the Gaelic majority and the Anglo-Irish, foretelling England's doomed involvement in the country. Long after its fortifications were dismantled, the idea of the Pale lived on as a state of mind. The expression "beyond the pale" survives as a definition of those outside the bounds of civilized society.

diamond dealing in Kimberley, South Africa. The Beit family donated Russborough to the Beit Foundation, opening the house to the public while living in one of the wings of the house.

In 1974, 1986, 2000 and 2001, several masterpieces were stolen from the house, but all were later retrieved. Only a selection of paintings is on view at any one time, while others are on permanent loan to the National Gallery in the centre of Dublin (see pp48–51). Other paintings from the National Gallery are also on view in the house from time to time.

Russborough enjoys a fine position near the village of **Blessington**, which has a good view of the Wicklow Mountains. The house lies in the midst of wooded parkland rather than elaborate gardens. As Alfred Beit said of Irish Palladianism, "Fine architecture standing in a green sward was considered enough". Adjoining the house is a maze.

Environs
The **Poulaphouca Reservoir**, formed by the damming of the River Liffey, extends south from Blessington. The placid lake is popular with watersports enthusiasts, while others come simply to enjoy the view of the nearby Wicklow Mountains.

Avondale House, with its colourful gardens in the foreground

Browne's Hill Dolmen ❼

Co Carlow. 🚉 🚌 to Carlow. ◯ daily.

In a field 3 km (2 miles) east of Carlow, along the R726, stands a huge dolmen boasting the biggest capstone in Ireland. It stands in the area of Browne's Hill, where there is a stone house dating from 1763. Weighing a reputed 100 tonnes, this massive stone is embedded in the earth at one end and supported at the other by three much smaller stones. Dating back to 2000 BC, the Dolmen is thought to mark the tomb of a local chieftain. A path from the road skirts the field before reaching it.

Parnell's chair in Avondale House

Avondale House ❽

Co Wicklow. **Tel** 0404 46111. 🚉 🚌 to Rathdrum. **House and grounds** ◯ mid-Mar–Oct: 11am–6pm daily (last adm to house: 5pm). ◯ Mar–Apr, Sep–Oct: Mon, Good Fri. 🈳 🍽 🎁

Lying just south of Rathdrum, Avondale House was the birthplace of the 19th-century politician and patriot, Charles Stewart Parnell (see p17). Built in 1779, it passed into the hands of the Parnell family in 1795 and Charles Stewart was born here on 27 June 1846. The Georgian mansion now houses a museum dedicated to Parnell and the fight for Home Rule. The birthplace of Irish Forestry, Avondale is managed by the Irish Forestry Board but the public is free to explore the 200 ha (512 acres) of grounds, complete with picnic and children's play areas. Known as **Avondale Forest Park**, the former estate includes an impressive arboretum which was first planted in the 18th century and has had many additions made to it since 1900.

There are some lovely walks through the woods, including the magnificent Great Ride, which is one of the best, with pleasant views along the River Avonmore. There is also much wildlife in the area, including hares, rabbits and otters.

Browne's Hill Dolmen, famous for its enormous capstone

Glendalough ❾

Co Wicklow. 🚌 *St Kevin's bus from Dublin.* **Ruins** ◯ *daily.* 🎫 *in summer.* **Visitors' centre** *Tel 0404 45325/ 45352.* ◯ *Oct–mid-Mar: 9:30am– 5pm (last adm 4:15pm) daily; mid– Mar–Sep: 9:30am–6pm (last adm 5:15pm).* ● *24–27 Dec.* 🎫 🚻 🎥 *on request.* **www**.heritageireland.ie

The steep, wooded slopes of Glendalough, the "valley of the two lakes", harbour an atmospheric monastic site. Established by St Kevin in the 6th century, the settlement was sacked time and again by the Vikings but nevertheless flourished for over 600 years. Decline set in only after English forces partially razed the site in 1398, though it functioned as a monastic centre until the Dissolution of the Monasteries in 1539 *(see p14).* Pilgrims kept on coming to Glendalough even after that, particularly on St Kevin's feast day, 3 June.

The age of the buildings is uncertain, but most date from the 8th to 12th centuries. Many

View along the Upper Lake at Glendalough

were restored in the 1870s. The main group of ruins lies east of the Lower Lake, but other buildings associated with St Kevin are found by the Upper Lake. Here, where the scenery is much wilder, it is possible to enjoy more the tranquillity of Glendalough and to escape the crowds which inevitably descend on the site. Try to arrive as early as possible in the day, particularly during the peak tourist season. Enter the

Remains of the Gatehouse, the original entrance to Glendalough

monastery through the double stone arch of the **Gatehouse**, the only surviving example in Ireland of a gateway into a monastic enclosure.

A short walk leads to a graveyard with a **Round tower** in one corner. Reaching 30 m (100 ft) in height, this is one of the finest of its kind in the country. Its cap was rebuilt in the 1870s using stones found inside the tower. The roofless **Cathedral** nearby dates mainly

St Kevin's Kitchen

from the 12th century and is the valley's largest ruin. At the centre of the churchyard stands the tiny **Priests' House**, whose name derives from the fact that it was a burial place for local clergy. The worn carving of a robed figure above the door is thought possibly to be St Kevin, flanked by two disciples. East of here, **St Kevin's Cross** dates from the 8th century and is one of the best preserved of Glendalough's various High Crosses. Made of granite, the cross may once have marked the boundary of the monastic cemetery. Below, nestled in the lush valley, a tiny oratory with a steeply pitched stone roof is a charming sight. Erected in the 11th century or even earlier, it is popularly known as **St Kevin's Kitchen**; this is perhaps because its belfry, which is thought to be a later addition, resembles a chimney. One of the earliest churches at Glendalough, **St**

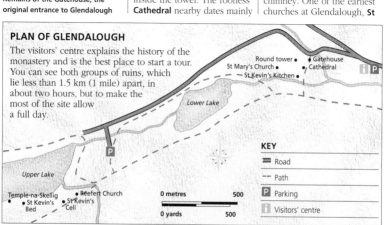

PLAN OF GLENDALOUGH

The visitors' centre explains the history of the monastery and is the best place to start a tour. You can see both groups of ruins, which lie less than 1.5 km (1 mile) apart, in about two hours, but to make the most of the site allow a full day.

Round tower ●
St Mary's Church ●   ● Gatehouse
── St Kevin's Kitchen ●   ● Cathedral

Lower Lake

Upper Lake

Temple-na-Skellig ●   ● Reefert Church
● St Kevin's   ● St Kevin's
Bed   Cell

0 metres   500

0 yards   500

KEY

▬ Road

-- Path

🅿 Parking

ℹ Visitors' centre

ST KEVIN AT GLENDALOUGH

St Kevin was born in 498, a descendant of the royal house of Leinster. He rejected his life of privilege, however, choosing to live instead as a hermit in a cave at Glendalough. He later founded a monastery here, and went on to establish a notable centre of learning devoted to the care of the sick and the copying and illumination of manuscripts. St Kevin attracted many disciples to Glendalough during his lifetime, but the monastery became more celebrated as a place of pilgrimage after his death in around 618.

Colourful legends about the saint make up for the dearth of facts about him. That he lived to the age of 120 is just one of the many stories told about him. Another tale claims that one day, when St Kevin was at prayer, a blackbird laid an egg in one of his outstretched hands. According to legend the saint remained in the same position until the bird was hatched.

have been used as a tomb in the Bronze Age, but it is more famous as St Kevin's favourite retreat. It was from this point that the saint allegedly rejected the advances of a naked woman by picking her up and throwing her into the lake.

Mount Usher Gardens ⑩

Ashford, Co Wicklow. *Tel 0404 40116.* 🚌 to Ashford. ☐ 1 Mar–31 Oct: 10:30am–6pm daily (last adm: 5:20pm). 🎫 🛍 🖥 (27 Apr–31 Oct). 🚻 limited. 📞 call to book. **www**.mount-usher-gardens.com

Set on the banks of the River Vartry, just east of Ashford, are the Mount Usher Gardens. They were designed in 1868 by a Dubliner, Edward Walpole, who imbued them with his strong sense of romanticism.

The 8 ha (20 acres) are laid out in a wild, informal style and contain around 4,000 different species of plants including rare shrubs and trees, from Chinese conifers and bamboos to Mexican pines and pampas grass. The Maple Walk is particularly glorious in the autumn, and in spring the rhododendron collection is brilliant with reds and pinks.

The river provides the main focus of the Mount Usher Gardens and, amid the exotic and lush vegetation, the visitor can usually catch a glimpse of herons standing on the many weirs and little bridges that cross the river.

Round tower at Glendalough

Mary's, lies across a field to the west. Some traces of hood moulding (intended to throw off water) are visible outside the east window. The path along the south bank of the river leads visitors to the Upper Lake. This is the site of more monastic ruins and is also the chief starting point for walks through the valley and to a number of abandoned lead and zinc mines.

Situated in a grove not far from the Poulanass waterfall are the ruins of the **Reefert Church**, a simple building. Its unusual name is a corruption of *Righ Fearta*, meaning "burial place of the kings"; the church may mark the site of an

ancient cemetery. Nearby, on a rocky spur overlooking the Upper Lake, stands **St Kevin's Cell**, the foundation of a beehive-shaped structure which is thought to have once been the home of the hermit.

There are two sites on the south side of the lake which cannot be reached on foot but are visible from the shore on the other side. **Temple-na-Skellig**, or the "church on the rock", was supposedly built on the site of the first church that was founded by St Kevin at Glendalough. To the east of it, carved into the cliff, is **St Kevin's Bed**. This small cave, in fact little more than a rocky ledge, is thought possibly to

Mount Usher Gardens, on the banks of the River Vartry

A Tour of the Military Road ⑪

The British built the Military Road through the heart of the Wicklow Mountains during a campaign to flush out Irish rebels after an uprising in 1798 *(see p16)*. Now known as the R115, this winding road takes you through the emptiest and most rugged landscapes of County Wicklow. Beautiful countryside, in which deer and other wildlife flourish, is characteristic of the whole of this tour.

Rare red squirrel

Powerscourt Waterfall ⑨
The River Dargle cascades 130 m (425 ft) over a granite escarpment to form Ireland's highest waterfall.

Glencree ①
The former British barracks in Glencree are among several found along the Military Road.

Great Sugar Loaf ⑧
The granite cone of Great Sugar Loaf Mountain can be climbed in under an hour from the car park on its southern side.

Sally Gap ②
This remote pass is surrounded by a vast expanse of blanket bog dotted with pools and streams.

Lough Tay ⑦
Stark, rocky slopes plunge down to the dark waters of Lough Tay. Though it lies within a Guinness-owned estate, the lake is accessible to walkers.

Glenmacnass ③
After Sally Gap, the road drops into a deep glen where a waterfall spills dramatically over rocks.

Roundwood ⑥
The highest village in Ireland at 238 m (780 ft) above sea level, Roundwood enjoys a fine setting. Its main street is lined with pubs, cafés and craft shops.

Glendalough ④
This ancient monastery *(see pp110–11)*, enclosed by wooded slopes, is the prime historical sight in the Wicklow Mountains.

Map labels:
DUBLIN · Glencree ① · Ennisberry · Powerscourt · R115 · Glencree · R760 · Great Sugar Loaf ⑧ · Dargle · ⑨ Powerscourt Waterfall · Sally Gap ② · R755 · Lough Tay ⑦ · R759 · Lough Dan · Glenmacnass ③ · R115 · Round-wood ⑥ · R755 · Vartry Reservoir · Annamoe · Glenmacnass · R756 · Laragh · Glendalough ④ · Avonmore · R755 · Vale of Clara ⑤ · Clara · RATHDRUM

TIPS FOR DRIVERS

Length: 96 km (60 miles).
Stopping-off points: There are several pubs and cafés in Enniskerry (including *Poppies*, an old-fashioned tearoom), and also in Roundwood, but this area is better suited for picnics. There are numerous marked picnic spots south of Enniskerry.

0 kilometres　　　5

0 miles　　　3

KEY

　Tour route

Other roads

⚡ Viewpoint

Vale of Clara ⑤
This picturesque wooded valley follows the River Avonmore. It contains the tiny village of Clara, which consists of two houses, a church and a school.

Wicklow Mountains ⑫

Co Wicklow. 🚌 to Rathdrum & Wicklow. 🚌 to Enniskerry, Wicklow, Glendalough, Rathdrum & Avoca. 🛈 Rialto House, Fitzwilliam Square, Wicklow, 0404 69117. www.eastcoastmidlands.ie

The inaccessibility of the rugged Wicklow Mountains meant that they once provided a safe hideout for opponents of English rule. Rebels who took part in the 1798 uprising sought refuge here. The building of the **Military Road**, started in 1800, made the area slightly more accessible, but the mountains are still thinly populated. There is little traffic to disturb enjoyment of the exhilarating scenery of rock-strewn glens, lush forest and bogland where heather gives a purple sheen to the land. Turf-cutting is still a thriving cottage industry, and you can often see peat stacked up by the road. Numerous walking trails weave through these landscapes. Among them is the **Wicklow Way**, which extends 132 km (82 miles) from Marlay Park in Dublin to Clonegal in County Carlow. It is marked but not always easy to follow, so do not set out without a good map. Although no peak exceeds 915 m (3,000 ft), the Wicklow Mountains can be dangerous in bad weather.

A good starting point for exploring the northern area is the picture-postcard estate village of **Enniskerry**, close to

View across the Long Ponds to Killruddery House

Powerscourt (see pp114–15). To the south, you can reach Glendalough (see pp110–11) and the **Vale of Avoca**. The beauty of this gentle valley was captured in the poetry of Thomas Moore (1779–1852): "There is not in the wide world a valley so sweet as that vale in whose bosom the bright waters meet" – a reference to the confluence of the Avonbeg and Avonmore rivers, the so-called **Meeting of the Waters** beyond Avondale House (see p109). Nestled among wooded hills at the heart of the valley is the hamlet of Avoca, where the **Avoca Handweavers** produce colourful tweeds in the oldest hand-weaving mill in Ireland, in operation since 1723.

Further north, towards the coast near Ashford, the River Vartry rushes through the deep chasm of the **Devil's Glen**. On entering the valley, the river falls 30 m (100 ft) into a pool known as the Devil's

Punchbowl. There are good walks around here, with fine views of the coast.

🏠 **Avoca Handweavers**
Avoca. **Tel** 0402 35105. 🕐 May–Oct: 9am–6pm daily, Nov–Apr: 9am–5pm daily. ● 25 & 26 Dec. **Weaving shed** 🕐 8am–4:30pm Mon–Fri, 10am–5pm Sat & Sun. 🅿 🛈 ♿ www.avoca.ie

Killruddery House and Gardens ⑬

Bray, Co Wicklow. **Tel** 0404 46024. **Gardens** 🕐 Apr: 1–5pm Sat, Sun; May–Sep: 1–5pm daily. **House** 🕐 May, Jun, Sep: 1–5pm daily. 📷 ♿ limited. www.killruddery.com

Killruddery House lies just to the south of Bray, in the shadow of Little Sugar Loaf Mountain. Built in 1651, it has been the seat of the Earls of Meath ever since, although it was remodelled in the 1800s.

The house contains some good carving and stuccowork. The real charm stems from its formal gardens. Laid out in the 1680s by a French gardener named Bonet, who also worked at Versailles, they feature romantic parterres and an array of hedges, trees and shrubs. The sylvan theatre, a small enclosure surrounded by a bay hedge, is the only known example in Ireland.

The garden centres on the Long Ponds, a pair of canals which extend 165 m (550 ft) and were once used to stock fish. Beyond, an enclosed pool leads to a Victorian arrangement of paths flanked by statues and hedges of yew, beech, lime and hornbeam.

Colourful moorland around Sally Gap in the Wicklow Mountains

Powerscourt ⑭

The gardens at Powerscourt are probably the finest in Ireland, both for their design and their dramatic setting at the foot of Great Sugar Loaf Mountain. The house and grounds were commissioned in the 1730s by Richard Wingfield, the first Viscount Powerscourt. The gardens fell into decline but, in 1840, the original scheme was revived. New ornamental gardens were completed in 1858–75 by the seventh Viscount, who added gates, urns and statues collected during his travels on the Continent. Gutted by an accidental fire in 1974, the ground floor and the ballroom on the first floor have been renovated.

Laocöon statue on upper terrace

Bamberg Gate
Made in Vienna in the 1770s, this gilded wrought-iron gate was brought to Powerscourt by the seventh Viscount from Bamberg Cathedral in Bavaria.

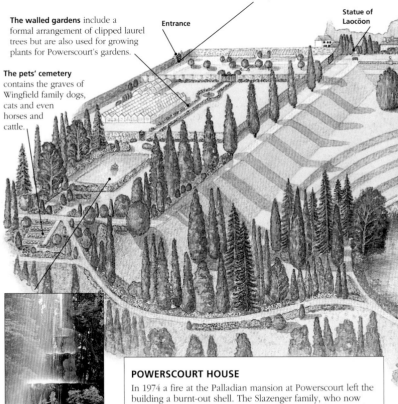

The walled gardens include a formal arrangement of clipped laurel trees but are also used for growing plants for Powerscourt's gardens.

Entrance

Statue of Laocöon

The pets' cemetery contains the graves of Wingfield family dogs, cats and even horses and cattle.

Dolphin pond
This pool, designed as a fish pond in the 18th century, is enclosed by exotic conifers in a lovely secluded garden.

POWERSCOURT HOUSE

In 1974 a fire at the Palladian mansion at Powerscourt left the building a burnt-out shell. The Slazenger family, who now own the estate, have restored part of the house; the ground floor now incorporates a terrace café, speciality shops and house exhibition describing the history of the estate. Originally built in 1731 on the site of a Norman castle, the house was designed by Richard Castle, also the architect of Russ-borough House *(see p108)*.

Powerscourt ablaze in 1974

★ **The Perron**
This superb Italianate stairway, added in 1874, leads down to the Triton Lake, which is guarded by two statues of the winged horse Pegasus and the emblem of the Wingfield family.

The Italian garden is laid out on terraces which were first cut into the steep hillside in the 1730s.

Pebble mosaic
Many tonnes of pebbles were gathered from nearby Bray beach to build the Perron and to make this mosaic on the terrace.

VISITORS' CHECKLIST

Enniskerry, Co Wicklow. *Tel 204 6000.* 🚌 185 from Bray DART station. 🅿 🕐 9:30am–5:30pm daily (gardens open until dusk in winter). ⬤ 25 & 26 Dec. 📷 ♿ 🍴 📷 www.powerscourt.ie

The Pepper Pot Tower was built in 1911.

★ **Triton Lake**
Made for the first garden, the lake takes its name from its central fountain, which is modelled on a 17th-century work by Bernini in Rome.

★ **Japanese gardens**
These enchanting Edwardian gardens, created out of bogland, contain Chinese conifers and bamboo trees.

STAR FEATURES

★ The Perron

★ Japanese gardens

★ Triton Lake

Bray ⓯

Co Wicklow. 🚶 *33,000.* 🚆 *DART.*
🅿 🛈 *Old Court House, Main St,*
286 7128/286 6796.
www.braytourism.ie

Once a refined Victorian resort,
Bray is nowadays a brash
holiday town, with amusement
arcades and fish-and-chip
shops lining the seafront. Its
beach attracts huge crowds in
summer, including many young
families. Anyone in search of
peace and quiet can escape to
nearby Bray Head, where there
is scope for bracing cliffside
walks. Bray also makes a good
base from which to explore the
Wicklow Mountains *(see p113),*
the delightful coastal villages of
Killiney and Dalkey *(see p91)*
and Powerscourt House and
Gardens *(see pp114–15).*

Tourist road train on the seafront
esplanade at Bray

Newbridge
Demesne ⓰

Donabate, Co Dublin. **Tel** *843 6534.*
🚆 *to Donabate.* 🚌 *33B from*
Swords. **House and Courtyard** 🕐
Apr–Sep: 10am–5pm Tue–Sat, noon–
6pm Sun & public hols; Oct–Mar:
noon–5pm Sat, Sun & public hols.
🔴 *25 & 26 Dec.* 🎟 🎫 *house only*
(obligatory). ♿ *courtyard only.* **Park**
🕐 *daily.* **www**.fingal-dublin.com

Newbridge is located on the
edge of the seaside village of
Donabate, 19 km (12 miles)
north of Dublin. The house
itself is a delight for enthusiasts
of Georgian architecture and
decor. The house was designed
by George Semple in 1737 for
Archbishop Charles Cobbe,
and it remained the family

Connemara Pony stabled at Newbridge House

home until 1986, when it was
bought by the local council.
The Cobbe family retains the
use of the upstairs quarters.

The highlight of the house
tour is the red drawing room,
one of the best-preserved
Georgian rooms in the country.
Its rich red decor is complemented by fine plasterwork
by Richard Williams and by
some impressive portrait and
landscape paintings. Its contents have remained unaltered
since at least the 1820s.

Also on view are the sizeable, airy dining room, a large
kitchen with a huge stock of
utensils, and the Museum of
Curiosities – a small room
filled to the rafters with
artifacts collected from 1790
onwards by Cobbe family
members on their foreign
travels. Housed in cabinets,
some of which date back to
the late 1700s, are unusual
and bizarre items such as
delicately carved ostrich eggs,
snakeskins and stuffed animals.

The cobbled courtyard has
been restored and now has
displays of aspects of late
18th-century life, including

dairy production,
carpentry and
forging. This
and the new
playground
make it a
popular spot
with families.
It also houses
rare goat and
pony breeds,
including the
native Conne-
mara pony, as
well as a pleasant tea room.
The Lord Chancellor's intricately detailed ceremonial
carriage which is on loan
from the National Museum
(see pp44–5) is an incongruous
exhibit but considered to be
one of the best examples of
carriagework in existence.

Footpaths wind through the
woodland, and the elegant,
rolling grounds of Newbridge,
which are attractively landscaped in the style of an
English estate.

Ardgillan
Demesne ⓱

Balbriggan, Co Dublin. **Tel** *849 2212.*
🚌 *33 via Skerries to Balbriggan.*
Castle 🕐 *Apr–Sep: 11am–6pm Tue–*
Sun & public hols (Jul–Aug: daily);
Oct–Mar: 11am–4:30pm Tue–Sun &
public hols. 🔴 *23 Dec–1 Jan.* 🎟 ♿
except kitchen. **Park and Gardens**
🕐 *daily.* **www**.visitdublin.com

In between the very likeable
resort towns of Skerries
and Balbriggan, the Ardgillan
Demesne is set on a high
stretch of coastline and offers

The elegant façade of Newbridge House

Stately drawing room in Ardgillan Castle

a particularly pleasant vantage point for stunning views over Drogheda Bay. Its sweeping and expansive grounds, which cover 78 ha (194 acres), incorporate various ornamental gardens, including a rose garden and a walled kitchen garden, as well as rolling pasture and dense woodland (the name Ardgillan means "high wooded area").

In the grounds stands Ardgillan Castle, which was built in 1737 by the Reverend Robert Taylor. The rooms on the ground floor are all furnished in Georgian and Victorian styles and the basement kitchen also retains its original decor. Upstairs there is an exhibition space which houses a permanent collection of old maps.

Gramophone in the Millmount Museum

Drogheda 🄳

Co Louth. 👥 28,000. 🚌 🚉
🛈 Bus Station, Donore Rd, 041 9837070, 9am–5pm Mon–Fri, 9am–4:30pm Sat. 🛒 Sat.

In the 14th century, this historic Norman port near the mouth of the River Boyne was one of Ireland's most important towns. It was first captured by the Danes in AD 911 and later heavily fortified by the Normans. However, the place seems never to have fully recovered from a vicious attack by the English general Oliver Cromwell in 1649, during which 3,000 citizens were killed after refusing to surrender. Although it looks rather dilapidated today, the town has retained its original street plan and has a rich medieval heritage. Little is left of Drogheda's Norman defences but **St Lawrence Gate**, a fine 13th-century barbican, has survived. The **Butter Gate** is the only other surviving gate. Near St Lawrence Gate there are two churches called **St Peter's**. The one belonging to the Church of Ireland, built in 1753, is the more striking and has some splendid gravestones. The Catholic church, on West Street and dating from 1791, is worth visiting just to see the embalmed head of Oliver Plunkett, an archbishop who was martyred in 1681. It is displayed in an elaborate glass case beside its certificate of authenticity, dated 1682.

South of the river you can climb Millmount, a Norman motte that is topped by a Martello tower. As well as providing a good view, this is the site of the **Millmount Museum**, which contains an interesting display of artifacts relating to the town and its history, as well as a number of craft workshops.

🏛 **Millmount Museum**
Millmount Square. **Tel** 041 983 3097.
🕐 daily. 🕐 10 days at Christmas.
📷 🎥 ♿ 🌐 www.millmount.net

Monasterboice 🄳

Co Louth. 🚉 to Drogheda. 🕐 daily.

Founded in the 5th century by an obscure disciple of St Patrick called St Buite, this monastic settlement is one of the most famous religious sites in Ireland. The ruins of the medieval monastery are enclosed within a graveyard in a lovely secluded spot to the north of Drogheda. The site includes a roofless round tower and two churches, but Monasterboice's greatest treasures are its 10th-century High Crosses, carved to help educate an illiterate populace.

Muiredach's High Cross is the finest of its kind in Ireland, and its sculpted biblical scenes are still remarkably fresh. They depict the life of Christ on the west face, while the east face features mainly Old Testament scenes. These include Moses striking the rock to get water for the Israelites and David struggling with Goliath. The cross is named after an inscription on the base which reads: "A prayer for Muiredach by whom this cross was made", which, it is thought, may refer to the abbot of Monasterboice.

The 6.5-m (21-ft) West Cross, also known as the Tall Cross, is one of the largest in Ireland. The carving has not lasted as well as on Muiredach's Cross, but scenes from the Death of Christ can still be made out. The North Cross, which is the least notable of the three, features a Crucifixion illustration and a carved spiral pattern.

Round tower and West High Cross at Monasterboice

Thatched cottage in Carlingford on the mountainous Cooley Peninsula

Carlingford ⓴

Co Louth. 🏠 650. 🚌
🛈 **Holy Trinity Heritage Centre**
Churchyard Rd, 042 9373454. 🕐
10am–12:30pm, 2–4pm Mon–Fri.
www.carlingfordheritagecentre.
com **Carlingford Adventure
Centre** *Tholsel St.* **Tel** *042 9373100.*
🕐 *9am–5:30pm daily.* ● *two
weeks at Christmas.* **www**.
carlingfordadventure.com

This is a picturesque fishing
village, located between the
mountains of the Cooley
Peninsula and the waters of
Carlingford Lough. The border
with Northern Ireland runs
right through the centre of this
drowned river valley, and from
the village you can look across
to the Mountains of Mourne on
the Ulster side. Carlingford is
an interesting place, with its
pretty whitewashed cottages
and ancient buildings clustered
along medieval alleyways. The
ruins of **King John's Castle**,
built by the Normans to protect
the entrance to the lough, still
dominate the village. The **Holy
Trinity Heritage Centre**, which
is housed in a medieval
church, tells the history of the
port from Anglo-Norman times.
Carlingford is the country's
oyster capital, and its oyster
festival in August draws large
crowds. The lough is popular
for watersports and in summer
cruises leave from the quay.
Carlingford is well placed for
hikes on the Cooley Peninsula. The **Carlingford Adventure
Centre** provides information
on walking and water activities.

Environs
A scenic route weaves around
the **Cooley Peninsula**, skirting
the coast and then cutting

through the mountains. The
section along the north coast
is the most dramatic: just
3 km (2 miles) northwest
of Carlingford, in the
**Slieve Foye Forest
Park**, a road climbs to
give a breathtaking
view over the hills
and lough.
The **Táin Trail**,
which you can join
at Carlingford, is a 30-
km (19-mile) circuit
through some of the
peninsula's most rug-
ged scenery, with cairns and
other prehistoric sites dotted
over the moorland. Keen
hikers can walk it in a day.

Dundalk ⓶

Co Louth. 🏠 30,000. 🚉 🚌 🛈
Jocelyn St, 042 9335484. 🚩 *Thu.*

Dundalk once marked the
northernmost point of the
Pale, the area controlled by
the English during the Middle
Ages *(see p108).* Now, lying
midway between Dublin and
Belfast, it is the last major
town before you reach the
Northern Ireland border.
Dundalk is the gatewayto
the Cooley Peninsula, but
there is little worth stopping
for in the town itself.
However, the **County
Museum**, which is housed
in an 18th-century distillery,
gives an insight into some of
Louth's traditional industries,
such as beer-making.

🏛 **County Museum**
Jocelyn St. **Tel** *042 9327056.*
🕐 *10:30am–5:30pm Tue–Sat (Mon
in May–Sep), 2–6pm Sun & public
hols.* 🈂 🚻 **www**.louthcoco.ie

Mellifont Abbey ㉒

Cullen, Co Louth. **Tel** *041 9826459.*
🚉 *to Drogheda.* 🚌 *to Drogheda
or Slane.* 🕐 *May–Oct: 10am–6pm
daily (last adm: 5:15pm).* 🈂
www.heritageireland.ie

On the banks of the River
Mattock, 10 km (6 miles) west
of Drogheda, lies the first
Cistercian monastery built in
Ireland. Mellifont was founded
in 1142 on the orders of St
Malachy, the Archbishop of
Armagh. He was influenced by
St Bernard, who was behind
the success of the Cistercian
Order in Europe. St Malachy
introduced not only Cistercian
rigour to Mellifont, but also
the formal style of
monastic architecture
used on the conti-
nent. In 1539, the
abbey was closed
and turned into a for-
tified house. William
of Orange used it as
his headquarters
during the Battle of
the Boyne in 1690.

**Glazed medieval tiles
at Mellifont Abbey**

It is now a ruin, but it is still
possible to appreciate the
scale and plan of the original
complex. Little survives of the
abbey church but, to the south
of it, enclosed by what is left
of the Roman-
esque cloister,
is the most
interesting
building at
Mellifont: a
13th-century
lavabo where
monks came
to wash

Ruined lavabo at Mellifont Abbey

THE BATTLE OF THE BOYNE

In 1688, the Catholic King of England, James II, was deposed from his throne, to be replaced by his Protestant daughter, Mary, and her husband, William of Orange. Determined to win back the crown, James sought the support of Irish Catholics, and challenged William at Oldbridge by the River Boyne west of Drogheda. The Battle of the Boyne took place on 12 July 1690, with James's poorly trained force of 25,000 French and Irish Catholics facing William's hardened army of 36,000 French Huguenots, Dutch, English and Scots. The Protestants triumphed and James fled to France, after a battle that signalled the beginning of total Protestant power over Ireland. It ushered in the confiscation of Catholic lands and the suppression of Catholic interests, sealing the country's fate for the next 300 years.

William of Orange leading his troops at the Battle of the Boyne, 12 July 1690

their hands before meals. Four of the building's original eight sides survive, each with a graceful Romanesque arch. On the eastern side of the cloister stands the 14th-century chapter house. It has an impressive vaulted ceiling and a floor laid with glazed medieval tiles taken from the abbey church.

The Boyne Valley ㉓

Co Meath. 🚌 to Drogheda.
🚌 to Slane or Drogheda. 🚻 Brú
na Bóinne interpretive centre, 041
9880300. 🕐 9:30am–5:30pm
(May–Sep: to 6:30pm; Nov–Feb:
to 5pm). **www**.heritageireland.ie

Known as Brú na Bóinne, the "Palace of the Boyne", this river valley was the cradle of Irish civilization. The fertile soil supported a sophisticated society in Neolithic times. Much evidence survives, in the form of ring forts, passage graves and sacred enclosures. The most important Neolithic monuments in the valley are three passage graves: supreme among these is **Newgrange** (see pp120–21), but **Dowth** and **Knowth** are significant too. The Boyne Valley also encompasses the Hill of Slane and the Hill of Tara (see p122), both major sites in Celtic lore.

With monuments pre-dating Egypt's pyramids, the Boyne Valley has been dubbed the Irish "Valley of the Kings".

Knowth and Newgrange can only be seen on a tour run by the interpretive centre near Newgrange, which also details the area's Stone Age heritage.

🏠 Dowth

Off N51, 3 km (2 miles) E of Newgrange. ● to the public. This passage grave was plundered in Victorian times by souvenir hunters and has not been fully excavated since. Visitors cannot approach the tomb, but may walk around the outside of the monument.

🏠 Knowth

1.5 km (1 mile) NW of Newgrange.
🖸 as Newgrange (see pp120–21). Knowth outdoes Newgrange in several respects, above all in the quantity of its treasures – Europe's greatest concentration of megalithic art. In addition, the site was occupied for a much longer period – from Neolithic times to about 1400.

Unusually, Knowth has two passage tombs rather than one. The excavations begun in 1962 are now complete and the site is open. The tombs can only be viewed externally to prevent further decay and visitors must sign up for tours via Brú na Bóinne (see p120).

River Boyne near the site of the Battle of the Boyne

Newgrange

**Tri-spiral carving
in chamber**

The origins of Newgrange, one of the most important passage graves in Europe, are steeped in mystery. According to Celtic lore, the legendary kings of Tara *(see p122)* were buried here, but Newgrange predates them. Built in around 3200 BC, the grave was left untouched by all invaders (though not by tomb robbers) and was eventually excavated in the 1960s. Archaeologists then discovered that on the winter solstice (21 December), rays of sun enter the tomb and light up the burial chamber – making it the oldest solar observatory in the world. All visitors to Newgrange and Knowth are admitted through the visitors' centre *(see p119)* from where tours of the historic sight are taken; early arrival is advised in summer to avoid long queues.

Basin stone
The chiselled stones, found in each recess, would have once contained funerary offerings and the bones of the dead.

The chamber has three recesses or side chambers: the north recess is the one struck by sunlight on the winter solstice.

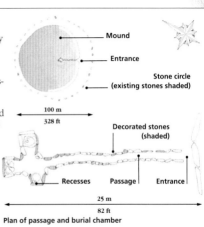

Chamber ceiling
The burial chamber's intricate corbelled ceiling, which reaches a height of 6 m (20 ft) above the floor, has survived intact. The overlapping slabs form a conical hollow, topped by a single capstone.

CONSTRUCTION OF NEWGRANGE

The tomb at Newgrange was designed by people with clearly exceptional artistic and engineering skills, who had use of neither the wheel nor metal tools. About 200,000 tonnes of loose stones were transported to build the mound, or cairn, which protects the passage grave. Larger slabs were used to make the circle around the cairn (12 out of a probable 35 stones have survived), the kerb and the tomb itself. Many of the kerbstones and the slabs lining the passage, the chamber and its recesses are decorated with zigzags, spirals and other geometric motifs. The grave's corbelled ceiling consists of smaller, unadorned slabs and has proved almost completely waterproof for the last 5,000 years.

Mound

Entrance

Stone circle
(existing stones shaded)

100 m
328 ft

Decorated stones
(shaded)

Recesses   Passage   Entrance

25 m
82 ft
Plan of passage and burial chamber

Restoration of Newgrange

Located on a low ridge north of the Boyne, Newgrange took more than 70 years to build. Between 1962 and 1975 the passage grave and mound were restored as closely as possible to their original state.

The standing stones in the passage are slabs of slate which would have been collected locally.

Passage

At dawn on 21 December, a beam of sunlight shines through the roof box (a feature unique to Newgrange), travels along the 19-m (62-ft) passage and hits the central recess in the burial chamber.

The retaining wall around the front of the cairn was rebuilt using the white quartz and granite stones found scattered around the site during excavations.

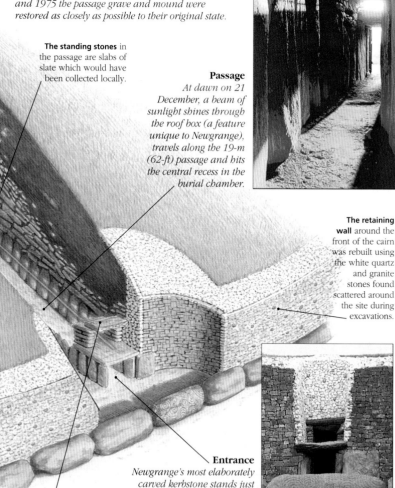

Roof box

Entrance

Newgrange's most elaborately carved kerbstone stands just in front of the entrance, forming part of the kerb of huge slabs around the cairn.

Trim Castle, set in water meadows beside the River Boyne

Slane ㉕

Co Meath. 🏠 950. 🚌 🛈 041 988 0305. www.eastcoastmidlands.ie

Slane is an attractive estate village, centred on a quartet of Georgian houses. The Boyne river flows through it and skirts around **Slane Castle Demesne**, set in glorious grounds laid out in the 18th century by the renowned landscape gardener, Capability Brown. The castle, dating from 1785, incorporates the designs of James Wyatt, Francis Johnson and James Gandon and is famous for its Gothic Revival ballroom designed by Thomas Hopper. The castle was badly damaged by fire in 1991 but reopened in 2001 after a decade of restoration. Just to the north rises the **Hill of Slane** where, in AD 433, St Patrick is said to

have lit a Paschal (Easter) fire as a challenge to the pagan High King of Tara. The local priest still marks this event by the lighting of a fire at Easter.

Hill of Tara ㉖

Nr Killmessan Village, Co Meath. **Tel** May–Oct: 046 25903; Nov–Apr: Brú na Bóinne 041 9880300. 🚌 to Navan. 🕐 May–Oct: 10am–6pm daily (last adm: 5:15pm). 🎫 for interpretive centre. 🅿 www.heritageireland.ie

A site of mythic importance, Tara was the political and spiritual centre of Celtic Ireland and the seat of the High Kings until the 11th century. The spread of Christianity, which eroded the importance of Tara, is marked by a statue of St Patrick. Tara's symbolism was not lost on Daniel O'Connell (*see p16*), who chose the site

for a rally in 1843, attended by more than a million people.

Tours from the interpretive centre point out a Stone Age passage grave and Iron Age hill forts though, to the untutored eye, these look like mere hollows and grassy mounds. Clearest is the Royal Enclosure, an oval fort, in the centre of which is Cormac's House containing the "stone of destiny" (*Liath Fáil*), an ancient fertility symbol and inauguration stone of the High Kings. However, all this is secondary to the views over the Boyne Valley and the site's sense of history.

Trim ㉗

Co Meath. 🏠 6,500. 🚌
🛈 Mill St, 046 9437111. 🚆 Fri.
www.eastcoastmidlandsireland.ie

Trim is one of the most pleasing Midlands market towns. A Norman stronghold on the River Boyne, it marked a boundary of the Pale (*see p108*). Trim runs efficient heritage and genealogy centres, including a visitors' centre next door to the tourist office.

Trim Castle was founded in 1173 by Hugh de Lacy, a Norman knight, and is one of the largest medieval castles in Europe. It makes a spectacular backdrop so is often used as a film set, most famously seen in Mel Gibson's *Braveheart* (1995). The castle is currently closed for renovation, but visitors can peer in from a barbican tower that is still open. In the summer, the Nun Run, a bizarre horse race with nuns as jockeys, takes place near the castle.

Aerial view of Iron Age forts on the Hill of Tara

Over the river is **Talbot Castle**, an Augustinian abbey converted to a manor house in the 15th century. Just north of the abbey, **St Patrick's Cathedral** incorporates part of a medieval church with a 15th-century tower and sections of the original chancel.

Butterstream Gardens, on the edge of town, are the best in the county. A luxuriant herbaceous bed is the centrepiece, but equally pleasing are the woodland, rose and white gardens. The design is enhanced by pergolas, pools and bridges.

🌿 **Butterstream Gardens**
Kildalkey Rd. *Tel 046 9436017.*
⭕ *Apr–Sep: 11am–6pm daily.* 🔲

Mullingar ㉘

Co Westmeath. 🏠 *14,000.* 🚌 🚲
ℹ️ *Market Sq, 044 9348650.* 🏪 *Sat.*

The county town of Westmeath is a prosperous market town encircled by the Royal Canal *(see p85)*, which links Dublin with the River Shannon. Although Mullingar's main appeal is as a base to explore the surrounding area, pubs such as Con's and cheery Canton Casey's can make a pleasant interlude. In addition, the 20th-century cathedral features unusual mosaics of St Anne and St Patrick.

Environs
Recent restoration of the Dublin to Mullingar stretch of the Royal Canal has resulted in attractive towpaths for canal-side walks, as well as good

The remains of the Jealous Wall at Belvedere House, near Mullingar

Lighting votive candles in Mullingar Cathedral

angling facilities. South of Mullingar, just off the road to Kilbeggan, stands **Belvedere House**, a romantic Palladian villa overlooking Lough Ennel. Built in 1740 by architect Richard Castle, Belvedere is decorated with Rococo plasterwork and set in wonderful gardens. Shortly after the house was built, the first Earl of Belvedere accused his wife of having an affair with his brother, and imprisoned her for 31 years in a neighbouring house. He sued the brother and had him jailed for life. In 1760, the Earl built a Gothic folly – the Jealous Wall – in order to block the view from another brother's more opulent mansion. The Jealous Wall still remains, as does an octagonal gazebo and other follies.

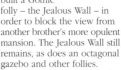
Miniature whiskey bottles at Locke's Distillery in Kilbeggan

Charming terraces, framed by urns and yews, descend to the lake; on the other side of the house is a pretty walled garden, enclosed by an arboretum and rolling parkland. There is also an animal sanctuary next to the visitor centre.

🏚️ **Belvedere House**
6 km (4 miles) S of Mullingar. *Tel 044 9349060.* **Gardens** ⭕ *daily. May, Apr, Sep–Feb: 10:30am–7pm (Nov–Feb: to 4:30pm); May–Aug: 9:30am–9pm (last adm: 1hr before closing).* 🔲 🔲 *of estate by tram.* 🦽 *visitor centre only.* 🔲 🔲 *www.belvedere-house.ie*

Kilbeggan ㉙

Co Westmeath. 🏠 *600.* 🚌

Situated between Mullingar and Tullamore, this pleasant village has a small harbour on the Grand Canal. However, the main point of interest is **Locke's Distillery**. Founded in 1757, it claims to be the oldest licensed pot still distillery in the world. Unable to compete with Scotch whisky manufacturers, the company went bankrupt in 1954, but the aroma hung in the warehouses for years and was known as "the angels' share". The distillery was reopened as a museum in 1987. The building is authentic, a solid structure complete with a water wheel and an indoor steam engine. A tour traces the process of Irish whiskey-making, from the mash tuns through to the fermentation vats and creation of wash (rough beer) to the distillation and maturation stages. At the tasting stage, workers would sample the whiskey in the can pit room. Visitors can still taste whiskeys in the bar but, unlike the original workers, cannot bathe in the whiskey vats.

🏛️ **Locke's Distillery**
Museum Main St. *Tel 057 9332134.* ⭕ *Apr–Oct: 9am–6pm daily; Nov–Mar: 10am–4pm daily.* 🔲 🔢 *www.lockesdistillerymuseum.ie*

TRAVELLERS' NEEDS

WHERE TO STAY 126–133

RESTAURANTS, CAFES AND PUBS 134–147

SHOPS AND MARKETS 148–153

ENTERTAINMENT IN DUBLIN 154–161

WHERE TO STAY

Doorman at the Conrad Hotel

Whether you are staying in exclusive luxury or modest bed-and-breakfast accommodation, one thing you can be certain of in Dublin is that you will receive a warm welcome. The Irish are renowned for their friendliness and even in big corporate hotels, where you might expect the reception to be more impersonal, the staff go out of their way to be hospitable. The choice is enormous: you can stay in an elegant, refurbished Georgian house, a comfortable bed-and-breakfast, a Victorian townhouse, an old-fashioned commercial hotel or a cosy pub. Details are given here of the various types of accommodation available. The listings on pages 128–33 recommend around 60 hotels in both central Dublin and outside the city – all places of quality, ranging from basic to luxury – and should help you decide upon your choice of accommodation. Fáilte Ireland (the Irish Tourist Board) and Dublin Tourism also publish comprehensive guides to recommended accommodation in the area.

Main entrance to the fashionable Clarence Hotel (see p131)

HOTELS

At the top of the price range there are quite a few expensive, luxury hotels in the heart of Dublin. Magnificently furnished and run, they offer maximum comfort, delicious food and often have indoor facilities, such as a gym and swimming pool. As well as luxurious individual hotels there are also the modern hotel chains, such as **Bewleys** and **Irish Welcome**, which offer a high standard of accommodation. However, these establishments can lack the charm and individuality of privately run hotels.

There are also numerous very moderate hotels in the centre of Dublin, providing a good standard of accommodation.

If you prefer to stay outside Dublin, there are some wonderful castles and stately homes which offer the same standards as the top city hotels but which have the bonus of being set in beautiful countryside. They can often also arrange outdoor pursuits such as fishing, riding and golf.

The shamrock symbol of **Fáilte Ireland** is displayed by hotels (and other forms of accommodation) that have been inspected and approved.

BED-AND-BREAKFAST ACCOMMODATION

Ireland has a reputation for the best B&Bs in Europe. Your welcome will always be friendly and the food and company excellent. Even if the house is no architectural

The entrance to the grand Shelbourne Hotel (see p130) on St Stephen's Green

A contemporary deluxe bedroom in the Brooks Hotel (see p130)

beauty, the comfort and atmosphere will more than compensate. Not all of the bedrooms have bathrooms *en suite*. When one is available, you may possibly have to pay a little extra but, considering the generally cheap rates, the surcharge is negligible.

The Irish swear by their B&Bs and many stay in them by choice rather than paying to stay in the luxurious surroundings of some of the big hotels. **Town and Country Homes** will provide details of bed-and-breakfast accommodation throughout Ireland.

GUESTHOUSES

Most guesthouses are found in cities and large towns. They are usually converted family homes and have an atmosphere all of their own. Most offer a good-value evening meal and all give you a delicious full Irish breakfast (see p136). Top-of-the-range guesthouses can be just as good, and sometimes even better, than hotels. You will see a much more personal side of a town or city while

◁ View of Ha'Penny Bridge from O'Connell Bridge

staying at a guesthouse. There are plenty to choose from in the Dublin area and the prices are usually reasonable. The **Irish Hotels Federation** publishes a useful booklet with guesthouse listings that cover the whole of Ireland, including Dublin and its environs.

PRICES

Room rates advertised are inclusive of service and tax. Hotel rates can vary by as much as 40 per cent depending on the time of year. Prices in guesthouses are influenced more by their proximity to tourist sights and public transport. Dublin offers a complete range of accommodation, from youth hostels through very reasonably priced bed-and-breakfasts to lavish five-star hotels such as the Merrion, Morrison and the Clarence.

TIPPING

Tipping in Dublin is a matter of personal discretion but is not common practice, even at the larger hotels. Tasks performed by staff are considered part of the service. Tipping is not expected for carrying bags to your room or for serving drinks. However, it is usual to tip the waiting staff in hotel restaurants: the standard tip is around 10–15 per cent of the bill – anything in excess of that would be considered particularly generous.

The elegant and modern reception at The Morrison hotel *(see p131)*

BOOKING

It is wise to reserve your accommodation during the peak season and public holidays *(see p29)*, particularly if your visit coincides with a local festival such as the St Patrick's Day celebrations *(see p26)* when the city can get booked up.
Dublin Tourism *(see p164)* can offer advice and make reservations through its accommodation service. Central reservation facilities are available at the hotel chains listed here.

Fáilte Ireland accommodation sign

YOUTH HOSTELS

There are 31 youth hostels registered with **An Óige** (the Irish Youth Hostel Association), with one in the Dublin area. Accommodation is provided in dormitories with comfortable beds and basic cooking facilities. You can only use these hostels if you are a member of An Óige or another organization affiliated to the International Youth Hostel Federation.

There are also independent hostels, and places such as universities that offer similar inexpensive accommodation in Dublin. The tourist board has listings of those places that are recommended.

DISABLED TRAVELLERS

A fact sheet for disabled visitors is produced by Fáilte Ireland and their accommodation guide indicates wheelchair accessibility. Dublin Tourism and **Citizens Information Board** are also helpful. *Accommodation for Disabled Persons* and *Dublin: A Guide for Disabled Persons* are useful leaflets which are available at the tourist office.

DIRECTORY

CHAIN HOTELS

Bewleys Hotel
Merrion Rd, Ballsbridge, Dublin 4.
Tel 668 1111. *Fax* 293 0221.
www.bewleyshotels.com

Irish Welcome
Bracken Court, Bracken Rd, Sandyford, Dublin 18.
Tel 293 3000. *Fax* 293 3001.
www.irishwelcometours.com

OTHER USEFUL ADDRESSES

An Óige (Irish Youth Hostel Association)
61 Mountjoy St, Dublin 7.
Tel 830 4555. *Fax* 830 5808.
www.anoige.ie

Citizens Information Board
George's Quay House, 43 Townsend St, Dublin 2.
Tel 1890 777 121.
www.citizensinformationboard.ie

Irish Hotels Federation
13 Northbrook Rd, Dublin 6.
Tel 497 6459. *Fax* 497 4613.
www.irelandhotels.com

Town and Country Homes
Beleek Rd, Ballyshannon, Co Donegal. *Tel* 071 982 2222.
www.townandcountry.ie

The stately charm of Dunbrody Country House *(see p133)*

Choosing a Hotel

The hotels in this guide have been selected across a wide price range for their good value, facilities and location. These listings highlight some of the factors that may influence your choice. Hotels are listed by area, beginning with the Southeast. For information on restaurants in the area, see pages 138–145.

PRICE CATEGORIES
For a standard double room per night, including tax, service charges and breakfast.

€ Under 120 euros
€€ 120–160 euros
€€€ 160–190 euros
€€€€ 190–250 euros
€€€€€ Over 250 euros

SOUTHEAST DUBLIN

Davenport

€€   Map F4

Merrion Square, Dublin 2 **Tel** *01 607 3500* **Fax** *01 661 5663* **Rooms** *114*

This hotel lies in the heart of Georgian Dublin, and its Neo-Classical façade dates from 1863. Mahogany, brass and marble furnishings give the Davenport the feel of a gentleman's club. The ample bedrooms are well appointed, with a warmly coloured decor. A fitness suite and a business centre are available. **www.ocallaghanhotels.ie**

Harcourt Hotel

€€   Map D5

60 Harcourt Street, Dublin 2 **Tel** *01 478 3677* **Fax** *01 475 2013* **Rooms** *104*

Just off St Stephen's Green, the Harcourt boasts a beautifully central location. Although the interior is fairly unremarkable, bedrooms are modern and well equipped. A popular nightclub, D-Two, is situated in the basement of the hotel and is a draw for late-night revellers. **www.harcourthotel.ie**

Kilronan House

€€

70 Adelaide Road, Dublin 2 **Tel** *01 475 5266* **Fax** *01 478 2841* **Rooms** *12*

Situated on a leafy street near St Stephen's Green, around the corner from the National Concert Hall, this listed townhouse dates back to 1834. Although it retains its Georgian character, it is newly refurbished with all modern comforts, including orthopaedic beds. Delicious breakfasts and friendly hosts. **www.dublinn.com**

Leeson Court Hotel

€€   Map E5

27 Leeson Street Lower, Dublin 2 **Tel** *01 676 3380* **Fax** *01 661 8273* **Rooms** *20*

Close to St Stephen's Green, this cheerfully decorated hotel is spread across two Georgian buildings. The ambience is relaxed and informal, but the service is of a high quality. The hotel bar, Kobra, is elegant, with wood furnishings. Bedrooms are tidy and comfortable, if somewhat on the small side. **www.theleesonhotel.com**

Longfields

€€   Map F5

10 Fitzwilliam Street Lower, Dublin 2 **Tel** *01 676 1367* **Fax** *01 676 1542* **Rooms** *26*

Two interconnected Georgian buildings make up this small, stylish hotel, situated between the appealing Fitzwilliam and Merrion squares. Furnished with antiques and tasteful reproduction pieces, Longfields exudes the warmth of a private home. Rooms have an individual character, and there is a good restaurant on site. **www.longfields.ie**

Russell Court

€€   Map D5

21–25 Harcourt Street, Dublin 2 **Tel** *01 478 4066* **Fax** *01 478 4994* **Rooms** *46*

Lively and welcoming, the Russell Court is a good choice for younger visitors. The hotel's main attraction lies in its upbeat nightclubs: Bojangles for the 30-plus set and Krystle for a younger crowd. At the rear, Dicey's Garden is a popular beer garden. Bedrooms are neat and tidy, and trams stop near the front. **www.russellcourthotel.ie**

Temple Bar Hotel

€€   Map D3

Fleet Street, Dublin 2 **Tel** *01 677 3333* **Fax** *01 677 3088* **Rooms** *129*

Its location in the heart of Temple Bar – a lively area with several pubs and restaurants – makes this modern hotel popular for stag and hen parties. Bedrooms are clean and adequate, if a little on the small side and lacking in character. A multi-storey car park is available nearby. **www.dublin-hotels.com**

Harrington Hall Guesthouse

€€€   Map D5

70 Harcourt Street, Dublin 2 **Tel** *475 3497* **Fax** *475 4544* **Rooms** *28*

Just off St Stephen's Green, this hotel is housed in two adjoining Georgian buildings. Careful restoration has retained many original features, including high ornamental ceilings and marble bathrooms. Guests can relax in the elegant drawing room, which has an open fire and comfy armchairs. Good breakfast. **www.harringtonhall.com**

Molesworth Court Suites

€€€   Map E4

Molesworth Court, Schoolhouse Lane, Dublin 2 **Tel** *01 676 4799* **Fax** *01 676 4982* **Rooms** *12*

Tucked away in a quiet lane off Molesworth Street, this four-star hotel comprises 12 self-contained apartments and penthouses. Equipped with modern conveniences, the lodgings are stylish and cosy, making this establishment ideal for businesspeople and families alike. Enclosed parking is provided. **www.molesworthcourt.ie**

Key to Symbols *see back cover flap*

Maldron Hotel
Sir John Rogerson's Quay, Cardiff Lane, Dublin 2 **Tel** *643 9500* **Fax** *643 9510* **Rooms** *303*

€€€

Located in a modern building in the Docklands, the Quality is part of the Choice Hotels chain. Its leisure centre offers a pool, sauna and spa therapies. Rooms are clean, modern and spacious. The hotel's affordability makes up for the 15-minute walk into city centre. **www.maldronhotels.com**

Stauntons on the Green
83 St Stephen's Green, Dublin 2 **Tel** *01 478 2300* **Fax** *01 478 2263* **Rooms** *57*　　　　**Map** D5

€€€

Located beside the Ministry of Foreign Affairs, this guesthouse offers comfortable and modest accommodation in three terraced Georgian houses. While bedrooms are reasonably equipped and en suite, those to the rear are quieter, with views of the private garden and Iveagh Gardens. Valet parking is available. **www.castlegroup.ie**

Trinity Lodge
12 South Frederick Street, Dublin 2 **Tel** *01 617 0900* **Fax** *01 617 0999* **Rooms** *23*　　　　**Map** E4

€€€

Close to Grafton Street and Trinity College, this Georgian townhouse enjoys one of the best locations in town. Though traditional in style, it is furnished with all modern conveniences, and the warmly coloured en-suite bedrooms are well maintained. Spend some time at Georges, the in-house bistro and wine bar. **www.trinitylodge.com**

Mont Clare
Merrion Square, Dublin 2 **Tel** *01 607 3800* **Fax** *01 661 5663* **Rooms** *74*　　　　**Map** F4

€€€€

Though not as grand as its sister hotel the Davenport *(see p128)*, Mont Clare is traditionally furnished in mahogany and brass. The well-appointed bedrooms are air conditioned and tastefully decorated. The popular bar serves food and the restaurant serves carvery lunches. Guests may use the gym across the road for free. **www.ocallaghanhotels.com**

Morgan Hotel
10 Fleet Street, Dublin 2 **Tel** *01 643 7000* **Fax** *01 643 7060* **Rooms** *121*　　　　**Map** D3

€€€€

In the heart of Temple Bar, this self-styled boutique hotel is contemporary in design, with clean lines and uncluttered public spaces. The minimalistic bedrooms have beech furnishings, cotton linen and CD systems. The ambience is relaxing, though the rooms overlooking the street can be noisy. There is a fine bar on site. **www.themorgan.com**

St Stephen's Green Hotel
St Stephen's Green, Dublin 2 **Tel** *01 607 3600* **Fax** *01 661 5663* **Rooms** *78*　　　　**Map** D4

€€€€

Warm and friendly, this hotel is superbly located on the southwest corner of St Stephen's Green. It consists of two splendid Georgian townhouses with a modern glass atrium. The spacious bedrooms are clean and well equipped, with comfortable beds and nice views of the green. **www.ocallaghanhotels.com**

Stephen's Hall Hotel
14–17 Leeson Street Lower, Dublin 2 **Tel** *01 638 1111* **Fax** *01 638 1122* **Rooms** *30*　　　　**Map** E5

€€€€

Situated close to St Stephen's Green, the recently refurbished Stephen's Hall provides suites that include an attached kitchen. Its proximity to the vibrant city centre makes this hotel a very good value family option. Underground parking is available. **www.stephens-hall.com**

Alexander Hotel
Fenian Street, off Merrion Square, Dublin 2 **Tel** *607 3700* **Fax** *661 5663* **Rooms** *102*　　　　**Map** F4

€€€€€

Located beside the National Gallery, the Alexander is a recent build that is tastefully sympathetic to the Georgian surroundings of Merrion Square. Modern rooms have climate control, wireless internet access and large beds. Residents can use the facilities of three sister hotels nearby. **www.ocallaghanhotels.com**

Bentley's
22 St Stephen's Green, Dublin 2 **Tel** *01 638 3939* **Fax** *01 638 3900* **Rooms** *10*　　　　**Map** D4

€€€€€

Set in a Georgian house overlooking St Stephen's Green, this charming and intimate boutique hotel is stylishly furnished with antiques. Each of the bedrooms is individually designed with comfort and character in mind. The sophisticated Bentley's Oyster Bar & Grill restaurant serves outstanding food. **www.bentleysdublin.com**

Buswell's
25 Molesworth Street, Dublin 2 **Tel** *01 614 6500* **Fax** *01 676 2090* **Rooms** *67*　　　　**Map** E4

€€€€€

Comprising five Georgian townhouses, this slightly old-fashioned hotel has been in operation since 1882. It is frequented by political figures, perhaps due to its location beside the government buildings, on a street renowned for commercial art galleries. The sophisticated interior is decorated in warm colours. **www.buswellshotel.com**

Conrad Hotel
Earlsfort Terrace, Dublin 2 **Tel** *01 602 8900* **Fax** *01 676 5424* **Rooms** *192*　　　　**Map** D5

€€€€€

Opposite the National Concert Hall, this international-style hotel is geared towards business people. The decor is tasteful and the atmosphere airy. Bedrooms are fitted out in a contemporary style with light wood furnishings and comfortable beds. The higher floors have good views. Professional service. **www.conraddublin.com**

Fitzwilliam Hotel
St Stephen's Green, Dublin 2 **Tel** *478 7000* **Fax** *478 7878* **Rooms** *139*　　　　**Map** D4

€€€€€

This five-star hotel features a fresh contemporary design by Sir Terence Conran, including a glass drawbridge in the entrance hall. Rooms are modern and unfussy, except for the penthouse, which boasts a grand piano. Voted one of the Top 20 Hottest Hotels in the World by *Condé Nast Traveller* magazine. **www.fitzwilliamhotel.com**

Merrion
🖼🍴🏊🏋🛗   €€€€€

Merrion Street Upper, Dublin 2 **Tel** *01 603 0600* **Fax** *01 603 0700* **Rooms** *143*   **Map** *E4*

In the heart of Georgian Dublin, the Merrion is an elegant and stylish oasis, with open log fires, opulent interiors and a collection of Irish art and antiques. It is a landmark hotel, comprising four listed townhouses from the 1760s, all sensitively restored to their original grandeur. Guests can use the excellent Tethra Spa. **www.merrionhotel.ie**

Number 31
€€€€€

31 Leeson Close, Leeson Street Lower, Dublin 2 **Tel** *01 676 5011* **Fax** *01 676 2929* **Rooms** *21*   **Map** *E5*

Reputedly the most stylish guesthouse in the city, this elegant establishment is more of a boutique hotel than a B&B, with individually decorated, luxurious bedrooms in two houses. The Coach House is decorated in contemporary style and the Georgian house is grand and formal. Delicious breakfasts are served in the plant-filled conservatory. **www.number31.ie**

Shelbourne Renaissance Hotel
🖼🍴🏋🛗   €€€€€

27 St Stephen's Green, Dublin 2 **Tel** *01 663 4500* **Fax** *01 661 6006* **Rooms** *265*   **Map** *D4*

The five-star Shelbourne, part of the Marriott empire, has been the city's most distinguished hotel since it first opened in 1824. Now extensively restored, the Shelbourne remains a haven of sophistication, featuring Egyptian-cotton bedding, flat-screen TVs and marble bathrooms. **www.theshelbourne.ie**

Westbury Hotel
🖼🍴🏋🛗   €€€€€

Grafton Street, Dublin 2 **Tel** *01 679 1122* **Fax** *01 679 7078* **Rooms** *205*   **Map** *D4*

Enjoying possibly the most convenient location in the city, the Westbury is only seconds from Dublin's main shopping street. The first floor lobby of this smart, ritzy, yet traditionally styled hotel, is a popular meeting place for afternoon tea. Underground parking comes with free valet service. There is also a small gymnasium. **www.doylecollection.com**

Westin Hotel
🖼🍴🏋🛗   €€€€€

College Green, Dublin 2 **Tel** *01 645 1000* **Fax** *01 645 1234* **Rooms** *163*   **Map** *D3*

Two 19th-century landmark buildings and part of the former Allied Irish Bank were reconstructed to create this sizeable hotel, across the street from Trinity College. The well-appointed bedrooms are furnished to a high standard; the beds are particularly comfortable. The former vaults of the bank are now a bar, The Mint. **www.westin.com/dublin**

SOUTHWEST DUBLIN

Avalon House
🖼   €

55 Aungier Street, Dublin 2 **Tel** *01 475 0001* **Fax** *01 475 0303* **Rooms** *70*   **Map** *C4*

One of the longest established hostels in the city, the centrally located Avalon House provides cheap and cheerful accommodation in a restored red brick Victorian building. Rooms are clean, with pine and tile floors, high ceilings and an open fire. Popular with young travellers, Avalon House also has a café. **www.avalon-house.ie**

Barnacles Hostel
🏋   €

Temple Lane, Temple Bar, Dublin 2 **Tel** *01 671 6277* **Fax** *01 671 6591* **Rooms** *32*   **Map** *C3*

Directly in the middle of Temple Bar, this award-winning hostel is bright, spacious, lively and clean, with a sunny lounge and a self-catering kitchen. There is a variety of rooms, including doubles, twins and dormitories sleeping from four to 12 people. All rooms are en suite. Staff are friendly and helpful. Open 24 hours. **www.barnacles.ie**

Blooms Hotel
🖼🍴   €€

Anglesea Street, Dublin 2 **Tel** *01 671 5622* **Fax** *01 671 5997* **Rooms** *100*   **Map** *D3*

The location – on the fringes of Temple Bar and close to Trinity College – is the main selling point of the Blooms. The hotel has an appealing modern exterior, and its compact bedrooms are adequate, if bland – the ones at the front are preferable. There is live music in the busy Vat House Bar, while Club M is a popular nightclub. **www.blooms.ie**

Central Hotel
🖼🍴🏋   €€

1–5 Exchequer Street, Dublin 2 **Tel** *01 679 7302* **Fax** *01 679 7303* **Rooms** *70*   **Map** *D5*

Established in 1887, this three-star hotel is aptly named, given its convenient location, very close to Grafton Street. Recently refurbished with modern facilities, the Central retains a somewhat old-fashioned atmosphere, with traditional yet cosy decor. Bedrooms are neat, functional and reasonably priced. **www.centralhotel.ie**

Jury's Inn Christchurch
🖼🍴🏋   €€

Christchurch Place, Dublin 8 **Tel** *01 454 0000* **Fax** *01 454 0012* **Rooms** *182*   **Map** *B4*

Opposite Christ Church Cathedral, in the old Viking centre of Dublin, this modern hotel lies within easy walking distance of the Temple Bar area. Rooms are neat and well equipped. Bathrooms are adequate, if a little on the small side. Prices per room are particularly good value for families. **www.jurysdoyle.com**

Brooks
🖼🍴🛗   €€€€

59–62 Drury Street, Dublin 2 **Tel** *01 670 4000* **Fax** *01 670 4455* **Rooms** *98*   **Map** *D4*

This immaculately maintained boutique hotel, located just minutes from Grafton Street, has a club-like feel and a welcoming ambience. It was built in 1997 and remodelled in 2003 with contemporary flourishes and warm colours, though the decor is tastefully traditional. Brooks enjoys a great reputation. **www.brookshotel.com**

Key to Price Guide *see p128* **Key to Symbols** *see back cover flap*

Mercer Hotel
Lower Mercer Street, Dublin 2 **Tel** *01 478 2179* **Fax** *01 672 9926* **Rooms** *41*   **Map** *C5*

Well located in the city centre, this three-star hotel combines the traditional with the contemporary, as witnessed in its wooden floors, subtle colour scheme and modern furnishings. Bedrooms are clean and comfortable and include all modern conveniences. There is a newly refurbished bar, as well as a restaurant, Cusacks. **www.mercerhotel.ie**

Clarence Hotel
6–8 Wellington Quay, Dublin 2 **Tel** *01 407 0800* **Fax** *01 407 0820* **Rooms** *49*   **Map** *C3*

Overlooking the Liffey, this 1852 Dublin landmark was bought by the rock band U2 in 1992. Extensively refurbished, it has now acquired cult status. With original wood panelling in the Arts and Crafts style, and luxuriously furnished rooms, this establishment successfully combines contemporary cool and old-style comfort. **www.theclarence.ie**

NORTH OF THE LIFFEY

Clifden Guest House
32 Gardiners Place, Dublin 1 **Tel** *01 874 6364* **Fax** *01 874 6122* **Rooms** *15*

This three-star family-run guesthouse is set in a four-storey Georgian townhouse, just a few minutes' walk from the centre of the city. The high-ceilinged rooms are functional, yet comfortably furnished and cheerfully decorated. They come in varying sizes – one accommodating up to five people. **www.clifdenhouse.com**

Harvey's Hotel
11 Upper Gardiner Street, Dublin 1 **Tel** *01 874 8384* **Fax** *01 874 5510* **Rooms** *16*

This hospitable family-run Georgian townhouse, north of the Liffey, is ten minutes' walk from the top of O'Connell Street. Rooms are clean and pleasant; while some are a little jaded, most are nicely decorated. Those at the back are quieter. The atmosphere is friendly and relaxed. **www.harveysguesthouse.com**

Cassidy's Hotel
Cavendish Row, Upper O'Connell Street, Dublin 1 **Tel** *01 878 0555* **Fax** *01 878 0687* **Rooms** *113*   **Map** *D2*

This hotel is conveniently located at the top of O'Connell Street, opposite the Gate Theatre, in three adjoining red brick Georgian townhouses. The generously proportioned rooms have been modernized, but they retain some period features. Spacious bedrooms are all en suite, with contemporary furnishings. **www.cassidyshotel.com**

Clarion IFSC
International Financial Service Centre, North Wall Quay, Dublin 1 **Tel** *01 433 8800* **Rooms** *163*   **Map** *F2*

A short stroll from the centre, the Clarion IFSC offers well-designed and decent accommodation overlooking the River Liffey, in the heart of the financial district. This hotel opened in 2001 and is becoming as popular with tourists as it is with business travellers. Public spaces are bright, airy and minimalist in style. **www.clarionhotelifsc.com**

Gresham Hotel
23 Upper O'Connell Street, Dublin 1 **Tel** *01 874 6881* **Fax** *01 878 7175* **Rooms** *288*   **Map** *D1*

One of Dublin's oldest and best known hotels, the Gresham is a popular rendezvous spot with ever-lively public areas. It has been recently refurbished, with pleasant furnishings that combine classic and contemporary styles. The well-equipped bedrooms are cheerfully decorated. A good business hotel. **www.gresham-hotels.com**

Royal Dublin
40–42 O'Connell Street, Dublin 2 **Tel** *01 873 3666* **Fax** *01 873 3120* **Rooms** *120*   **Map** *D1*

The modern Royal Dublin is located in one of city's most famous and historic streets. O'Connell Street has been extensively upgraded in recent times, making it much more pleasant than in the past. This hotel may be lacking in atmosphere, but the rooms are self-sufficient. Those at the rear are quieter. Friendly staff. **www.royaldublin.com**

The Morrison
Ormond Quay, Dublin 1 **Tel** *01 887 2400* **Fax** *01 878 3185* **Rooms** *138*   **Map** *C3*

Located on the quay overlooking the river, this luxurious hotel was built in 1999, with John Rocha as design consultant. The interior is a mix of high ceilings, dark woods, pale walls, dim lighting, handcrafted Irish carpets and original art. Bedrooms have a modern design. There is also a stylish restaurant, Halo. **www.morrisonhotel.ie**

FURTHER AFIELD

Clara House
23 Leinster Road, Rathmines, Dublin 6 **Tel** *01 497 5904* **Fax** *01 497 5580* **Rooms** *13*

Built in 1840, this listed red brick Georgian house is a favoured B&B. It is a 15-minute walk from the city centre, and there is also a good bus route into town. The atmosphere is relaxed and friendly. Secure private car park is available at the rear. The pleasant waterside walks along the canal are an added attraction.

Donnybrook Hall   €

6 Belmont Avenue, Donnybrook, Dublin 4 **Tel** *01 269 1633* **Fax** *01 269 2649* **Rooms** *10*

This family-run guesthouse is located on a quiet residential street near the Royal Dublin Society showgrounds and Landsdowne Road stadium. The interior is light and elegant, and all rooms have orthopaedic mattresses. Three of them open on to a garden. Great breakfasts include pancakes, French toast and fresh fruit. **www.donnybrookhall.com**

Druid Lodge   🏃   €

Killiney Hill Road, Killiney, Co Dublin **Tel** *01 285 1632* **Fax** *01 285 8504* **Rooms** *4*

Situated on picturesque Killiney Hill, overlooking the bay, Druid Lodge is 11 km (7 miles) south of Dublin city centre. A charming ivy-clad guesthouse, it was built in 1832 and named after the adjoining sacred site of Druid's Chair. Exuding a peaceful, old-world charm, it is well furnished and comfortable. **www.druidlodge.com**

Glenogra Guesthouse   🏃   €

64 Merrion Road, Ballsbridge, Dublin 4 **Tel** *01 668 3661* **Fax** *01 668 3698* **Rooms** *12*

This stylish and award-winning guesthouse provides pleasant and good value B&B accommodation in a leafy, upmarket area of Dublin. The owners create a welcoming atmosphere for their guests: bedrooms are pleasantly appointed, and the breakfast is good. **www.glenogra.com**

Marble Hall Guest Accommodation   📋   €

81 Marlborough Road, Donnybrook, Dublin 4 **Tel** *01 497 7350* **Rooms** *3*

This much-loved guesthouse is set in a leafy residential area, 20 minutes' walk from town and on a well-serviced bus route. Victorian in style, it is meticulously maintained by Shelagh Conway, who is renowned for her excellent breakfasts. Bedrooms are spacious and tastefully decorated with antique furniture. **www.marblehall.net**

Mount Herbert Hotel   📋 🔧 🍴 🏃 🛎   €

7 Herbert Road, Ballsbridge, Dublin 4 **Tel** *01 668 4321* **Fax** *01 660 7077* **Rooms** *168*

Established for more than 50 years, the Mount Herbert is located in a residential area close to the Landsdowne Road stadium. It consists of a terrace of interconnecting houses decorated with modern furnishings. The en-suite bedrooms are equipped with good facilities. There is free access to a nearby gym. **www.mountherberthotel.ie**

Tara Towers Hotel   🔧 🍴 🏃   €

Merrion Road, Booterstown, Dublin 4 **Tel** *01 269 4666* **Fax** *01 269 1027* **Rooms** *111*

South of the city centre, this three-star hotel is situated on the coastal road. Dun Laoghaire is a 15-minute drive away, and there is a well-serviced bus route and a DART station nearby. The ambience is relaxed, and bedrooms are comfortable and spacious, if rather basic in decor. There is a traditional restaurant on site. **www.taratowers.com**

Belcamp Hutchinson   €€

Carrs Lane, Malahide Road, Balgriffin, Dublin 17 **Tel** *01 846 0843* **Fax** *01 848 5703* **Rooms** *8*

Only 15 minutes' drive from the airport, this secluded, creeper-clad Georgian house offers B&B accommodation. The friendly and welcoming hosts and large, high-ceilinged rooms make for a pleasant stay. Nearby, the picturesque seaside village of Malahide offers golf, tennis, sailing and horse-riding facilities. **www.belcamphutchinson.com**

Butlers Town House   🏃 🛎   €€

44 Landsdowne Road, Ballsbridge, Dublin 4 **Tel** *01 667 4022* **Fax** *01 667 3960* **Rooms** *20*

Furnished in a country-house style, this Georgian guesthouse offers four-star accommodation in individually designed bedrooms with Egyptian cotton sheets. Good breakfasts are served in the Conservatory Restaurant, which features an all-day menu, making this more of a small hotel than a B&B. **www.butlers-hotel.com**

Crowne Plaza Hotel   🔧 🍴 🏃 🛎   €€

Northwood Park, Santry Demesne, Santry, Dublin 9 **Tel** *01 862 8888* **Fax** *01 862 8800* **Rooms** *204*

Set in mature parkland, just five minutes from Dublin Airport and 15 minutes from the city centre, the Crowne Plaza offers all modern comforts. Rooms are well equipped, and there is an on-site fitness centre. A 24-hour courtesy coach for the airport is available. Located close to the M1 and M50 motorways. **www.cpdublin-airport.com**

The Red Bank   🍴 🏃   €€

6–7 Church Street, Skerries, Co Dublin **Tel** *01 849 1005* **Fax** *01 849 1598* **Rooms** *18*

On the premises of a former bank, in the heart of the village of Skerries, this guesthouse offers comfortably furnished rooms with good facilities. The award-winning Red Bank Restaurant has great character and specializes in seafood. Warm hospitality is guaranteed. Dublin Airport is just a short drive away. **www.redbank.ie**

Waterloo House   🔧 🏃   €€

8–10 Waterloo Road, Ballsbridge, Dublin 4 **Tel** *01 660 1888* **Fax** *01 667 1955* **Rooms** *17*

A short walk from St Stephen's Green, this lovely guesthouse comprises two adjoining Georgian buildings on a tree-lined road, away from the bustle of the city. The ambience is informal, and the bedrooms cosy. A good, hearty breakfast is served in a cheerful dining room. Off-street parking is available. **www.waterloohouse.ie**

Ballsbridge Court   🔧 🍴 🏃   €€€

Landsdowne Road, Ballsbridge, Dublin 4 **Tel** *01 668 4468* **Rooms** *188*

In the heart of the embassy belt, this five-star hotel is conveniently located for the Royal Dublin Society showground and Landsdowne Road stadium. Beyond the unappealing exterior, the chandeliered lobby sets the tone for a plush ambience. Rooms are well appointed and there is a jazz bar and bistro. **www.d4hotels.com**

Key to Price Guide *see p128* **Key to Symbols** *see back cover flap*

Grand Canal Hotel

Grand Canal Street, Ballsbridge, Dublin 4 **Tel** *01 646 1000* **Fax** *01 646 1001* **Rooms** *142*

Winner of the New Hotel of the Year award in 2005, the Grand Canal is spacious and modern, with a friendly staff. The on-site pub, Kitty O'Sheas, is one of the best in town. There is also a new restaurant, Epic. It is conveniently located between Trinity College and Landsdowne Road. **www.grandcanalhotel.com**

Herbert Park Hotel

Ballsbridge, Dublin 4 **Tel** *01 667 2200* **Fax** *01 667 2595* **Rooms** *153*

Overlooking the park after which it is named, this big contemporary hotel is bright and airy. Materials used to enliven the interiors include polished granite, Irish abstract art, Irish furniture and glass walls. Bedrooms are well appointed and stylishly designed. **www.herbertparkhotel.ie**

The Burlington

Upper Leeson Street, Dublin 4 **Tel** *01 618 5600* **Fax** *01 660 8086* **Rooms** *500*

This four-star hotel is a genuine Dublin institution at the heart of the city's south side. The rooms are smartly appointed, and there is a choice of two restaurants, The Sussex or The Diplomat. Bellini's bar is contemporary and stylish and has a relaxed atmosphere for an afternoon drink. **www.burlingtonhotel.ie**

Portmarnock Hotel & Golf Links

Portmarnock, Co Dublin **Tel** *01 846 0611* **Fax** *01 846 2422* **Rooms** *135*

Famous for their Irish whiskey, the Jameson family originally owned this house with a lovely beachside location. Close to Dublin Airport, the Portmarnock is tastefully decorated, with bright public spaces. Rooms are excellently furnished, with views of the sea or the championship golf course. There is also a spa. **www.portmarnock.com**

Dylan

Eastmoreland Place, Dublin 4 **Tel** *01 660 3000* **Fax** *01 660 3005* **Rooms** *44*

Awarded the title of Best Boutique Hotel 2008 by Hospitality Ireland, the Dylan boasts a plush interior with sumptuous rooms, each of which has been individually designed. Dine in the hotel's elegant but informal restaurant, or sip cocktails in the bar. **www.dylan.ie**

Four Seasons

Simmonscourt Road, Ballsbridge, Dublin 4 **Tel** *01 665 4000* **Fax** *01 665 4099* **Rooms** *196*

The luxurious Four Seasons combines period-style elegance with contemporary comfort. The large public spaces are opulently decorated with deep-pile rugs and rich furnishings. Bedrooms are large and lavish, and service is exceptional. The Ice Bar is a magnet for fashionistas. There are also 25 apartments. **www.fourseasons.com**

BEYOND DUBLIN

Beaufort House

Ghan Road, Carlingford, Co Louth **Tel** *042 937 3879* **Rooms** *6*

Michael Caine (not the film star) is a fantastic chef. Along with their core business of sailing courses and yacht charter, he and wife Glynis run this award-winning guesthouse in medieval Carlingford, halfway between Dublin and Belfast. En-suite rooms enjoy sea and mountain views. Great breakfasts. **www.beauforthouse.net**

Smarmore Castle

Ardee, Co Louth **Tel** *041 685 7167* **Fax** *041 685 7650* **Rooms** *5*

This 1320 castle-mansion is a hidden gem. The Mullen family offer a warm welcome and impeccable service, then leave you to enjoy the peaceful garden, rooms – all different – and the drawing room. The spa offers massages, Jacuzzi and sauna. Smarmore Castle is one hour from Dublin, close to Newgrange. **www.smarmorecastle.com**

Castle Leslie Estate

Glaslough, Co Monaghan **Tel** *047 88 100* **Fax** *047 88 256* **Rooms** *50*

Located within a thousand acres of rolling countryside, this castle is owned and run by the colourful Leslie family. The castle and a hunting lodge provide accommodation for 50, and two self-catering apartments and five houses in the village are also available. The Organic Spa and equestrian centre are open to visitors. **www.castleleslie.com**

Brooklodge Hotel

Macreddin Village, Co Wicklow **Tel** *0402 36444* **Fax** *0402 36580* **Rooms** *90*

Not so much a hotel as a village complex. Standard rooms have four-poster beds; the suites are even more luxurious. The renowned spa offers a flotation tank and hammam massages. There is an equestrian centre, an organic food fair on Sundays and live jazz on Saturday nights. **www.brooklodge.com**

Dunbrody Country House Hotel

Arthurstown, Co Wexford **Tel** *051 389 600* **Fax** *051 389 601* **Rooms** *22*

Set in parkland on the dramatic Hook Peninsula, this 1830s Georgian manor (home to the world-renowned Dunbrody cookery school) offers a relaxing, elegant atmosphere complemented by log fires and a luxury spa. Rooms are individually styled. **www.dunbrodyhouse.com**

RESTAURANTS, CAFES AND PUBS

The Dublin of today is a modern, cosmopolitan city, something which is reflected in its vast array of restaurants. The Temple Bar area is good for modern international cuisine, and also has a large number of pubs as well as a few traditional Irish restaurants. There are many Italian, Chinese and Indian restaurants, and in recent years Thai, Indonesian, Japanese, Mexican and Cuban places have proliferated. Seafood and fish is abundant in

The Bad Ass Café, Temple Bar

Dublin, in particular smoked salmon and oysters; the latter is famously often consumed with Guinness. Popular for a light lunch is smoked salmon on delicious dark rye bread, with a pint of Guinness. Wherever you eat, portions will be generous, especially in pubs, whose platefuls of roast meat and vegetables offer excellent value for money. Takeaway food, from fish and chips to pizzas and kebabs, is also widely available.

IRISH EATING PATTERNS

Traditionally, the Irish have started the day with a huge breakfast: bacon, sausages, black pudding, eggs, tomatoes and brown bread. The main meal, dinner, was served at midday, with a lighter "tea" in the early evening.

Although Continental breakfasts are now available, the traditional breakfast is still included in almost all hotel and B&B rates. Most of the Irish today settle for a light lunch and save their main meal for the evening. Vestiges of the old eating patterns remain in the huge midday meals still served in pubs.

EATING OUT

Elegant dining becomes considerably more affordable when you make lunch your main meal of the day. In many of the top restaurants in Dublin, the fixed-price lunch

and dinner menus offer much the same, but the bill at lunchtime will usually amount to about half the price. If you like wine to accompany your meal, the house wines are quite drinkable in most restaurants and can reduce the total cost of your meal. If you are travelling with children, look out for one of the many restaurants that offer a children's menu. Lunch in Dublin is invariably served between noon and 2:30pm, with dinner between 6:30 and 10pm, although many ethnic and city-centre restaurants stay open later. If you are staying in a bed-and-breakfast, your hosts may provide a home-cooked evening meal if given advance notice. Visa and MasterCard are the most commonly accepted credit cards in Ireland, with American Express and Diners Club also in use.

An Irish coffee

GOURMET AND ETHNIC DINING

Once considerably lacking in gourmet establishments, Dublin now offers many restaurants that rank among Europe's very best, with chefs trained in outstanding domestic and Continental institutions.

Increasingly it is the hotels which house the city's award-winning restaurants. There is an enormous range of cuisines to be found in and around Dublin. Locations vary as widely as the cuisine, from conventional hotel dining rooms, townhouse basements and city mansions to romantic castle hotels and tiny village cafés tucked away by the sea.

In the city centre, the eating areas with the widest choice tend to be located in Temple Bar or between St Stephen's Green and Merrion Square and between Grafton Street and South Great Georges Street. Outside the city, Malahide and Howth have a good selection of restaurants, and Dun Laoghaire is worth a special visit for fresh fish and seafood.

BUDGET DINING

It is quite possible to eat well on a moderate budget in Dublin. Both in the city and outside it, there are small

The Mermaid Café, with its floor-to-ceiling windows *(see p142)*

La Stampa's luxurious bar, Samsara *(see p139)*

cafés, tea rooms and family-style restaurants which offer reasonably priced meals. Sandwiches are usually made with thick, delicious slices of fresh, rather than processed, cheese or meat; salad plates feature chicken, pork, beef and the ever-popular smoked salmon; and hot meals usually come with generous helpings of vegetables, with the beloved potato often showing up in different forms, including roasted and mashed, sometimes all on one plate.

Another cheap alternative is to take picnics when you go out. Farmhouse cheeses and homegrown tomatoes make delicious sandwiches, and the beautiful countryside, fine beaches and breathtaking mountains make ideal locations for a picnic. Phoenix Park and Powerscourt both have their own picnic areas.

Whelan's, renowned for its live music programme *(see p155)*

PUB FOOD

Ireland's pubs have moved into the food field with a vengeance. In addition to bar snacks (soup, sandwiches and so on), available from noon until late, salads and hot meals are served from midday to 2:30pm. At rock-bottom prices, hot plates all come heaped with mounds of fresh vegetables, potatoes, and good portions of local fish or meat. Particularly good value are the pub carveries that offer a choice of joints, sliced to your preference. In recent years, the international staples of spaghetti, lasagne and quiche have also appeared on pub menus, along with more Mediterranean dishes such as *bruschetta* in the trendier pubs. For a list of recommended pubs, see pages 146–7.

PUB OPENING HOURS

Many people come to Dublin for its endless pubs and bars and its excellent stouts and whiskeys. Opening hours are Monday to Wednesday 10:30am until 11:30pm; Thursday to Saturday 10:30am until 12:30pm. Sunday opening times have changed to become more flexible. Pubs used to close for "holy hour" between 2pm and 4pm. Now most pubs are open on a Sunday from 12:30pm until 11pm. Late bars tend to stay open until 1am or 2am, the nightclubs even later. Alcohol is not served past 2am, however, and off-licences must close at 10pm.

FISH AND CHIPS AND OTHER FAST FOODS

The Irish, from peasant to parliamentarian, love their "chippers", immortalized in Roddy Doyle's novel *The Van*, and any good pub night will often end with a visit to the nearest fish-and-chip shop. At virtually any time of day, however, if you pass by Leo Burdock's in Dublin, there will be a long queue for this international institution *(see p141)*. With Ireland's long coastline, wherever you choose, the fish will usually be the freshest catch of the day – plaice, cod, haddock, whiting or ray (a delicacy). As an alternative to fish and chips, there are numerous good pasta and pizza restaurants around the city, including the Steps of Rome, Pasta Fresca and Milano, which also does takeaways. In addition Dublin has become home to the ubiquitous burger chains, including McDonald's, as well as other forms of fast food outlets such as KFC.

Picnickers enjoying the sunshine outside at Dublin Zoo *(see p81)*

VEGETARIAN FOOD

As with most western European cities, there is plenty of scope for vegetarians to eat well in Dublin. Although much traditional Irish food is meat-based, most restaurants will have vegetarian dishes on the menu, particularly in the modern international and Italian restaurants, but there are also some excellent exclusively vegetarian restaurants in the city. If you happen to go somewhere to eat and realize that there is no vegetarian option, most restaurants will be more than happy to make something up for you, such as a salad or a vegetable stir fry.

The Flavours of Ireland

Boxty, barm brack, champ, coddle, cruibins, colcannon – the basic dishes that have nourished Ireland are spiced with fancy names. But the secret of their success is their ingredients, which are nurtured in a warm, damp climate on lush hills that brings them flavour. Beef and dairy cattle can stay out all year and produce abundant butter, cheese and cream. Pork and pork products, such as ham and bacon, are a mainstay, though lamb is traditional, too. Potatoes, the king of vegetables, turn up in soup, pies, cakes, bread and scones that are piled on breakfast and tea tables. And the rivers, lakes and shores are rich in seafood.

Oysters

Sea trout, plucked fresh from the Atlantic Ocean

THE BASIC DISHES

Irish stews are thick and tasty, traditionally featuring lamb or mutton, onion and potatoes, while beef and Guinness (see pp82–3) make a darker casserole, sometimes with the addition of oysters. Carrots and turnips are the first choice of vegetables. Pork is the basis of many dishes. Trotters, called cruibins or crubeens, are sometimes pickled, while bacon can be especially meaty. Dublin coddle, a fill-me-up after the pub on a Saturday night, relies on sausages and potatoes as well as bacon. Ham is sometimes smoked over peat and, for special occasions, it is baked with cloves and brown sugar and served with buttered cabbage. Cabbage is the basis of colcannon, with mashed potato and onions, sometimes with butter and milk. Boxty is a bake of raw and cooked potato mashed with butter, buttermilk and flour; champ is potatoes mashed with milk, butter and onions.

FISH AND SEAFOOD

The Atlantic Ocean and Irish Sea have a rich variety of shellfish, from lobsters and Dublin Bay prawns to

Barm brack   White soda bread   Brown soda bread   Potato bread

Potato farls

Wheaten bread

Selection of the many traditional Irish breads

TRADITIONAL IRISH FOOD

If your heart is up to it, start the day with a "Full Irish Fry". This breakfast fry-up includes thick, tasty bacon, plus black pudding, soda farls and potato cake. A "lady's breakfast" will have one egg, a "gentleman's" two. Gooseberry jam will be spread on fried bread, and mugs of tea will wash it down. Irish stews traditionally use mutton, not so common today, while Spiced Beef uses up brisket, which is covered in a various spices then left for a week before being cooked slowly with Guinness and vegetables. A high tea in the early evening is the major meal in many homes; a main course will be followed by a succession of breads and cakes.

Gubbeen cheese

Irish Stew *Traditionally, neck of mutton, potatoes, carrots and onions are slowly cooked together for hours.*

Delivery in time-honoured style at Moore Street Market, Dublin

mussels and oysters, clams, scallops, and razor-shells. Herring, mackerel, plaice and skate are brought in from the sea, while the rivers and lakes offer up salmon, trout and eels, which are often smoked. Galway salmon and oysters are famous and are served throughout the city's restaurants. Salmon is usually smoked in oak wood kilns. Also traditional is a red seaweed called dulse, mixed with potatoes mashed in their skins to make dulse champ.

BAKED GOODS

Bread and cakes make up a large percentage of the Irish diet. Unleaven soda bread is ubiquitous in both white and brown varieties, and is great with Irish cheeses. Potato bread is fried or eaten cold, as cake. Farls ("quarters") are

made with wheat flour or oats, bicarbonate of soda and buttermilk, which goes into many recipes. Fruit breads include barm brack, which is traditionally eaten at Hallowe'en and on All Saints' Day, while rich porter cake is made with Guinness or

A range of Ireland's finest farmhouse cheeses

other stout. White, brown and fruit scones will never be far from tea and breakfast tables.

DAIRY PRODUCTS

Creamy butter, usually salted, is applied generously. Cream, too, is used in cooking, stirred into soups and whipped for puddings. The variety and quality of Irish farmhouse cheeses has given them a worldwide reputation, and a farmhouse St Killian took the crown of "Best Irish Cheese" from Irish Cheddar at the 2007 World Cheese Awards. The winner in 2008 was Wicklow Blue Cheese.

IRISH CHEESES

Carrigaline Nutty-tasting, Gouda-like cheese from Cork.

Cashel Blue The first Irish blue cheese. Soft and creamy. Unpasteurized; from Tipperary.

Cooleeny Small, Camembert-style unpasteurized cheese from Tipperary.

Durrus Creamy, natural-rind unpasteurized cheese from West Cork. May be smoked.

Gubbeen Semi-soft washed rind cheese. Rich, milky taste.

Mileens Soft, rich rind-washed cheese. Unpasteurized; from the Beara peninsula, Cork.

St Killian Hexagonal Brie-like creamy cheese from Wexford.

Dublin Coddle *This is a comforting mixture of sausages, bacon, potatoes and onions, stewed in ham stock.*

Galway Salmon *Top quality fish can be simply served with an Irish butter sauce, watercress and colcannon.*

Irish Coffee *This is a chilled soufflé of coffee, cream and Irish whiskey, topped with crushed walnuts.*

Choosing a Restaurant

The restaurants in this guide have been selected across a wide range of price categories for their good value, exceptional food or interesting location. These listings highlight some of the factors that may influence your choice, such as whether you can eat outdoors or if the venue offers live music. Entries are listed by area.

PRICE CATEGORIES
For a three-course evening meal for one including a half bottle of house wine, service and taxes.

€ Under 25 euros
€€ 25–35 euros
€€€ 35–45 euros
€€€€ 45–55 euros
€€€€€ Over 55 euros

SOUTHEAST DUBLIN

Cornucopia   €
19 Wicklow Street, Dublin 2 **Tel** *01 677 7583*   **Map** *D3*

Small and often crowded, Cornucopia is one of the few exclusively vegetarian restaurants in the city, open for breakfast, lunch and dinner. It serves delicious, cheap and wholesome food – such as salads, soups, pasta dishes, casseroles and quiches – to an army of bookworm bachelors and earthy students. Open until 8pm (9pm on Thursdays and 7pm Sundays).

Nude   €
21 Suffolk Street, Dublin 2 **Tel** *01 672 5577*   **Map** *D3*

Bono's brother, Norman Hewson, has created a very successful, hip and intimate restaurant that serves freshly prepared food, organic where possible. Soups, panini, wraps, salads and freshly squeezed juices are ordered at the counter. Then, take a seat at the long wooden tables and enjoy these colourful snacks in an upbeat atmosphere.

Steps of Rome   €
1 Chatham Street, Dublin 2 **Tel** *01 670 5630*   **Map** *D4*

This tiny Italian café, selling great coffee, is always abuzz with people coming and going to collect tasty slices of pizza. The reasonably priced menu includes pasta dishes and bruschettas. Service is brisk, if a little brusque. Steps of Rome is popular with students and fast-moving shoppers pausing for breath. Open all day and into the evening.

Yamamori Noodles   €
71 South Great George's Street, Dublin 2 **Tel** *01 475 5001*   **Map** *C4*

Very popular with the young crowd, this lively and informal Japanese restaurant specializes in *yamamori ramen* (a noodle dish with meat and vegetables), sushi and sashimi. Try the interesting bento box for variety. Dishes are good value, service is prompt, and the atmosphere is friendly. Evenings are very busy. Open for lunch and dinner.

Avoca Café   €€
11–13 Suffolk Street, Dublin 2 **Tel** *01 672 6019*   **Map** *D3*

Climb to the top floor of the renowned Irish craft shop Avoca, and you will be rewarded with creative, wholesome and colourful cooking in a bright and airy room. The queues get longer during lunch hour. Such popularity is testament to the delicious salads, panini, hot dishes and wonderful desserts on offer. Open daytime only.

Café Bar Deli   €€
18 South Great George's Street, Dublin 2 **Tel** *01 677 1646*   **Map** *C4*

Vibrant and modestly priced, Café Bar Deli is decorated in a European café style, with bentwood chairs and a mahogany and brass interior. The imaginative and colourful menus feature pizzas, pasta dishes and salads. Service is prompt and enthusiastic, and the place is particularly popular with 20- and 30-somethings.

Dunne & Crescenzi   €€
14 South Frederick Street, Dublin 2 **Tel** *01 677 3815*   **Map** *E4*

This delightful Italian wine bar serves authentic food and wine in a stylishly rustic atmosphere. Enjoy the excellent minestrone, antipasti platters, bruschettas, panini, pasta dishes, delicious fruit tartlets and excellent coffee. There is also a superb collection of wines, many of them served by the glass, too. Open all day and into the evening.

Good World Chinese Restaurant   €€
18 South Great George's Street, Dublin 2 **Tel** *01 677 5373*   **Map** *C4*

This restaurant's popularity with the Chinese community is witness to the superlative and authentic quality of the food on offer. The dim sum selection is a popular choice. Authentic beef, chicken and fish dishes are also on the menu, along with the standard range of Westernized dishes. Friendly and efficient service.

Gotham Café   €€
8 South Anne Street, Dublin 2 **Tel** *01 679 5266*   **Map** *D4*

Always abuzz with activity, this lively and colourful spot offers bistro-style food at affordable prices. With covers of *Rolling Stone* magazine lining the walls, it is popular with the young – and the young-at-heart. Gotham Café is renowned for its tasty and imaginative pizzas, but it also serves delectable pasta dishes and salads.

Key to Symbols *see back cover flap*

Kilkenny Restaurant and Café
5–6 Nassau Street, Dublin 2 **Tel** *01 677 7066*
€€ Map E4

Situated on the first floor of a high quality craft shop, the Kilkenny overlooks the grounds of Trinity College. Wholesome, freshly prepared soups, sandwiches, panini, salads, quiches, hot casseroles and pies are available in this self-service restaurant. Lovely desserts include baked cheesecake, carrot cake and fruit tarts.

La Maison des Gourmets
15 Castle Market Street, Dublin 2 **Tel** *01 672 7258*
€€ Map D4

This boulangerie has a stylish and intimate room upstairs, where high-quality snacks are served. French onion soup, home-baked breads, *tartines* (open sandwiches), salads, a hot special and delicious pastries are on the menu. Takeaway is available from the downstairs shop. In fine weather, you can sit outside and watch the world go by.

The Cedar Tree
118 South Andrew Street, Dublin 2 **Tel** *01 677 2121*
€€€ Map D3

This restaurant has been serving genuine Lebanese food for almost 20 years. The wide *meze* selection includes hummus, mussels, quails, prawns, baba ganoush, tabbouleh and spiced potatoes. Belly dancing shows take place on Friday and Saturday evenings. The ground floor restaurant, Byblos, serves lighter fare.

Chilli Club
Anne's Lane, South Anne Street, Dublin 2 **Tel** *01 677 3721*
€€€ Map D4

Knock on the door to be let into this award-winning Thai restaurant just off Grafton Street. Do not let the very small, intimate setting and simple decor put you off: the standard of cooking is very high, and the service is great. Thai curries are particularly tasty and the set lunches are good value. AmEx is not accepted.

Ely Wine Bar and Café
22 Ely Place, Dublin 2 **Tel** *01 676 8986*
€€€ Map E5

Erik and Michelle Robson's unusual wine bar and café, just off St Stephen's Green, has been stylishly converted. The menu features delicious cheese dishes, fish cakes, Kilkee oysters, lamb stew and home-made sausages. The atmosphere is cosy and lively, and the imaginative wine list features some truly exceptional labels.

Jaipur
41–46 South Great George's Street, Dublin 2 **Tel** *01 677 0999*
€€€ Map C4

Often acclaimed as the best Indian restaurant in the city, Jaipur offers high-quality, innovative dishes. The decor, stylish and with a contemporary feel, features warm, tasteful colours. The restaurant is superbly managed by a well-informed and charming staff. Vegetarians are well catered for. Branches have now opened in Malahide and Dalkey.

La Peniche
Grand Canal, Mespil Road, Dublin 4 **Tel** *087 790 00 77*
€€€

This floating French/Italian bistro and wine bar is moored on a lovely stretch of the Grand Canal. Each table has an attention light that you can switch on, rather than having to catch the waiter's eye. Every Tuesday, Wednesday and Thursday, cruise dinners are available for an extra 10 euros – be sure to book early. La Peniche can also be chartered privately.

La Stampa
35 Dawson Street, Dublin 2 **Tel** *01 677 4444*
€€€ Map D4

The main attraction of the brasserie-style La Stampa is its dining room, arguably the most romantic in the city, set in a charming 19th-century mirrored ballroom. Given the food's modest quality, the experience is rather pricey. However, the pleasing ambience and cordial staff more than make up for any shortcomings on your plate.

Pearl Brasserie
20 Merrion Street Upper, Dublin 2 **Tel** *01 661 3572*
€€€ Map D4

This refurbished basement brasserie exudes a cool, contemporary French ethos. It combines charming service with good food at affordable prices. Lunch is particularly good value. Seafood features prominently on the menu, and the impressive wine list is heavy on French labels. The separate Oyster Bar offers lighter fare, including a fish platter.

Trocadero
3–4 St Andrew Street, Dublin 2 **Tel** *01 677 5545*
€€€ Map D3

This much-loved restaurant has been in operation since 1956. A favourite haunt of actors and the literati, it has deep red walls lined with black and white images of the notables who have passed through its doors. Traditional classics include rack of lamb, steak, Dublin Bay prawns and tempting desserts. The service is intimate and welcoming.

Bang Café
11 Merrion Row, Dublin 2 **Tel** *01 676 0898*
€€€€ Map E5

This hip restaurant is the essence of stylish minimalism; a fact that is reflected in its cuisine, as well as in the decor of natural tones and dark wood furnishings. The contemporary fare includes great fish dishes, mouth-watering scallops and excellent bangers and mash. The service is highly professional.

Bentley's Oyster Bar & Grill
22 St Stephen's Green, Dublin 2 **Tel** *01 638 3939*
€€€€ Map D4

Celebrity chef Richard Corrigan has restored the once-legendary Bentley's to its former glory. The venue is a stunning Georgian townhouse, and the menu is big on seafood. Meat-eaters are also well-catered for, with dishes including *weiner schnitzel* and natice lamb. A baby grand piano provides musical accompaniment throughout the evening.

Diep le Shaker
55 Pembroke Lane, Dublin 2 **Tel** *01 661 1829*   €€€€   **Map** *E5*

Superb food and efficient service await at this bright, cheery Asian diner. Try prawn red curry served in the shell of a baby coconut, or the popular spicy beef curry. The layout is open-plan, and you can eat on the balcony overlooking the lower floor. Excellent exotic cocktails can be enjoyed at the bar. Live jazz Tuesdays and Wednesdays.

FXB
Pembroke Street, Dublin 2 **Tel** *01 676 4606*   €€€€   **Map** *E5*

This quality traditional steakhouse and seafood chain enjoys a long-standing reputation of excellence. Meat is supplied by reliable butchers in Offaly. Sip a bubbly champagne cocktails as you wait for your meaty order to arrive. The popularity of this restaurant has led to other branches being opened in Temple Bar and Christchurch.

La Cave
28 South Anne Street, Dublin 2 **Tel** *01 679 4409*   €€€€   **Map** *D4*

Descend the stairs from street level into a tiny cavernous wine bar that is also a restaurant offering French food of a high standard, sometimes with a North African flavour. The owner, Margaret, is one of Ireland's leading wine experts and offers an impressively extensive wine list, sourced everywhere from France to Uruguay. The wine bar is open late.

L'Gueuleton
1 Fade Street, Dublin 2 **Tel** *01 675 3708*   €€€€   **Map** *C4*

Come to this popular French bistro for everything from snail and Roquefort Pithivier to duck with sweetened chicory, all accompanied by smooth jazz music in the background. Although it is not possible to make reservations in advance, there is a bar area where you can wait for a table. AmEx and Diner cards not accepted.

Nico's
53 Dame Street, Dublin 2 **Tel** *01 677 3062*   €€€€   **Map** *D3*

Traditional Italian fare from a restaurant that has maintained a quiet, dignified presence on the scene for more than 30 years. Plush red drapes set the tone for the decor and for the traditional menu. For dessert, try the Italian *cassata* with Galliano. A piano player performs Tuesday to Saturday evenings, and there is an excellent wine list.

Dobbins Wine Bistro
15 Stephen's Lane, Dublin 2 **Tel** *01 661 9536*   €€€€€   **Map** *F5*

Popular since 1978, this cheerful bistro has a sleek, modern look, with leather banquettes and cool lighting. Given the good and extensive wine list, Dobbins is a popular spot for a leisurely liquid lunch. Among the highlights on the menu are Dublin Bay prawns and organic pork served with crackling.

Il Posto
10 St Stephen's Green, Dublin 2 **Tel** *01 679 4769*   €€€€€   **Map** *D4*

Il Posto is an oasis of calm from the bustle of Stephen's Green. Although the atmosphere is relaxed, this restaurant offers very formal dining. The food is of the highest standard, a mix of traditional and contemporary Italian, coupled with excellent service. In summer, try to get one of the tables on the terrace, with views of St Stephen's Green.

L'Ecrivain
109a Lower Baggot Street, Dublin 2 **Tel** *01 661 1919*   €€€€€   **Map** *F5*

One of the best restaurants in Dublin, L'Ecrivain combines classic formality with contemporary cool. Authentic French cuisine with an Irish flavour includes delicacies such as Galway Bay oysters and caviar. Seasonal game and seafood, as well as tasty desserts and cheeses, also figure prominently on the menu. The service is highly polished and efficient.

Peploe's Wine Bistro
16 St Stephen's Green, Dublin 2 **Tel** *01 676 3144*   €€€€€   **Map** *D4*

Located in the basement of a Georgian building, Peploe's is a glamorous, cosy and immensely popular restaurant. It is also always rushed, due to the consistently high-quality food available. It provides an extensive wine list – more than 30 varieties of wine are served by the glass. Book in advance.

Shanahan's on the Green
119 St Stephen's Street, Dublin 2 **Tel** *01 407 0939*   €€€€€   **Map** *D5*

The most succulent steaks in Dublin are found at this renowned steakhouse, set in an elegantly furnished Georgian house. Though steeply priced, the food is consistently of the highest quality. The portions are gargantuan, so it is wise to skip the starter if you hope to finish your main. Seafood, too, is available at this superbly managed establishment.

Thorntons
128 St Stephen's Green, Dublin 2 **Tel** *01 478 7008*   €€€€€   **Map** *D4*

Haute cuisine is on the menu at this Michelin-starred restaurant in the Fitzwilliam Hotel *(see p129)*. Its small dining room gives it a sense of privacy, while the cream and gold decor adds to the cosy, bright atmosphere. Chef Kevin Thornton offers signature dishes such as braised suckling pig, loin of venison or roast quail with brioche.

Unicorn
12B Merrion Court, Dublin 2 **Tel** *01 662 4757*   €€€€€   **Map** *E4*

Situated around the corner from St Stephen's Green, Unicorn has maintained an excellent standard since it first opened in 1938. Its casual atmosphere is unparalleled and enhanced by the friendly waiting staff. The Italian-Mediterranean food served here is utterly delicious, and the veal is particularly appetizing.

Key to Price Guide *see p138* **Key to Symbols** *see back cover flap*

SOUTHWEST DUBLIN

Govinda's

4 Aungier Street, Dublin 2 **Tel** 01 475 0309   **Map** C4

Bright, cheerful and bustling with energy, Govinda's is run by Hare Krishnas and offers filling and tasty vegetarian fare, such as samosas, pizzas and moussaka, not to mention vegan options. For dessert, try the upside-down pineapple cake. Sinead O'Connor is a regular here. Another branch can be found at 83 Middle Abbey Street, and a third on Merrion Row.

Leo Burdock's

2 Werburgh Street, Dublin 8 **Tel** 01 454 0306   **Map** B4

The patrons of Leo Burdock's, the oldest fish-and-chip takeaway in Dublin, include the ordinary folk of Dublin, as well as the stars. The chips are made from top-grade Irish potatoes, and there is a wide choice of fish, including smoked cod, haddock and lemon-sole goujon. Service is efficient. There is another branch on Liffey Street.

Queen of Tarts

4 Cork Hill, Dame Street, Dublin 2 **Tel** 01 670 7499   **Map** C3

Opposite Dublin Castle and Dublin City Hall, this charming little café is cosy and welcoming. In addition to freshly prepared soups, sandwiches and hot savoury tarts, there is a dazzling array of mouth-watering desserts, including chocolate fudge cake, fruit tarts and home-made biscuits. A new, roomier branch has opened on Cow's Lane.

Gruel

68a Dame Street, Dublin 2 **Tel** 01 670 7119   **Map** C3

This tiny, quirky café blends the rustic with the innovative in its light snacks, soups and hot specials. The "roast in a roll" is delicious and a firm favourite among the colourful patrons. Good pizzas and tasty sweet dishes make it an ideal spot for a quick bite at affordable prices. Eat in or take away.

Buenos Aires Grill

Unit 2, Castle Way, Golden Lane, Dublin 2 **Tel** 01 475 9616 **Map** C4

This authentic Argentinian restaurant has floor to ceiling windows, an open kitchen and contemporary decor in cool, neutral tones. There are good lunch deals and an evening menu specialising in beef, but also offering pork and chicken dishes, and good vegetarian and seafood options. Popular with people working in the area and tourists.

Chez Max

1 Palace Street, Dublin 2 **Tel** 01 633 7215   **Map** C3

This cosy French diner at the gates of Dublin Castle is so authentic that it is hard to get a seat on account of all the French clients who come here for lunch. There is a covered back garden and a little terrace out front for alfresco dining. The good, simple French cuisine is classic; the signature dish is *boeuf bourguignon*.

Eden

Meeting House Square, Temple Bar, Dublin 2 **Tel** 01 670 5372 **Map** C3

Featuring an outside terrace on the square, this split-level restaurant is bright and modern in design, with cool blue tiled walls and an open kitchen. Eden is famed for its sirloin steaks, cleverly arranged fish dishes and imaginative use of seasonal vegetables. The early evening menu provides excellent value for money.

Elephant & Castle

18 Temple Bar, Dublin 2 **Tel** 01 679 3121   **Map** D3

Very lively, this American-style brasserie in the heart of Temple Bar is invariably crowded. Have the mouth-watering chicken wings to start, and continue with the good omelettes, steaks, hamburgers and salads, all available at affordable prices. Weekend brunches are also popular. Telephone bookings are not accepted.

Lord Edward

23 Christchurch Place, Dublin 8 **Tel** 01 454 2420   **Map** B4

The oldest seafood restaurant in the city, Lord Edward is located above a cosy and traditional pub that serves lunch downstairs. It has changed little over the years and maintains an authentic, old-fashioned feel. The long-established waiters are renowned for their charming service.

Mongolian Barbecue

7 Anglesea Street, Dublin 2 **Tel** 01 670 4154   **Map** D3

Mix your own meat and spices, and bring the resulting patty to a shared, massive, hot metal plate to sizzle to your satisfaction. And go back for seconds, thirds and fourths. Veggies follow the same steps using tofu instead of meat – they also get a free starter of samosa or a spring roll. Excellent value.

Monty's of Kathmandu

28 Eustace Street, Dublin 2 **Tel** 01 670 4911   **Map** C3

This friendly Nepalese restaurant serves tasty and interesting fish, chicken and lamb dishes at affordable prices. Vegetarians are also well catered for. Try the dumplings or the tandoori butter chicken in a deliciously creamy sauce. Upstairs is more cheerful than the basement dining room. The service is good and the atmosphere relaxed.

Saba

26–28 Clarendon Street, Dublin 2 **Tel** *01 679 2000*   **Map** *D4*

This slick Thai/Vietnamese eatery is a cut above the norm. Chef Trakoolwattana has previously cooked for the Thai royal family. Herbs, vegetables and fruit arrive weekly from Bangkok, ensuring fresh authentic flavours. The extensive menu features hake and banana leaf, red curry sauce, and crispy whole sea bass. Good vegetarian selection, too.

Darwin's

16 Aungier Street, Dublin 2 **Tel** *01 475 7511*   **Map** *C4*

Specializing in steaks made from certified organic meat from the proprietor's own butcher shop, this is a carnivore's dream. The menu also includes crab cakes and duck spring rolls, not to mention some vegetarian options. Dishes are prepared using quality ingredients and presented with flair. Unpretentious ambience, with warm, friendly service.

Les Frères Jacques

74 Dame Street, Dublin 2 **Tel** *01 679 4555*   **Map** *C3*

This elegant restaurant is French in style, cuisine, atmosphere and service. Seafood and game feature prominently on the balanced seasonal menus. Try the grilled lobster fresh from the tank, or the roast lamb casserole with courgette, aubergine (eggplant) and thyme. Classic desserts are also on the menu. The good wine list favours French labels.

The Mermaid Café

69–70 Dame Street, Dublin 2 **Tel** *01 670 8236*   **Map** *C3*

A bright, contemporary restaurant with large windows and wooden furniture, The Mermaid Café is a firm favourite for weekend brunches. There is a certain American East Coast ambience about it, which is also evident in specialities such as New England crab cakes. The chef makes creative use of high quality Irish artisanal produce.

Fallon & Byrne

11–17 Exchequer Street, Dublin 2 **Tel** *01 472 1010*   **Map** *D3*

A New York-style food hall combined with a French restaurant and a superlative wine cellar. There is also a food shop on the ground floor and a restaurant upstairs. The restaurant is open, spacious and bright, and serves particularly tasty breads. The wines are incredible, but beware – you can pay in excess of 1,000 euros a bottle here.

The Tea Room

The Clarence Hotel, 6–8 Wellington Quay, Dublin 2 **Tel** *01 407 0800*   **Map** *C3*

The Clarence Hotel is owned by rock band U2. Come in by the Essex Street entrance, opposite the Project Theatre, and savour excellent cuisine served in a stylish dining room. High ceilings and large windows create a bright and airy atmosphere. The food is innovative and seasonal, and the lunch menu is particularly good value.

NORTH OF THE LIFFEY

The Cobalt Café

16 North Great George's Street, Dublin 1 **Tel** *01 873 0313*   **Map** *D3*

This daytime café offers a range of home-made soups, sandwiches and cakes, as well as the delicious signature dish, Chicken Cobalt. The café doubles as a gallery exhibiting the works of up-and-coming Irish artists; as a result, it is a popular venue for art lovers.

Epicurean Food Hall

Lower Liffey Street, Dublin 1   **Map** *D2*

This food hall comprises a number of outlets serving international light meals and snacks. There is a communal dining area in the centre, or you can take your food away and enjoy it on a seat on the boardwalk overlooking the Liffey. Itsabagel's snacks and Burdock's fish and chips are on offer, as well as Turkish, Italian and Mexican cuisines.

Kingfisher Restaurant

166 Parnell Street, Dublin 1 **Tel** *01 872 8732*   **Map** *C2*

Modestly decorated but immaculately maintained, Kingfisher Grill is a no-frills diner. Prompt service and cheap prices make it a good spot for the simple dishes many of us long for. Potato wedges and prawn cocktail are two of the more popular starters. Finish your meal with jelly or ice cream.

Panem

Ha'penny Bridge House, 21 Lower Ormond Quay, Dublin 1 **Tel** *01 872 8510*   **Map** *C3*

This tiny café and bakery offers Italian and French food, freshly prepared using only high quality ingredients. The menu includes delicious croissants and focaccia with savoury fillings, sweet brioches with chocolate, home-baked biscuits and good coffee. The mouth-watering hot chocolate is made from dark Belgian chocolate. Friendly staff.

Alilang

102 Parnell Street, Dublin 1 **Tel** *01 874 6766*   **Map** *D1*

This cheerful and buzzing Chinese/Korean eatery is one of many emerging along Parnell Street, the fledgling Chinatown of Dublin. The food is tasty, filling and fantastic value. A great option for a group of friends is the Korean barbecue, where you cook strips of lean, tasty meat on a hot dish in the centre of the pine table.

Key to Price Guide *see p138* **Key to Symbols** *see back cover flap*

Cactus Jacks

Millennium Walkway, Middle Abbey Street, Dublin 1 **Tel** *01 874 6198*

€€

Map *C3*

A recent addition to the popular chain begun in Galway, this restaurant is modern and slick, with a low-lit setting. Cactus Jacks is one of few Mexican restaurants in Dublin that succeed by keeping food simple but tasty, with steak, fish and vegetarian dishes that are lighter versions of traditional Mexican recipes. Nice frozen margaritas, too.

Milano

Unit 6, Excise Walk, Clarion Quay, Dublin 1 **Tel** *01 611 9012*

€€

Map *F2*

Milano is the chain run by the popular British eatery Pizza Express in Ireland. It is family-friendly, with a play area and face painter on Sundays, and features mainly Italian fare such as pizzas, pastas, and chicken dishes. Lunchtime is buzzing, and evenings see concert goers to the nearby O2 area stopping in.

101 Talbot

100–102 Talbot Street, Dublin 2 **Tel** *01 874 5011*

€€

Map *E2*

A Mediterranean approach is reflected in the decor as much as the cuisine at 101 Talbot, livening up the rather drab street on which it is located. The early-bird menu is good value and attracts many theatre-goers. Vegetarians are spoiled for choice at this restaurant, which will also do its utmost to meet any other dietary requirements.

Stillroom Restaurant

Old Jameson Distillery, Bow Street, Dublin 1 **Tel** *01 807 2355*

€€

Map *A2*

This restaurant is part of the Old Jameson Distillery complex, which lies on the site of the original 18th-century distillery. At lunchtime the legal eagles from the nearby Courts swoop in here to savour the comfort food on offer. Traditional dishes include a daily roast, as well as delicious sandwiches and soups.

Nancy Hands

30–32 Parkgate Street, Dublin 8 **Tel** *01 677 0149*

€€€

Traditional Irish cuisine is on the menu at this restaurant next to Phoenix Park and the zoo. The open fireplace and wood and stone decor give an old-world atmosphere to this relatively new pub. The fare is of a good standard, a mix of traditional bar food, carvery and more international offerings. The chowder is particularly good.

Bar Italia

Quartier Bloom, Lower Ormond Quay, Dublin 1 **Tel** *01 874 1000*

€€€€

Map *C3*

The popular Bar Italia, specializing in Italian fare, is always a hive of activity around lunchtime, when patrons stream in for freshly prepared antipasti, risottos, grilled vegetables or the pasta specials. Desserts are also an attraction, as is the excellent – and strong! – espresso.

Rhodes D7

Capel Building, Mary's Abbey, Dublin 7 **Tel** *01 804 4444*

€€€

Map *C2*

Celebrity chef Gary Rhodes's first Irish restaurant features his unique cuisine, which has already earned him five Michelin stars. On the walls is commissioned art by renowned Irish artist Deborah Donnelly. Try eel for starters, or a plate of three tomato soups. Finish your meal with Bailey's crème brûlée. No kids after 9pm. Closed on Mondays.

Winding Stair

40 Ormond Quay, Dublin 1 **Tel** *01 872 7320*

€€€€

Map *D3*

At this slick and popular contemporary Irish restaurant, dishes include smoked haddock poached in milk with onions and white cheddar mash, or boiled Irish bacon collar with buttered new-season organic cabbage, mash and parsley sauce. Ingredients are organic and local where possible – even the chorizo is made in Ireland. No Diner or AmEx.

Chapter One

18–19 Parnell Square, Dublin 1 **Tel** *01 873 2266*

€€€€€

Map *C1*

In the basement of the Dublin Writers' Museum, Chapter One is often cited by critics as the best restaurant north of the Liffey. Relish the imaginative European cuisine, with an Irish twist, in a dining room of great character and comfort. The pre-theatre menu is a favourite among regulars who frequent the nearby Gate Theatre.

Ely chq

Stack A, Mayor Street, IFSC, Dublin 1 **Tel** *01 672 0010*

€€€€€

Map *F2*

This offshoot of the Ely Wine Bar *(see p139)* boasts a stylish and contemporary decor. The food – whether from the bar or à la carte menu – is fresh and tasty, and there is an exceptional wine list, with almost 100 wines by the glass. Eat alfresco on the covered terrace, in the cavernous basement or in the spacious, ground floor interior.

FURTHER AFIELD

Angler's Rest

Knockmaroon Hill, Strawberry Beds, Chapelizod, Dublin 20 **Tel** *01 820 4351*

€€

Long known as a watering hole for fishermen along the river, the Angler's Rest has an open fire, timber ceilings and floors, and comfortable seating. Specials include seafood chowder and platter – fish is delivered daily from Howth. At weekends there is live music, featuring a mix of artists. Michael Collins used to be a regular in the Salmon Bar.

Aqua Restaurant

1 West Pier, Howth, Co Dublin **Tel** *01 832 0690*

This first floor restaurant, with lovely views over the sea and harbour, was formerly a yacht club, now converted into a bright contemporary space. The cuisine betrays a Californian-Italian influence; prominent on the menu are steaks, as well as fish and chicken dishes. The set menus are good value. Sunday brunch is accompanied by live jazz.

Independent Pizza

28 Lower Drumcondra Road, Dublin 7 **Tel** *01 830 2044*

This pizza house, owned by Gotham Café crew *(see p139)*, serves delicious, surprising and light American-style pizza, said to be the best in Dublin. Try the Texas Chicken, the Thai Spice or the Pizza of the Month. A good wine list is also available. Book ahead if you can: the place is extremely popular and always busy.

Johnnie Fox's

Glencullen, Co Dublin **Tel** *01 295 5647*

About 30 minutes' drive south of the city, on the way up to the Dublin Mountains, this friendly pub has good Irish food, open fires, traditional music and dancing. Pan-seared scallops, crab salad, smoked salmon and sirloin steak are on the menu. The "Hooley Night", featuring dinner and a traditional show, attracts overseas visitors. Book ahead.

Beaufield Mews Restaurant, Gardens & Antiques

Woodlands Ave, Stillorgan, Co Dublin **Tel** *01 288 0375*

One of County Dublin's oldest restaurants, Beaufield Mews is beautifully set in an 18th-century cobbled courtyard with a rose garden to the rear. Good modern European food is served in an elegant dining room decorated with Irish art and antiques. An inviting atmosphere prevails throughout.

Bon Appetit

9 St James Terrace, Malahide, Co Dublin **Tel** *01 845 0314*

Under the direction of new chef-patron Oliver Dunne, this restaurant has retained its reputation as Malahide's fine dining choice. With a smart reception area and new basement bistro, the restaurant takes a sophisticated, modern approach. Dishes include Aberdeen Angus beef with slow-roasted tomato and Bordelaise onion pomme purée.

Dali's Restaurant

63–65 Main Street, Blackrock, Co Dublin **Tel** *01 278 0660*

At this chic, small restaurant with a distinctive contemporary feel, menus are appealingly light and colourful. Highlights include variations on classic themes, such as seared scallops and Dublin Bay prawns. The set lunch menus offer particularly good value for money. There is also a good wine list and a varied cheese selection.

Expresso Bar Café

1 St Mary's Road, Ballsbridge, Dublin 4 **Tel** *01 660 0585*

This restaurant is decorated in a contemporary, minimalist style. Open from breakfast, it is popular for lunch and weekend brunches. The traditional Irish fare, featuring chicken, fish, steaks and Irish beefburgers, uses high quality ingredients. The bread-and-butter pudding makes a perfect dessert. The service could be friendlier, though.

The Forty Foot

Pavilion Centre, Dun Laoghaire, Co Dublin **Tel** *01 284 2982*

After a walk on the pier, relax in this very modern upstairs restaurant and watch the day fade over Dublin Bay. The views are the main attraction at The Forty Foot, but the food is also appealing. Try the tian of crab and salmon with crème fraîche. Pleasant and competent staff.

Nosh

111 Coliemore Road, Dalkey, Co Dublin **Tel** *01 284 0666*

Nosh is contemporary in style, with light wood furniture. The well-balanced menus feature good fish and vegetarian dishes, as well as succulent steaks. Cod and chips, pea and asparagus risotto, and seared scallops also make appearances. The home-made desserts are good. The weekend brunch is very popular, as is the early-bird menu.

The Queens

Castle Street, Dalkey **Tel** *01 285 4569*

Established in 1745, The Queens is one of Ireland's oldest hostelries, right in the centre of Dalkey. It has grown into an award-winning restaurant serving everything from hamburgers to steamed mussels, or bacon and cabbage. The most pleasant tables are those located out front, with a view of the battlements of Goat's Castle, next door.

Abbey Tavern

Abbey Street, Howth, Co Dublin **Tel** *01 839 0307*

Open fires, linen-clad tables, fresh flowers and a slightly old-fashioned atmosphere define this restaurant on the first floor of a characteristic pub. Good, uncomplicated fish and meat dishes are served. The traditional Irish evening downstairs, featuring set dinners, is popular with visitors.

Hartley's

1 Harbour Road, Dun Laoghaire, Co Dublin **Tel** *01 280 6767*

Conveniently located beside the harbour, ferry terminal and DART station, this welcoming restaurant is housed in a graceful period building. Seafood is a speciality, but the extensive menu makes room for steaks and a variety of pasta dishes too. The home-made desserts are delicious.

Key to Price Guide *see p138* **Key to Symbols** *see back cover flap*

Caviston's Seafood Restaurant

59 Glasthule Road, Dun Laoghaire, Sandycove, Co Dublin **Tel** *01 280 9245*

Stunning seafood, prepared with simple flair, is on the menu at Caviston's. Sadly, this culinary cult address is only open for lunch, so be sure to book early and reserve the last sitting so that you can enjoy a leisurely afternoon lingering over coffee and dessert. The adjoining delicatessen sells delectable fare great for a picnic.

King Sitric Fish Restaurant and Accommodation

East Pier, Howth, Co Dublin **Tel** *01 832 5235*

Named after the medieval Norse king of Dublin, this restaurant is acclaimed for good seafood and game. The dining room is stylishly modern, with scenic views. Specialities include crab bisque, Balscadden Bay lobster, black sole meunière and fillet steak with forest mushrooms. Excellent wine cellar.

The Lobster Pot

9 Ballsbridge Terrace, Ballsbridge, Dublin 4 **Tel** *01 660 9170*

This long-established upstairs restaurant deservedly commands a loyal following. High-quality food is well presented and served by professional, charming waiters. Specialities feature dressed Kilmore crab, Dublin Bay prawns in Provençal sauce, generously sized sole on the bone, delicious steaks, and chicken and game dishes.

Roly's Bistro

7 Ballsbridge Terrace, Ballsbridge, Dublin 4 **Tel** *01 668 2611*

In the heart of Ballsbridge, this lively, bustling bistro offers reliable, colourful and delicious food. Try the Kerry lamb pie or the Dublin Bay prawns Provençal. Other delicacies include fish and game dishes and succulent steaks. Sit upstairs, if possible, and take home the delicious home-made breads, which are for sale. Reservations are advised.

The Washerwoman's Hill Café

62a Glasnevin Hill, Dublin 9 **Tel** *01 837 9199*

A short stroll from the Botanic Gardens, this cosy restaurant is housed in an 18th-century building, one of the oldest in Glasnevin. It serves traditional food made from locally sourced ingredients. Try the pork belly with cider sauce, and the delicious chocolate brownies. While you eat, enjoy the original artworks on the walls – they are all for sale.

Mint

47 Ranelagh Village, Dublin 6 **Tel** *01 497 8655*

This acclaimed French restaurant uses both rustic and luxurious ingredients to create food that looks like a work of art, as well as tasting divine. Try the lasagne of rabbit or the roasted John Dory. The meal usually comes with delicious little extras. An extensive wine list and a wide range of cheeses, mostly Irish, complete the picture.

BEYOND DUBLIN

O'Brien's Good Food and Drink House

The Village, Johnstown, Navan, Co Meath **Tel** *046 902 0555*

The menu at this award-winning gastropub with wood panelling, brick walls and a rustic feel includes spring rolls and pizzas. Seafood dishes are a speciality: try the Seafood Surprise, a pie dish full of prawns, salmon, monkfish and other sea creatures. Leave some room for the ginger and honeycomb pudding. Live music on Friday nights.

Franzini O'Briens

French's Lane, by Trim Castle, Co Meath **Tel** *046 943 1002*

Modern and crisp in both decor and cuisine, this restaurant beside Trim Castle offers contemporary European cuisine. Food is prepared simply but to a high standard, and includes chicken and pasta dishes, pizzas and steaks. Vegetarians will have plenty of choice, too. The staff are very welcoming, and there is a good wine list.

The Harvest Room

Arthurstown, Co Wexford **Tel** *051 389 600*

TV chef Kevin Dundon, one of Ireland's best, runs a cookery school at this award-winning restaurant at the Dunbrody Country House Hotel. The understated dishes rely on the freshness and quality of locally sourced seasonal ingredients – some from the kitchen garden and orchard. The airy dining room overlooks the garden. No children after 8pm.

The Strawberry Tree

Brooklodge Hotel, Macreddin Village, Co Wicklow **Tel** *0402 36444*

Ireland's only certified organic restaurant, at the Brooklodge Hotel, serves only wild and organic foods sourced from local artisan suppliers. Large feasts can be arranged for parties of eight or more. Try the wild wood pigeon terrine with strawberry and green pepper jam, or the carrot and orange sorbet, described by critics as "a slice of heaven".

Wineport Lodge

Glasson, Athlone, Co Westmeath **Tel** *090 643 9010*

Ireland's first wine hotel is housed in a modern, cedar-clad structure on the shores of Lough Ree – you can even arrive by boat if you wish. The mission statement says they believe in good food, great wine and relaxation, and they certainly deliver on all three. Seasonal local food is creatively mastered. The wine list is extensive.

Pubs, Bars and Cafés

Dublin's pubs are a slice of living history, famous as the haunts of literary figures, politicans and rock stars alike. Today, as well as the memorabilia on the walls, it is the singing, dancing, talk and laughter that make a pub tour of Dublin a necessity (see p156).

There are nearly 1,000 pubs inside the city limits. Some excel in entertainment, others in the quality of their Guinness and their pub food, but there are also many modern bars to match the best in Europe.

In recent years Dublin has become very cosmopolitan and, as well as the pubs, there is a wide range of cafés offering quick and inexpensive food. The ones listed here are good for those on a busy sightseeing schedule.

TRADITIONAL PUBS

Each Dublin pub has its own character and, while many of them are rather touristy, they retain a trademark clientèle: **Doheny & Nesbitt** and the **Horseshoe Bar** attract politicians, journalists and lawyers while **Neary's** pulls in a theatrical crowd. Others have a strong literary connection; Brendan Behan drank at **McDaid's** while **Davy Byrne's** was featured in Joyce's *Ulysses*. Some of the best and most ornate interiors include **The Brazen Head**, the **Stag's Head**, the **Long Hall** and **Kehoe's** with its great snugs. **Mulligan's**, founded in 1782, claims to have the best Guinness. If you fancy something different, **Porter House** in Parliament Street brews its own, including an excellent oyster stout.

MUSIC PUBS

Regular traditional music sessions take place all over Dublin. **The Brazen Head, O'Donoghue's** and the **Cobblestone** are popular venues. The **International Bar** focuses on singers and comedians, while **Whelan's** has a proper venue room next door with an eclectic range of acts for a cover charge of under 10 euros.

MODERN BARS

Recently, a number of Continental-style bars have cropped up which cater to a young and fashionable crowd. **Hogan's**, and the **Globe** are on the edge of Temple Bar. The main bar at the **Clarence Hotel** does great cocktails. Inventive drinks are also on the menu at the trendy **Tripod. Café en Seine** near Trinity College has a wide choice of food and offers a live jazz brunch on Sunday.

PUB FOOD

Many of Dublin's grand old pubs offer tasty and good-value pub lunches. Just off Grafton Street are **O'Neill's** and the very traditional **Old Stand**. In Temple Bar, **Oliver St John Gogarty** is probably the best option.

MUSEUM AND SHOP CAFES

Many of Dublin's tourist attractions offer good-quality cafés and snack bars. One of the best is at the **National Gallery**: it serves mainly Mediterranean food and is operated by the Fitzer's chain. Food at the **National Museum** has more of a traditional Irish choice while the **Irish Film Institute** offers an eclectic range. Food at **Avoca** is modern and delicious: go early if you want to get in. For a unique place to eat, try the upstairs café at the **Winding Stair Bookshop**.

BREAKFAST

Most hotels and B&Bs in the city serve reasonable breakfasts, an essential start to a full day's sightseeing. A particular favourite of Dubliners is **Café Java**, while **Heavenly Café** serves great-value food and a nice variety of breakfasts. **Café Kylemore** also makes a good breakfast.

COFFEE AND CAKES

In an attractive setting among the stalls at Powerscourt Townhouse, **Mimo** offers coffee, fresh food and a good wine selection in a relaxed, spacious environment.

PIZZA AND PASTA

Irish-Italian cafés and restaurants offer some of the best-value meals in the city. Two very popular ones, the family-oriented **Little Caesar's Palace** and the tiny **Steps of Rome**, lie off Grafton Street, as does the excellent **Pasta Fresca**. Temple Bar's **Bad Ass Café** has a youthful feel and serves pizza, pasta and salads. Sinéad O'Connor worked here before making it in music. **Milano**, currently with two branches in the city, is a branch of the popular British chain Pizza Express.

TRADITIONAL FOOD

For traditional food with a modern slant, **Gallagher's Boxty House**, specialising in Irish pancakes, is a popular choice. However, some might prefer the even simpler fare at **Café Kylemore** which is run by a major city bakery. For good honest fish and chips try the venerable **Leo Burdock's** or **Beshoff's**.

VEGETARIAN

One of the great favourites is the long-running café, **Cornucopia**, also open for breakfast and lunch. **Café Fresh** is a fun place to eat in the Powerscourt Townhouse while **Juice** offers a cool, modern feel. The **Alamo Café** is the pick of the city's Mexican restaurants and offers lots of choice for vegetarians but also serves meat dishes. Temple Bar's Saturday market has a good organic selection.

DIRECTORY

TRADITIONAL PUBS

The Brazen Head
20 Bridge St Lower.
Map A3.
Tel 679 5186.

Davy Byrne's
21 Duke St.
Map D4.
Tel 677 5217.

Doheny & Nesbitt
5 Lower Baggot St.
Map F5.
Tel 676 2945.

Horseshoe Bar
Shelbourne Hotel,
27 St Stephen's Green.
Map E4.
Tel 663 4500.

John Kehoe's
9 Anne St South.
Map D4.
Tel 677 8312.

The Long Hall
51 South Great George's
St. **Map** C4.
Tel 475 1590.

McDaid's
3 Harry St.
Map D4.
Tel 679 4395.

Mulligan's
8 Poolbeg St.
Map E3.
Tel 677 5582.

Neary's
1 Chatham St.
Map D4.
Tel 677 8596.

Porter House
16–18 Parliament St.
Map C3.
Tel 679 8847

Stag's Head
1 Dame Court,
off Dame St. **Map** C3.
Tel 679 3687.

MUSIC BARS

Cobblestone
77 North King St.
Map A2.
Tel 872 1799

International Bar
23 Wicklow St.
Map D3.
Tel 677 9250.

O'Donoghue's
15 Merrion Row.
Map E5.
Tel 676 2807.

Whelan's
25 Wexford St.
Map C5.
Tel 478 0766.

MODERN BARS

The Café Bar
Morrison Hotel,
Ormond Quay.
Map C3.
Tel 887 2400.

Café en Seine
40 Dawson St.
Map D4.
Tel 677 4567.

The Globe
11 South Great George's
St. **Map** C4.
Tel 671 1220.

Hogan's
35 South Great George's
St. **Map** C4.
Tel 677 5904.

Octagon Bar
Clarence Hotel,
6–8 Wellington Quay.
Map C3.
Tel 670 9000.

Tripod
Harcourt St, at Hatch St
Lower. **Map** D5.
Tel 476 3374.

PUB FOOD

The Old Stand
37 Exchequer St.
Map D3.
Tel 677 7220.

Oliver St John Gogarty
57 Fleet St.
Map D3.
Tel 671 1822.

O'Neill's
2 Suffolk St.
Map D3.
Tel 679 3656.

MUSEUM AND SHOP CAFÉS

Avoca Café
11–13 Suffolk St.
Map D3.
Tel 286 7466.

Irish Film Institute
6 Eustace St,
Temple Bar.
Map C3.
Tel 679 3477.

National Gallery
Merrion Square West.
Map E4.
Tel 661 5133.

National Museum
Kildare St.
Map E4.
Tel 677 7444.

Winding Stair Bookshop
40 Ormond Quay Lower.
Map C3.
Tel 872 7320.

BREAKFAST

Café Java
145 Leeson St.
Map E5.
Tel 660 0675.

Heavenly Café
87 Lower Camden St.
Map C5.
Tel 405 3990.

COFFEE AND CAKES

Mimo
Powerscourt Townhouse,
South William St.
Map D4.
Tel 679 4160.

PIZZA AND PASTA

Bad Ass Café
9 Crown Alley,
Temple Bar.
Map D3.
Tel 671 2596.

Little Caesar's Palace
1–3 Balfe St. **Map** D4.
Tel 670 4534.

Milano
38 Dawson St.
Map D4.
Tel 670 7744.
19 Essex St East.
Map C3.
Tel 670 3384.

Pasta Fresca
4 Chatham St.
Map D4.
Tel 679 2402.

Steps of Rome
Unit 1, Chatham Court,
Chatham St.
Map D4.
Tel 670 5630.

TRADITIONAL FOOD

Beshoff's
O'Connell St.
Map D2.
Tel 462 4181.

Café Kylemore
O'Connell St.
Map D2.
Tel 872 2138.

Gallagher's Boxty House
Temple Bar.
Map D3.
Tel 677 2762.

Leo Burdock's
2 Werburgh St.
Map C4.
Tel 454 0306.

VEGETARIAN

Alamo Café
22 Temple Bar.
Map C3.
Tel 677 6546.

Café Fresh
Powerscourt Townhouse,
South William St.
Map D4.
Tel 671 9669.

Cornucopia
19 Wicklow St.
Map D3.
Tel 677 7583.

Juice
9 Castlehouse
South Great George's St.
Map C4.
Tel 475 7856.

SHOPS AND MARKETS

Dublin is a paradise for shoppers, with its wide streets, indoor markets, craft stores and out-of-town shopping centres. Popular buys include chunky Aran sweaters, Waterford crystal, Irish linen, hand-loomed tweed from Donegal and tasty farmhouse cheeses. The thriving crafts industry is based on traditional products with an innovative twist. Typical of contemporary Irish crafts are good design, quality craftsmanship and a range spanning Celtic brooches and bone china, knitwear and designer fashion, carved bogwood and books of Irish poetry. Kitsch souvenirs also abound, from leprechauns and shamrock emblems to Guinness tankards and garish religious memorabilia. Irish whiskeys and liqueurs are always popular and very reasonable to buy in Dublin.

In the directory on page 151, a map reference is given for each address that features on the Dublin Street Finder map on pages 180–81.

Modern Irish pottery

Johnson's Court alley behind Grafton Street in southwest Dublin

WHERE TO SHOP

There are two major shopping quarters in Dublin. The north side of the Liffey, centred on O'Connell and Henry streets, has several shopping centres and department stores. The famous Moore Street fruit and vegetable market is held Monday to Saturday just off Grafton Street. More upmarket shops can be found on the south side, around Grafton and Nassau streets. The Temple Bar area contains a number of trendy craft shops.

WHEN TO SHOP

Most shops are open from Monday to Saturday, 9am to 5:30 or 6pm. Shops open late on Thursday nights. Shops are closed at Easter and Christmas and on St Patrick's Day but are open on most other public holidays.

HOW TO PAY

Major credit cards such as VISA and MasterCard are accepted in most large stores, but smaller shops may prefer cash. Traveller's cheques are accepted in major stores with a passport as identification. Eurocheques are generally no longer acceptable.

SALES TAX AND REFUNDS

Most purchases are subject to VAT (sales tax) at 21 per cent, a sum included in the sales price. However, visitors from outside the European Union (EU) can reclaim VAT prior to departure. If you are shipping goods overseas, refunds can be claimed at the point of purchase. If taking your goods with you, look for the CashBack logo in shops, fill in the special voucher, then visit the CashBack offices at Dublin airport.

SHOPPING CENTRES

Dublin has several large shopping centres, including the **Dundrum Shopping Centre**, voted the best in Europe in 2007. The **Dun Laoghaire Shopping Centre** is on several floors and has a huge range of clothes shops, bookshops and electronics shops. In central Dublin are the **St Stephen's Green Shopping Centre** and the **Jervis Shopping Centre**, both offering the comfort of covered shopping. A more unusual centre is the **Powerscourt Townhouse** (see p60), more of an indoor market than a shopping centre, selling various Irish crafts. **Kildare Village**, on the outskirts of town, is good for outlet shopping.

BOOKS

Bookshops abound in Dublin. **Eason and Son**, on O'Connell Street, is the biggest bookseller in the city with a wide

The Ha'penny Bridge Galleries on Bachelors Walk

Brown Thomas department store on Grafton Street

range of Irish literature and national and international newspapers. For antiquarian books, **Cathach Books** on Duke Street is excellent.

Foreign-language books are available in Dublin – try **International Books** for the best range. **Hodges Figgis** specializes in Irish literature and academic publications. They also have a coffee shop in the store. One of the best for general books is the **Dublin Bookshop** on Grafton Street (part of the Dubray Books chain). On two floors, they have an extensive Irish section and a good range of tourist guides as well as general fiction and children's books. **Waterstone's** and **Hughes & Hughes** are also both good general booksellers.

MUSIC

Traditional musical instruments are made in many regions of Ireland, but Dublin has a history of specializing in hand-made harps. Several shops sell musical instruments, such as hand-crafted bodhráns (traditional goatskin hand-held drums) and uilleann pipes (bagpipes). **Waltons** sells traditional instruments and sheet music, while **Claddagh Records** is a specialist folk shop, selling Irish folk and ethnic music. For a standard range of pop and classical music there are two branches of the **HMV** music store in Dublin.

ANTIQUES

Dublin has its own antiques centre, in the form of Francis Street in the south west of the city. **Lantern Antiques** specializes in old pub fittings such as mirrors and old advertisements. For rugs and carpets try **Forsyth Antiques**. For 20th-century decorative arts visit **Johnston Antiques. The Ha'penny Bridge Galleries** sell everything from furniture through to cast iron and marble. **Courtville Antiques** in the Powerscourt Townhouse has a beautiful collection of antique jewellery, silver, paintings and objets d'art. On Grafton Street, **McCormack** is particularly good for antique jewellery.

Sign outside Eason and Son

CRAFTS

Whichcraft at the Designyard Gallery in Cow's Lane and the **Irish Celtic Craftshop** in Lord Edward Street have a great

range of contemporary Irish crafts. The Crafts Council also recommends other good outlets for Irish crafts, and the tourist offices have lists of local workshops, where you can often watch the production process. **The Kilkenny Shop** sells tiles, rugs, metal-, leather- and woodwork.

JEWELLERY

In its golden age, Celtic metalwork was the pride of Ireland. Many contemporary craftspeople are still inspired by traditional designs on Celtic chalices and ornaments. Silver and gold jewellery is made all over Ireland in many designs and widely available in Dublin. The Claddagh ring is the most famous of all – the lovers' symbol of two hands cradling a heart with a crown. In the Powerscourt Townhouse, shops have handmade and antique jewellery on display and gold- and silversmiths can be seen at work. **McDowell** jewellers specialize in handcrafted gold and silver Irish jewellery.

CHINA, CRYSTAL AND GLASSWARE

Ireland's most famous make of crystalware is Waterford Crystal. Still made today in the town of Waterford, south of Dublin, this beautiful crystal and glassware is known all over the world for its outstanding quality.

Dublin Crystal, in Blackrock, south of the city, makes and sells on the premises fine-quality hand-cut crystal.

There are many producers of fine china in Ireland. Royal Tara China in Galway is Ireland's leading fine bone china manufacturer, with designs incorporating Celtic themes. The best place to buy china and glassware is in department stores, such as Clery's and Brown Thomas.

Bodhráns of perfect pitch for sale in Dublin

LINEN

Damask linen was brought to Armagh in Northern Ireland by Huguenot refugees fleeing French persecution. Linen is widely available all over Ireland today, and fine Irish linen can be bought at many outlets in Dublin, including the **Brown Thomas** department store, which has an excellent linen shop. Another good supplier is **Murphy, Sheehy and Co**, who are located behind the Powerscourt Townhouse. As well as being famous for fine-quality Irish linen, they also sell tweeds.

Sign for the linen department at Brown Thomas store

KNITWEAR AND TWEED

Aran sweaters are sold all over Ireland, but originate in County Galway and the Aran Islands themselves, off the west coast of Ireland. One of Dublin's best buys, these oiled, off-white sweaters used to be handed down through generations of Aran fishermen. Legend has it that each family used its own motifs so that, if a fisherman were lost at sea and his body unidentifiable, his family could recognize him by his sweater. Warm and rain-resistant clothes are generally of good quality, from waxed jackets and duffel coats to sheepskin jackets. **House of Ireland** offer an excellent selection of quality Irish clothing. Knitwear is sold everywhere in Dublin.

Good buys include embroidered waistcoats and handwoven scarves. **The Sweater Shop** has woollens and tweeds at reasonable prices. The Suffolk Street branch of **Avoca** has a good mix of traditional and trendy.

Donegal tweed is noted for its texture and subtle colours (originally produced by local plant and mineral dyes). Tweed caps, scarves, ties, jackets and suits are sold in outlets such as **Kevin & Howlin** in Dublin. For menswear specialists, try **Kennedy & McSharry**.

FASHION

Inspired by a predominantly young population, Ireland is fast acquiring a name for fashion. Conservatively cut tweed and linen suits continue to be models of classic good taste, while younger designers are increasingly experimental, using bold lines and mixing traditional fabrics.

A-Wear is an Irish chain store that has a branch in Dublin. The Design Centre in Powerscourt Townhouse Shopping Centre features the best Irish designers including Paul Costelloe, Louise Kennedy, Quin and Donnelly and Mariad Whisker. The Loft Market at Powerscourt showcases up-and-coming design talent (Thu, Sat, Sun). The department stores **Brown Thomas** and **Clery's** have an excellent selection of men's, women's and children's clothing.

Fresh cheeses in Meetinghouse Square

FOOD AND DRINK

Smoked salmon, home-cured bacon, farmhouse cheeses, preserves, soda bread and handmade chocolates make perfect last-minute gifts. **Butlers Chocolate Café**, sells particularly delicious handmade Irish chocolates. Several shops will package and send Irish salmon overseas.

Bewley's teas and coffees are sold in supermarkets like Tescos, **Dunnes** and Super Value all over Ireland. Guinness travels less well and is best drunk in Ireland. Irish whiskey is hard to beat as a gift or souvenir. Apart from the cheaper Power and Paddy brands, the big names are Bushmills and Jameson. Irish liqueurs to enjoy include Irish Mist and Bailey's Irish Cream.

Fresh fruit stall off O'Connell Street

DIRECTORY

SHOPPING CENTRES

Dundrum Shopping Centre
Sandyford Rd, Dundrum, Dublin 16.
Tel 299 1700.
www.dundrum.ie

Dun Laoghaire Shopping Centre
Marine Rd, Dun Laoghaire.
Tel 280 2981.

Jervis Shopping Centre
125 Abbey St Upper.
Map C2.
Tel 878 1323.

Kildare Village Outlet Shopping
Nurney Rd, Kildare Town, Co. Kildare.
Tel 455 20501.

Powerscourt Townhouse Shopping Centre
South William St.
Map D4.
Tel 671 7000.
www.powerscourtcentre.com

St Stephen's Green Shopping Centre
St Stephen's Green West.
Map D4.
Tel 478 0888.

BOOKS

Cathach Books
10 Duke St.
Map D4.
Tel 671 8676.
www.rarebooks.ie

Dublin Bookshop
36 Grafton St.
Map D4.
Tel 677 5568.

Eason and Son
80 Middle Abbey St.
Map D2.
Tel 858 3881.
www.eason.ie

Hodges Figgis
56–58 Dawson St.
Map D4.
Tel 677 4754.

Hughes & Hughes
St Stephen's Green Shopping Centre.
Map D4.
Tel 478 3060.
Also at Dublin Airport.
Tel 704 4034.

International Books
18 Frederick St South.
Map E4.
Tel 679 9375.
www.international books.ie

Waterstone's
7 Dawson St.
Map D4.
Tel 679 1415.
Also at
Jervis Shopping Centre.
Map C2.
Tel 878 1311.
www.waterstones.co.uk

MUSIC

Claddagh Records
2 Cecilia St, Temple Bar.
Map C3.
Tel 677 0262.

HMV
18 Henry St.
Map D2.
Tel 873 2899.
Also at
Grafton St.
Map D4.
Tel 679 5334.

Waltons
3–5 Frederick St North.
Map C1.
Tel 874 7805.

JEWELLERY

McDowell
3 Upper O'Connell St.
Map D2.
Tel 874 4961.

ANTIQUES

Courtville Antiques
Powerscourt Townhouse Shopping Centre.
Map D4.
Tel 679 4042.

Forsyth Antiques
108 Francis St.
Map B4.
Tel 473 2148.

The Ha'penny Bridge Galleries
15 Bachelors Walk.
Map D3. *Tel 872 3950.*

Johnston Antiques
69–70 Francis St.
Map B4.
Tel 473 2384.
www.johnston antiques.net

Lantern Antiques
56 Francis St.
Map B4.
Tel 453 4593.

McCormack
51 Grafton St.
Map D4.
Tel 677 3737.

CRAFTS

The Irish Celtic Craftshop
10–12 Lord Edward St.
Map C3.
Tel 679 9912.

The Kilkenny Shop
6 Nassau St.
Map E4.
Tel 677 7066.
www.kilkenny group.com

Whichcraft
Designyard Gallery, Cow's Lane, Temple Bar.
Map C3.
Tel 474 1011.
www.whichcraft.com

CERAMICS, CHINA AND CRYSTAL

Dublin Crystal
Dundrum Shopping Centre.
Tel 298 7302.
www.dublincrystal.com

LINENS

Brown Thomas Linen Department
Grafton St.
Map D4.
Tel 605 6666.
www.brownthomas.com

Murphy, Sheehy and Co
14 Castle Market.
Map D4.
Tel 677 0316.
www.murphysheehy fabrics.com

KNITWEAR AND TWEED

Avoca
11-13 Suffolk St.
Map D3.
Tel 677 4215.
www.avoca.ie

House of Ireland
37–38 Nassau St.
Map D4.
Tel 671 1111.
www.houseof ireland.com

Kennedy and McSharry
39 Nassau St.
Map D3.
Tel 677 8770.

Kevin and Howlin
31 Nassau St.
Map D3.
Tel 677 0257.

The Sweater Shop
9 Wicklow St.
Map D3.
Tel 671 3270.
www.sweatershop.ie

FASHION

A-Wear
26 Grafton St.
Map D4.
Tel 671 7200.
www.awear.ie

Brown Thomas
88–95 Grafton St.
Map D4.
Tel 605 6666.

Clery's
18–27 O'Connell St Lower.
Map D2.
Tel 878 6000.
www.clerys.ie

FOOD AND DRINK

Butlers Chocolate Café
51a Grafton St.
Map D4.
Tel 671 0599.

Dunnes
Henry St.
Map D2.
Tel 671 4629.

What to Buy in Dublin

St Brigid's cross

The many gift and craft shops scattered throughout Dublin make it easy to find Irish specialities to suit all budgets. The best buys include linen, tweeds and lead crystal. Local crafts make unique souvenirs, from delicate handmade silver jewellery and hand-thrown ceramics to traditional musical instruments. Religious artifacts are also widely available. Irish food and drink, especially whiskey, are evocative reminders of your trip.

Traditional hand-held drum (bodhrán) and beater

Connemara marble "worry stone"   **Traditional Claddagh ring**

Enamel brooch

Modern jewellery and metalwork *draw on a long and varied tradition. Craftspeople continue to base their designs on sources such as the* Book of Kells *(see p40) and Celtic myths. Local plants and wildlife are also an inspiration. Claddagh rings – traditional betrothal rings – originated in County Galway but are widely available in Dublin.*

Fuchsia earring from Dingle   **Celtic design enamel brooch**   **Celtic design silver pendant**

Donegal tweed jacket and waistcoat

Tweed jacket and skirt

Clothing *made in Ireland is usually of excellent quality. Tweed-making still flourishes in Donegal where tweed can be bought ready-made as clothing or hats or as lengths of cloth. Knitwear is widely available throughout Dublin in department stores and local craft shops. The many hand-knitted items on sale, including Aran jumpers, are not cheap but should give years of wear.*

Tweed cap

Tweed fisherman's hat

Aran jumper

Irish linen *is world-famous and the range unparalleled. There is a huge choice of table and bed linen, including extravagant bedspreads and crisp, formal tablecloths. On a smaller scale, tiny, intricately embroidered hand-kerchiefs make lovely gifts as do linen table napkins. Tea towels printed with colourful designs are widely available. You can also buy linen goods trimmed with fine lace, which is still hand-made in many parts of the country.*

Set of linen placemats and napkins

Fine linen handkerchiefs

Nicholas Mosse plate

Belleek teapot

Nicholas Mosse cup

Irish ceramics *come in traditional and modern designs. You can buy anything from a full dinner service by established factories, such as Royal Tara China or the Belleek Pottery, to a one-off contemporary piece from a local potter's studio.*

·IRISH· PROVERBS

ILLUSTRATED BY KAREN BAILEY

Book of Irish Proverbs

Books and stationery *are often beautifully illustrated. Museums and bookshops stock a wide range.*

Irish crystal, *hand-blown and hand-cut, can be ordered or bought in many shops in Dublin. Pieces from the principal manufacturers, such as Waterford Crystal, Tyrone Crystal and Jerpoint Glass, from glasses and decanters to elaborate chandeliers, are widely sold.*

Celtic design cards

Waterford crystal tumbler and decanter

Food and drink *will keep the distinctive tastes of Dublin fresh long after you arrive home. Whiskey connoisseurs should visit the Old Jameson Distillery (see p75) to sample their choice of whiskeys. The Guinness Storehouse (see p82) is a must for aficionados of the dark stout. Good regional food can be found all over the Dublin area.*

Jameson whiskey

Bushmills whiskey

Fruit cake made with Guinness

Jar of Irish marmalade

Packet of dried seaweed

ENTERTAINMENT IN DUBLIN

Although Dublin is well served by theatres, cinemas, night-clubs and rock venues, what sets the city apart from other European capitals is its pubs. Lively banter, impromptu music sessions and great Guinness are the essential ingredients for an enjoyable night in any one of dozens of lively, atmospheric hostelries in Dublin.

One of the most popular entertainment districts is the Temple Bar area. Along this narrow network of cobbled streets you can find

Traditional Irish dancer

everything from traditional music in grand old pubs to the latest dance tracks in a post-industrial setting. The variety of venues makes the centre south of the Liffey the place to be at night, although the north side does boast the two most illustrious theatres, the largest cinemas and the 7,000-seater Point Theatre, a converted 19th-century rail terminal beside the docks. It is now the venue for all major rock concerts and stage musicals as well as some classical music performances.

Monthly magazine *The Dubliner,* details local entertainment

ENTERTAINMENT LISTINGS

Entertainment listings can be found in the online directory www.dublin.ie. *The Dubliner* magazine also reviews bars and restaurants.

Hot Press, a national bimonthly newspaper, covers rock and traditional music, and has comprehensive listings for Dublin. The *Dublin Event Guide* is a free sheet available from pubs, cafés, restaurants and record shops. Published every two weeks, it is particularly strong on the city's music and nightclub scene.

Listings are also available in the free morning papers *Metro* and *Herald FM* and *Totally Dublin* magazine.

BOOKING TICKETS

Tickets for many events are available on the night, but it is safer to book in advance. The main venues accept payment over the telephone by all major

credit cards. **Ticketmaster** accepts phone bookings by credit card for many of the major shows in and around Dublin, while **HMV** and **Dublin Tourism** (Suffolk Street) sell tickets for theatres and gigs.

NIGHTCLUBS

Dublin's clublife offers plenty of choice. **POD** (Place of Dance) has great djs performing, whilst **Lillie's Bordello** is a magnet for celebrities, models and visiting stars. The more laid-back **Rí-Rá** (Gaelic for "uproar") is at the cutting edge of R&B and dance music.

For a lounge atmosphere, head for **The Sugar Club** which offers live music and cocktails. **Renards** is a hip three-tiered bar/nightclub attracting music and film stars. **Club M**, in the

The decadent interior of Lillie's Bordello, reminiscent of a boudoir

basement of Bloom's Hotel, plays chart, dance and R&B hits. Another popular basement club is **Boomerang**, with three bars, a state-of-the-art sound system and a different music mix each night.

Nightclubs in Dublin are being replaced by "super pubs" with dance floors. This has led to the rise of the "club night", which hosts a particular DJ or music genre on a given night of the week. Check out the club nights at POD, named Crawdaddy and Tripod, which involve a mix of electro, break beats, house and hip hop.

On Friday and Saturday nights, the **Gaiety Theatre** turns into a club; the music varies from soul, Motown and R&B to indie

Street entertainer in central Dublin

Buskers playing on Grafton Street in Southeast Dublin

and 80s hits. At **The Village**, DJs take to the decks every night, and there is karaoke on Sundays. The music at **Think-tank** covers everything from retro grooves to contemporary house.

The **Academy** is a live music venue and club, playing mainly indie, alternative and electro. Fridays at **The Vaults** see a mix of electro house, progressive and techno trance, while Saturdays host R&B, hip hop, soul and funk.

The **George**, a gay pub and club that has been running since 1985, stages popular drag shows, as well as Irish and international acts.

Wax hosts blues, house and garage tracks, as well as a popular electro-house club night on Thursdays. Friday's Sub Zero is a mix of indie, ska, alternative and funk downstairs in **Thomas Read's** pub.

CLASSICAL MUSIC, OPERA AND DANCE

Dublin has a great venue in the **National Concert Hall**, a 19th-century exhibition hall that was redesigned and acoustically adapted in the 1980s. It is where the National Symphony Orchestra plays most Friday evenings. The programme also includes jazz, dance, opera, chamber music and some traditional music.

The **Hugh Lane Municipal Gallery of Modern Art** *(see p73)* has regular Sunday lunchtime concerts. Other classical venues include the **Royal Hospital Kilmainham**

(see p84) and the **Royal Dublin Society (RDS)**. Opera Ireland performs every April and November at the Gaiety Theatre on King Street South.

COMEDY

The Laughter Lounge is one of Dublin's top comedy venues, attracting big names from the world of stand-up comedy. Other venues include the **Olympia Theatre** for international stars and **The Ha'penny Bridge Inn**, Tuesday to Thursday, for local talent.

The Laughter Lounge

TRADITIONAL MUSIC AND DANCE

To many Irish people, the standard of music in a pub is just as important as the quality of the Guinness. Central Dublin has a host of pubs reverberating to the sound of bodhráns, fiddles and uilleann pipes.

One of the most famous is **O'Donoghue's**, where the legendary Dubliners started out in the early 1960s. The long-established **Auld Dubliner** and **Cobblestone** are also renowned venues for local and foreign bands. **The Merry Ploughboy** hosts traditional nights with an exciting mix of music and dancing involving many of Ireland's finest talents. **The Farmhouse Bar** and the **Castle Inn** stage Irish cabaret featuring dancing, singing and lively, toe-tapping music.

ROCK, JAZZ, BLUES AND COUNTRY

Dublin has had a thriving rock scene ever since local band Thin Lizzy made it big in the early 1970s. U2's success acted as a further catalyst for local bands, and there is a gig somewhere in the city on most nights. **Whelan's** features the best new Irish bands nightly; the **International Bar** caters mostly for acoustic acts and singer-songwriters; and the **Ha'penny Bridge Inn** *(see Comedy)* has folk and blues on Fridays and Saturdays. Big names play at either **The O2** or, in summer, local sports stadia. **Slane Castle** hosts a big rock event every summer.

The Button Factory and **The Sugar Club** *(see Nightclubs)* offer jazz, blues, salsa, swing and latin throughout the year, with the **Heineken Green Energy Festival** in May. Country music also has a big following.

Crowds dancing at The Sugar Club

The glamorous Horseshoe Bar in the Shelbourne Hotel

HOTEL BARS

In recent years, the pubs of Dublin have become so popular, they have started to overflow. As a consequence, a new breed of bar has successfully taken off. The hotel bars are the city's sophisticated watering holes, appealing to those who wish to escape the raucous "craic" of the more traditional pubs.

The **Inn on the Green**, located in the Fitzwilliam Hotel, features Nineties cool metal decor. At the Merrion Hotel, you can hide from the hubbub of the city in the **Cellar Bar**. Trendy media types hang out at the mellow **Octagon Bar** at The Clarence Hotel, or at the **Lobo Bar** at the Morrison. However, if it is undiluted glamour you seek, head for a shot of whiskey in **The Horseshoe Bar**, located within the renowned Shelbourne Hotel.

PUB CRAWLS AND TOURS

There are a number of organized pub crawls in Dublin, most of which cover the character pubs and those with a long and colourful history. The **Dublin Literary Pub Crawl**, which starts in The Duke pub on Duke Street, is perhaps the most famous of these. The two-and-a-half-hour tours feature pubs once frequented by Ireland's most famous authors and playwrights.

Viking Splash Tours operate a land-and-water sightseeing tour of Dublin. This tour is carried out in an amphibious military vehicle decorated as a Viking ship and complete with Viking costumed driver.

A handful of tours around the city offer an insight into Dublin's dark and spooky history. **The Walk Macabre**, for example, visits scenes of murder and intrigue in the city. If you prefer to be driven around, the **Dublin Ghost Bus Tour** offers on-board entertainment as well as lessons in bodysnatching and the story behind Bram Stoker's *Dracula*.

If tracing Dublin's musical heritage is of more interest to you, join the **Music Hall of Fame**. This takes you to the sites where bands such as U2 and Thin Lizzy first found fame. The **Musical Pub Crawl** is another tour that traces the history of Irish music, with musicians performing from pub to pub.

The **Historical Walking Tour** of Dublin takes in many of the significant locations of the city's colourful past.

Record shop and ticket office in Crown Alley, Temple Bar

CINEMA

Dublin's cinemas have had a boost thanks to the success of Dublin-based films such as *My Left Foot* (1989), *The Commitments* (1991) and *Michael Collins* (1996) and a subsequent growth in the country's movie production industry. The **Irish Film Institute** *(see p58)* opened its doors in 1992 and was a most welcome addition to the city's entertainment scene. Housed in an original 17th-century building in Temple Bar, the centre shows mostly independent and foreign films, along with a programme of lectures, seminars and masterclasses. It boasts two screens, a bar, a restaurant and an archive of old film material.

"Mr Screen" cinema sign

Another two cinemas with repertoires of mostly art house are the **Screen** and **Lighthouse**. The large first-run cinemas, such as the **Savoy** and the multiplex **Cineworld**, are all located on the north side of the river. These usually offer reduced prices for their afternoon screenings and show late-night movies at the weekend.

Temple Bar Cultural Trust Summer Programme *(see p159)* offers free outdoor screenings of Irish and international films at Meeting House Square. Tickets are available from Temple Bar Information Centre.

One of the amphibious vehicles used by Viking Splash Tours

DIRECTORY

BOOKING TICKETS

HMV
18 Henry St. **Map** D2.
Tel 872 2095.
65 Grafton St. **Map** D4.
Tel 679 5334.

Ticketmaster
www.ticketmaster.ie

NIGHTCLUBS

The Academy
57 Middle Abbey St.
Map D2. *Tel 877 9999.*
www.theacademydublin.
com

Boomerang
Fleet Street. **Map** D3.
Tel 677 3333. www.
boomerangniteclub.com

Club M
Bloom's Hotel, Cope St.
Map D3. *Tel 671 5622.*
www.clubm.ie

Gaiety Theatre
South King St. **Map** D4.
Tel 677 1717.
www.gaietytheatre.ie

The George
South Great George's St.
Map C3. *Tel 478 2983.*

Lillie's Bordello
Adam Court, off Grafton
St. **Map** D4. *Tel 679 9204.*

POD
Old Harcourt St train
station, Harcourt St.
Map D5. *Tel 478 0225.*
www.pod.ie

Renards
South Frederick St.
Map E4. *Tel 677 5876.*
www.renards.ie

Rí-Rá
11 South Great George's
St. **Map** C3. *Tel 671 1220.*

Spy
Powerscourt Townhouse
Ctr, South William St.
Map D4. *Tel 677 0014.*
www.spydublin.com

The Sugar Club
8 Lower Leeson St.
Map E5. *Tel 678 7188.*

Thinktank
23–24 Eustace St.
Map C3. *Tel 670 7655.*

Thomas Reads
Parliament Street.
Map C3.
Tel 677 1487.

The Vaults
Harbourmaster Place.
Map F2. *Tel 605 4700.*
www.thevaults.ie

The Village
26 Wexford St. **Map** C5.
Tel 475 8555.
www.thevillagevenue.com

CLASSICAL MUSIC, OPERA AND DANCE

Hugh Lane Municipal Gallery of Modern Art
Charlemont House,
Parnell Sq North. **Map** C1.
Tel 222 5550.
www.hughlane.ie.

National Concert Hall
Earlsfort Terrace. **Map** D5.
Tel 417 0077.
www.nch.ie

The O2 Dublin
North Wall Quay. **Map** F2.
Tel 819 8888.
www.theO2.ie

Royal Dublin Society (RDS)
Ballsbridge. *Tel 668 0866.*
www.rds.ie

Royal Hospital Kilmainham
Kilmainham, Dublin 8.
Tel 612 9900.
www.modernart.ie

COMEDY

The Ha'penny Bridge Inn
Wellington Quay.
Map C3. *Tel 677 0616.*

The Laughter Lounge
4–6 Eden Quay. **Map** D2.
Tel 874 4611.

Olympia Theatre
Dame St. **Map** C3.
Tel 679 3323.

TRADITIONAL MUSIC & DANCE

Auld Dubliner
24–25 Temple Bar.
Map D3. *Tel 677 0527.*

Castle Inn
5–7 Lord Edward St.
Map C3. *Tel 475 1122.*

Cobblestone
77 King St North.
Map A2. *Tel 872 1799.*

The Farmhouse Bar
Rathfarnham, Dublin 16.
Tel 494 2311.

The Merry Ploughboy
Rockbrook, Rathfarnham,
Dublin 16.
Tel 493 1495.

O'Donoghue's
15 Merrion Row.
Map E5. *Tel 676 2807.*

ROCK, JAZZ, BLUES, SALSA AND COUNTRY

The Button Factory
Curved St, Temple Bar.
Map E4.*Tel 670 9202.*
www.buttonfactory.ie

Heineken Green Energy Festival
Tel 284 1747.
www.mcd.ie

International Bar
23 Wicklow St.
Map D3.*Tel 677 9250.*

Slane Annual Rock Concert
Slane Castle, Co Meath
Tel 041 988 4400.
www.slanecastle.ie

Whelan's
25 Wexford St.
Map C5.*Tel 478 0766.*
www.whelanslive.com

HOTEL BARS

Cellar Bar
Merrion Hotel
24 Merrion St Upper.
Map E5.*Tel 603 0600.*

The Horseshoe Bar
Shelbourne Hotel, 27 St
Stephen's Green North.
Map E4. *Tel 663 4500.*

Inn on the Green
Fitzwilliam Hotel, 12 St
Stephen's Green West.
Map D4. *Tel 478 7000.*

The Lobo Bar
The Morrison,
Ormond Quay. **Map** C3.
Tel 878 2999.

Octagon Bar
The Clarence,
6–8 Wellington Quay.
Map C3. *Tel 407 0800.*

PUB CRAWLS AND TOURS

Dublin Bus Ghost Tour
Tel 873 4222.

Dublin Literary Pub Crawl
Tel 670 5602.

Historical Walking Tour
Tel 878 0227.

Musical Pub Crawl
Tel 475 3313.

Music Hall of Fame
Tel 878 3345.

Viking Splash Tours
Tel 707 6000.

The Walk Macabre
Tel 087 677 1512.

CINEMA

Cineworld
Parnell Centre, Parnell St.
Map C2. *Tel 1520 880
444.* www.cineworld.ie

Irish Film Institute
6 Eustace St. **Map** C3.
Tel 679 5744.
www.irishfilm.ie

Lighthouse Cinema
Market Square, Smithfield.
Map A2. *Tel 679 5744.*

Savoy
O'Connell St. **Map** D2.
Tel 874 8487. www.
savoy.ie

Screen
D'Olier St. **Map** D3.
Tel 672 5500.
www.screencinema.ie

Theatre in Dublin

Dublin is synonymous with theatre, having produced some of the greatest practitioners of the art in both English and Gaelic. It is not surprising, therefore, that with the economic boom of the 1990s, theatre was one of the areas to flourish. These days there is almost always something worth seeing in the capital, whether it is a remake of an old favourite or cutting-edge work from an emerging talent. Productions are usually of a very high standard.

The splendid Victorian interior of the Olympia Theatre

INFORMATION SOURCES

Theatre listings can be found in the *Dublin Event Guide* *(see p154)*. A monthly publication, *The Dubliner*, also has theatre reviews, as does the free daily commuter newspaper, *Metro*, and the *Irish Times* Friday pullout, The Ticket. Online resources include www.indublin.ie and www.entertainment.ie, which also list music and cinema venues. Visit www.tickets.ie to book tickets in advance.

MAINSTREAM THEATRE

The most famous venue is Ireland's national theatre, the **Abbey** *(see p70)*, which concentrates on new Irish productions, as well as revivals of Irish classics by playwrights such as Brendan Behan, Oscar Wilde, JM Synge and Sean O'Casey. The smaller **Peacock Theatre** downstairs runs more experimental work.

Founded in 1928, the **Gate Theatre** *(see p72)* is still noted for its adventurous interpretations of well-known plays.

The **Gaiety** stages a mainstream mix of musicals, opera, ballet and plays, emphasizing the work of Irish playwrights. With its Victorian music hall interior, the **Olympia Theatre** *(see p60)* stages comedy and popular drama. It is also well known as a music venue.

Other venues include the **Liberty Hall Theatre**, which offers an eclectic mix of drama, musicals and pantomime, and the **Tivoli Theatre**, which focuses on drama.

CONTEMPORARY/ AVANT-GARDE THEATRE

Some of the best fringe theatre in Dublin can be seen at the **Project Arts Centre** in Temple Bar. During the Dublin Fringe *(see Festivals)*, many other venues are also used, including Crawdaddy and The Sugar Club *(see p154 for both)* and art galleries.

The **Smock Alley Theatre**, dating from 1662, plays host to many dynamic theatre companies, including the acclaimed Rough Magic and Team Theatre.

The **New Theatre**, a small venue behind Connolly Bookshop, provides a mix of established and up-and-coming writers and directors, often with an Irish flavour. New talent can also be found at university theatres. At the **Samuel Beckett Centre** at Trinity College, the standard is generally higher than you would expect from student theatre. **The Helix** at Dublin City University (DCU), near Glasnevin, has an excellent reputation for cutting-edge and diverse theatre and music. The **Teachers' Club** on Parnell Square is also a good spot to catch emerging talent. The **Axis** in Ballymun has a growing reputation for presenting politically-focused, socially relevant new work by emerging Irish playwrights.

Bewley's Café Theatre offers lunchtime performances of one-act plays or cabaret, usually by new writers, with a small cast. The shows cost €15 including lunch.

FESTIVALS

The **Dublin Theatre Festival** runs for two weeks between late September and early October, bringing together Irish and international talents to perform both new and classic works. An integral part of the festival is the Theatre Olympics, a programme of special events, forums, performances, exhibitions and workshops. Booking is highly recommended.

In mid-September, just ahead of the main theatre festival, is the **Dublin Fringe**, one of the country's largest contemporary performing arts festivals. The Fringe includes dance, street theatre, visual arts and comedy, with many performances taking place in the lush, mirrored Spiegeltent.

Also in mid-September, puppeteers from across the world come to take part in the **International Puppet Festival**.

The **Gay and Lesbian Theatre Festival** held each year in May is a platform for both serious work and outrageous fun, while the vibrant **Festival of World Cultures** (late Aug) in Dún Laoghaire features theatre performances from all around the world, as well as music, art and circus.

The Axis theatre in Ballymun

A performance at the Dublin Theatre Festival

The Temple Bar Cultural Trust Summer Programme, Dublin's free entertainment festival, includes circus and drama performances.

Free tours of the Abbey and Gate theatres are included in

Culture Night, one night in September when all cultural organizations open their doors to the general public. Visit www.templebar.ie for more details.

CHILDREN'S THEATRE

The Ark, a children's cultural centre in Temple Bar, has a packed programme of events, including drama. It is worth checking out, especially during the Dublin Theatre Festival. Around Christmas, the **Gaiety** (see Mainstream Theatre) and the **Olympia** (see p60) theatres attempt to outdo each other in lavishly produced pantomimes.

Eugene Lambert, a well loved puppeteer from Irish children's television in the 1980s, gives almost 30 performances a month in his famous **Lambert**

Puppet Theatre and museum in Monkstown.

In mid-June, the Draíocht theatre company runs the annual **Spréacha Festival**, a six-day event of theatre, puppetry, storytelling and visual art for children aged between three and 12.

OUT OF TOWN

Outside of town are many more theatres that offer a mix of local amateur drama groups and professional touring companies. They include the **Pavilion** in Dún Laoghaire; **Draíocht** in Blanchardstown; the **Civic Theatre** in Tallaght; the **Millbank Theatre** in Rush; the **Mill Theatre** in Dundrum; and the Axis in Ballymun (see Contemporary/Avant-Garde Theatre).

DIRECTORY

MAINSTREAM THEATRE

Gaiety Theatre
King Street South.
Map D4.
Tel 677 1717.
www.gaietytheatre.ie

Liberty Hall Theatre
Eden Quay. **Map** E2.
Tel 872 1122.
www.centralticket
bureau.com

Tivoli Theatre
Francis Street.
Map B4.
Tel 454 4472.

CONTEMPORARY/ AVANT-GARDE THEATRE

Axis
Main Street, Ballymun.
Tel 883 2100.
www.axis-ballymun.ie

Bewley's Café Theatre
Grafton Street. **Map** D4.
Tel 086 878 4001.
www.bewleyscafe
theatre.com

The Helix
Collins Avenue, Dublin City University, Glasnevin.
Tel 700 7000.
www.thehelix.ie

New Theatre
43 East Essex Street, Temple Bar.
Map C3.
Tel 670 3361.
www.thenewtheatre.com

Project Arts Centre
39 East Essex Street.
Map C3.
Tel 881 9613/14.
www.project.ie

Samuel Beckett Centre
Trinity College.
Map E3.
Tel 896 2461.
www.tcd.ie/drama

Smock Alley Theatre
Essex Street.
Map C3.
Tel 679 9277.
www.gaietyschool.com/
smock_alley_theatre

Teachers' Club
36 Parnell Square West.
Map C1.
Tel 872 6944.

FESTIVALS

Dublin Fringe
Tel 679 2320.
www.fringefest.com

Dublin Theatre Festival
44 East Essex Street.
Map C3.**Tel** 677 8439.
www.dublintheatre
festival.com

Festival of World Cultures
Dún Laoghaire.
Tel 230 1035.
www.festivalofworld
cultures.com

Gay and Lesbian Theatre Festival
179 South Circular Road.
www.gaytheatre.ie

International Puppet Festival
Tel 280 0974.

Temple Bar Cultural Trust Summer Programme
Tel 677 2255.
www.templebar.ie

CHILDREN'S THEATRE

The Ark
11a Eustace Street.
Map C3.**Tel** 670 7788.
www.ark.ie

Lambert Puppet Theatre
Clifton Lane, Monkstown.
Tel 280 0974.
www.lambertpuppet
theatre.com

Spréacha Festival
Draíocht, Blanchardstown.
Tel 885 2622.
www.draiocht.ie

OUT OF TOWN

Civic Theatre
The Square, Tallaght, Dublin 24.
Tel 462 7477.
www.civictheatre.ie

Draíocht
Blanchardstown, Dublin 15. **Tel** 885 2622.
www.draiocht.ie

Millbank Theatre
Chapel Green, Rush, Co. Dublin.
Tel 843 7475.
www.millbanktheatre.
com

Mill Theatre
Dundrum.
Tel 296 9340.
www.milltheatre.com

Pavilion
Marine Rd, Dún Laoghaire.
Tel 231 2929.
www.paviliontheatre.ie

Outdoor Activities

The city of Dublin is only minutes away from open countryside, and Ireland has many activities to tempt all lovers of the outdoors. The beautiful Wicklow Mountains are within easy reach for scenic walks, and the coastline from Dublin Bay to Dun Laoghaire offers a range of sports including sailing, fishing and windsurfing. There are plenty of opportunities to go horse riding and cycling in the Dublin area. Entire holidays can be based around outdoor activities. In addition to the contacts on page 161, Fáilte Ireland and Dublin Tourism *(see pp164–5)* have information on all sports and recreational activities in and around the city.

Backpackers walking in the Dublin area

Fishing in the canal at Robertstown, County Kildare

The beautiful gardens of Powerscourt House *(see pp114–15)*

WALKING

Walking in Ireland puts you in the very midst of some glorious countryside. The network of waymarked trails takes you to some of the loveliest areas, inaccessible by car. Information on long-distance walks is available from Fáilte Ireland. Routes include the Wicklow Way, which leads from the south of Dublin into the heart of the beautiful Wicklow Mountains *(see p113)*. All the walks may be split into shorter sections for less experienced walkers or those short of time.

Hill walking, rock climbing and mountaineering holidays are also available in Ireland. For specialized information, contact the **Mountaineering Council of Ireland**. When walking or climbing always make sure that you go well-equipped for the notoriously changeable Irish weather.

HORSE RIDING AND PONY TREKKING

A number of riding centres, both residential and non-residential, offer trail riding and trekking along woodland trails, deserted beaches, country lanes and mountain routes. **Equestrian Holidays Ireland** organizes holidays for riders of various abilities. There are two types of trail riding – post-to-post and based. Post-to-post trails follow a series of routes with accommodation in a different place each night. Based trail rides follow different routes in one area and you stay at the same place for the whole holiday. Lessons are available at many riding centres for beginners to more advanced riders. Fáilte Ireland publish details of riding centres and courses.

Horseriding in Phoenix Park

FISHING

The claim that Ireland is a paradise for anglers is no exaggeration. Coarse, game and sea fishing all enjoy wide-spread popularity. Coastal rivers yield the famous Irish salmon, and, among other game fish, sea trout and brown trout also offer a real challenge.

Flounder, whiting, mullet, bass and coalfish tempt the sea angler; deep-sea excursions chase abundant supplies of dogfish, shark, skate and ling. You can organize sea-angling trips from many places.

Maps and information on fishing locations are provided by the **Central Fisheries Board** and the **Irish Federation of Sea Anglers**.

CYCLING

Cycling is very popular both in central Dublin and in the countryside. If you prefer to bring your own bike, you can transport it fairly cheaply by train or bus. If not, you can always rent one from **Cycleways** or **Belfield Bike Shop** on the campus of University College Dublin. Also based here, **Irish Cycling Safaris** concentrate on trips outside Dublin, so you can enjoy the quiet country roads. The paths along Dublin Bay offer fun routes, while the Wicklow Mountains are more of a challenge. They also offer guided cycling tours of the city centre for groups.

WATER SPORTS

With a coastline of over 4,800 km (3,000 miles), it is small wonder that water sports are among Ireland's favourite recreational activities. Surfing, windsurfing, water-skiing, scuba-diving and canoeing are the most popular, and there are facilities for all of these along the Dublin coast and in Dublin Bay itself.

Windsurfing is a popular sport throughout Ireland and there are a number of clubs and schools operating around Dublin Bay. **Surfdock** at Grand Canal Dock Yard and **Wind & Wave** in Monkstown both offer advice, tuition and the latest equipment.

There is a wide range of diving conditions off the coast of Ireland and the **Irish Underwater Council** will give you details of courses and their facilities.

Dun Laoghaire harbour at dusk

CRUISING AND SAILING

A tranquil cruising holiday is an ideal alternative to the stress and strain of driving, and Ireland's many rivers and lakes offer a huge variety of conditions for those who want a waterborne holiday. Stopping over at waterside towns and villages puts you in touch with the Irish on their home ground. Hiring a boat and drifting down the Grand Canal *(see p85)* from Dublin to the Shannon gives a unique view of the countryside.

Another popular sailing area is the scenic Howth peninsula, and the harbour of Dun Laoghaire southeast of Dublin, where you will find sailing schools offering tuition at all levels. For details of these schools, contact the **Irish Sailing Association**.

SPORTS FOR THE DISABLED

Sports enthusiasts with a disability can obtain details of facilities for the disabled from the **Irish Wheelchair Association**. Central and local tourist boards, and many of the organizations listed in the directory under each sport, will be able to offer facilities for disabled visitors. To be sure of this, it is advisable to call the venue first to check what is available.

Cycling in the Irish countryside

DIRECTORY

WALKING

Mountaineering Council of Ireland
House of Sport, 13 Joyce Way, Parkwest Business Park, Dublin 12.
Tel 625 1115.
www.mountaineering.ie

HORSE RIDING

Association of Irish Riding Establishments
11 Moore Park, Newbridge, Co Kildare.
Tel 045 431584.
www.aire.ie

Equestrian Holidays Ireland
www.ehi.ie

FISHING

Central Fisheries Board
Swords Business Campus, Co Dublin.
Tel 884 2600.
www.cfb.ie

Irish Federation of Sea Anglers
Mr Hugh O'Rorke, 67 Windsor Drive, Monkstown, Co Dublin.
Tel 280 6873.
www.ifsa.ie

CYCLING

Cycleways
185–186 Parnell St, Dublin 1. *Tel 873 4748.*
www.cycleways.com

Irish Cycling Safaris
Belfield Bike Shop,
University College Dublin, Dublin 4. *Tel 260 0749.*
www.cyclingsafaris.com

WATER SPORTS

Irish Underwater Council
78a Patrick St, Dun Laoghaire, Co Dublin.
Tel 284 4601.
www.cft.ie

Surfdock Windsurfing
Grand Canal Dockyard, South Dock Rd, Ringsend, Dublin 4.
Tel 668 3945.
www.surfdock.ie

Wind & Wave
16a The Crescent, Monkstown, Co Dublin.
Tel 284 4177.
www.windandwave.ie

SAILING

Irish Sailing Association
3 Park Rd, Dun Laoghaire, Co Dublin.
Tel 280 0239.
www.sailing.ie

SPORTS FOR THE DISABLED

Irish Wheelchair Association
Áras Chúchulain, Blackheath Drive, Clontarf, Dublin 3.
Tel 818 6400.
www.iwa.ie

SURVIVAL
GUIDE

PRACTICAL INFORMATION 164–171

TRAVEL INFORMATION 172–177

DUBLIN STREET FINDER 178–181

PRACTICAL INFORMATION

In the past few years, Dublin has enjoyed a dramatic renaissance. The renovation of the vibrant Temple Bar area, combined with the city's numerous museums, galleries and shops, attracts visitors in their thousands all year round. The best time to visit the region is probably late spring, before the peak summer season. Dublin is generally a safe place, but it does have a wide mixture of districts. You can very quickly find yourself out of a tourist area and in a less desirable part of town. It is wise to avoid the rougher areas to the north of the Liffey, away from O'Connell Street, especially at night. Transport around the city is good and taxis are readily available in the town centre. Dublin Tourism has geared itself up to the increasing demands of the tourist, and their office (in a converted church) is well organized with helpful and friendly staff.

Dublin Tourism logo

Sign showing the way to Ardgillan Demesne

VISAS

Visitors from the EU, US, Canada, Australia and New Zealand require a valid passport but not a visa for entry into Ireland. All others, including those wanting to study or work, should check with their local embassy first. UK nationals do not strictly need a passport to enter Ireland but should take it with them for identification.

TOURIST INFORMATION

The tourist board for Ireland is **Tourism Ireland**, incorporating Faílte Ireland and the Northern Ireland Tourist Board. Its network of overseas offices offer brochures and information.

Dublin Tourism is the regional authority for the Dublin area. The main office is in a converted church on Suffolk Street. There are also walk-in information offices at 14 Upper O'Connell Street, Baggot Street and Dublin Airport. Tourist offices sell maps and guide books, provide local information and can arrange car rental and reserve accommodation. Their accommodation lists include only hotels and guesthouses approved by the tourist board. Museums and libraries often stock useful tourist literature.

ADMISSION CHARGES

Some of Dublin's major sights have an admission fee but many are free. For each place of interest in this guide, we specify whether or not there is a charge. Entrance fees are usually between 1 and 10 euros with discounts for students and the elderly. **The Heritage Service** maintains Ireland's parks, museums, monuments and gardens and issues a Heritage Card which allows unlimited access to more than 70 sites for a year.

Heritage card giving access to historic sites

Students at Trinity College, Dublin

STUDENT INFORMATION

Students with a valid ISIC card (International Student Identity Card) benefit from numerous travel discounts as well as reduced admission to museums and concerts. Buy a Travelsave stamp from any branch of **USIT** and affix it to your ISIC card to get a discount on various rail and bus services operated by Iarnród Éireann and Dublin Bus. You can also get a Temple Bar Culture stamp for discounts on cultural attractions in the area. ISIC cards can be obtained easily from any branch of USIT in Dublin.

USIT will also supply non-students under 26 with an EYC or IYC (European or International Youth Card) for discounts on airfares, and in restaurants, shops and theatres.

DUTY-FREE GOODS

In 1999 the duty-free allowances on goods bought by adults travelling between the Republic of Ireland and other countries were abolished.

However, a wide range of items may still be purchased at airport shops and on ferries, including goods that were previously duty-free, such as beers, wines, spirits, perfume and cigarettes. These shops can also be a useful source of souvenirs and last-minute gifts.

◁ **The main thoroughfare of O'Connell Street**

A selection of Ireland's quality daily newspapers

RELIGIOUS SERVICES

The Republic is 95 per cent Roman Catholic. For many people, churchgoing is a way of life; however, attendance is on the decline. Tourist offices, hotels and B&Bs keep lists of church service times.

IRISH TIME

The whole of Ireland is in the same time zone as Great Britain; five hours ahead of New York and Toronto, one hour behind Germany and France, and ten hours behind Sydney. Clocks go forward one hour for summer time.

NEWSPAPERS AND MAGAZINES

The Republic of Ireland has six national daily papers and five Sunday papers. Quality dailies include the *Irish Independent,* the *Examiner* and *The Irish*

Times. The broadsheets are useful for information on theatre and concerts.

Ireland's daily tabloid is the *Star,* and Irish editions of British tabloids such as *The Sun* and *The Daily Mail* are on sale throughout Dublin. Broadsheets such as *The Times* are also available.

OPENING TIMES

Increasing numbers of shops are now open on Sunday afternoons. Some museums are shut on Monday. Opening hours are generally between 10am and 5pm but phone to check before your visit.

METRICATION

This has been taking place for a few years. Most road signs and all speed limits are shown in kilometres. Fuel is sold in litres, but beer is still sold in pints.

RADIO AND TELEVISION

Ireland has four TV channels, RTE 1, RTE 2, TV3 and TG4, which is an Irish-language service, and a new commercial channel, Channel 6. There are six national radio stations and many local ones. The five British television channels can also be picked up in most parts of Ireland. Cable and satellite TV is quite common and is offered by most hotels.

FACILITIES FOR THE DISABLED

Most sights in Ireland have access for wheelchairs. However it is always worth phoning to check details. The Access Department of the **National Disability Association** provide useful information on amenities.

DIRECTORY

TOURIST INFORMATION

In Ireland
Tel 1850 230 330 (information).
Tel 1800 363 626 (reservations).
www.ireland.ie

In the UK
Tel 0800 039 7000 (info).
www.tourismireland.com

In the USA and Canada
Tel 1800 223 6470 (info).
Tel 1800 398 4376 (res).
www.tourismireland.com

EMBASSIES AND CONSULATES

Australia
Fitzwilton House, Wilton Terrace, Dublin 2. *Tel* 664 5300.
www.australianembassy.ie

Canada
65–68 St Stephen's Green, Dublin 2. *Tel* 417 4100.
www.canada.ie

UK
29 Merrion Rd, Dublin 4.
Tel 205 3700.
www.britishembassy.ie

United States
42 Elgin Rd, Ballsbridge, Dublin 4. *Tel* 668 7122.
www.usembassy.gov

USEFUL ADDRESSES

Dublin Tourism Centre
Suffolk St, Dublin 2.
Tel 605 7700.
www.visitdublin.com

The Heritage Service
6 Upper Ely Place, Dublin 2.
Tel 647 3000 or 1890 321421.
www.heritageireland.ie

National Disability Association
25 Clyde Rd, Ballsbridge, Dublin 4. *Tel* 608 0400.
www.nda.ie

USIT
19–21 Aston Quay, Dublin 2.
Tel 602 1904. www.usit.ie

LANGUAGE

The Republic of Ireland is officially bilingual – almost all road signs have names in English and Irish. English is spoken everywhere except for a few parts of the far west, an area known as the Gaeltacht, but now and then you may find signs only in Irish. On the right are some of the words you are most likely to come across when travelling around the Republic.

Sign using old form of Gaelic

USEFUL WORDS

an banc – **bank**
an lár – **town centre**
an trá – **beach**
ar aghaidh – **straight on**
bealach amach – **exit**
bealach isteach – **entrance**
dúnta – **closed**
fáilte – **welcome**
fir – **men**
gardaí – **police**
leithreas – **toilet**
mná – **women**
oifig an phoist – **post office**
oscailte – **open**
óstán – **hotel**
siopa – **shop**
sláinte! – **cheers!**
stop/stad – **stop**
ticéad – **ticket**
traein – **train**

Personal Security and Health

Although crime in Ireland has long been a relative rarity, in recent years bag-snatching, pickpocketing and car break-ins have become more and more prevalent on the streets of Dublin. Levels of crime are still low by international standards, but Dublin is a modern city with most of the accompanying problems, and visitors should not allow the fabled Irish friendliness to lull them into complacency. Tourist offices and hoteliers will gladly point out the areas to be avoided, but anyone who takes simple precautions should enjoy a trouble-free stay.

Police motorcyclist patrolling the busy Dublin streets

Garda station situated on Pearse Street, near the centre of Dublin

PERSONAL SECURITY

The police in Dublin and the rest of the Republic, should you ever need them, are called the **Gardaí**. Until recently, street crime was very rare in Dublin but, because of poverty and a degree of heroin addiction in certain areas of the city, it is now on a steady increase. However, if you use common sense when wandering around, there should be little cause for concern: avoid the backstreets or poorly lit areas at night; don't draw attention to yourself by wearing flashy jewellery; sit near the driver on buses; use a bag that can be held securely; be alert in crowded places.

You may be approached in the street by people asking for money. This rarely develops into a troublesome situation, but it is still best to avoid eye contact and leave the scene as quickly as possible. In general, safety in the city is about being alert to your surroundings. If you feel uncomfortable anywhere, especially at night, walk away confidently and head for well-lit, populated areas.

Light outside Garda station

PERSONAL PROPERTY

Before you leave home, make sure your possessions are insured, as it can be expensive and difficult to do so in Ireland. Travel insurance for the UK will not cover you in the Republic, so ensure your policy is adequate.

As pickpocketing and petty theft can be a problem in Dublin, it is best not to carry your passport, air tickets or large amounts of cash around with you, or even leave them in your room. Most hotels have a safe and it makes sense to take advantage of this facility. Visitors carrying large amounts of money around should use traveller's cheques rather than cash (see p168–9). When sitting in pubs and restaurants, keep your bag on your lap, if possible, and don't leave your wallet lying on the table. A money belt that can be worn under clothing is a good investment, as is a shoulder bag that can be carried across the chest with the opening facing inwards. When withdrawing money from cash machines, put the notes away as quickly as possible; don't stand around counting them.

Also, if there is a cash machine inside the bank, use that one in preference to one in the street.

If travelling by car, ensure that all valuables are out of sight and the car is locked, even when leaving it for just a few minutes. When you arrive at a hotel, ask the receptionist about secure parking in the area and, on trips out of Dublin to other towns, use guarded parking areas rather than street parking.

LOST PROPERTY

Report all lost or stolen items at once to the police. To make an insurance claim, you will need to get a copy of the police report. Most rail and bus stations in Dublin and the surrounding towns operate a lost property service.

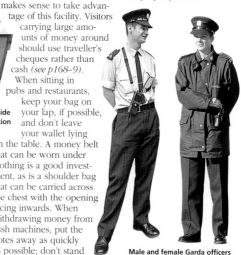

Male and female Garda officers in ordinary uniform

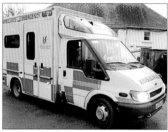

Dublin ambulance

Dublin fire engine

Garda patrol car

IN AN EMERGENCY

In an emergency, either call an ambulance (by dialling 999 or 112) or head for 24-hour accident and emergency departments at **Beaumont**, **St James** or **St Vincent's** hospitals. **Dublin Dental Hospital** serves emergency dental

needs. They are closed at weekends, but provide numbers of dentists on call. In a medical emergency which does not require an ambulance, you should visit a general practitioner (GP) or the outpatients, accident and emergency or casualty department of the nearest public hospital. If not referred to the hospital by a GP you may be asked for a fee of €100.

If you find yourself with no money, or sick and not speaking the language, call the nearest police station (Garda Síochána or PSNI) for practical advice, such as addresses of cheap accommodation. During the day, tourist offices will be helpful. Public hospitals are used to providing translation for patients of many nationalities.

PHARMACIES

A wide range of medical supplies is available over the counter at pharmacies. However, many medicines are available only with a prescription from a local doctor. If you are likely to require specialized drugs during your stay, take your own supplies or ask your

Pharmacy in the city showing old-fashioned snake and goblet symbol

doctor to write a letter specifying the generic name of the medicine you require. Always obtain a receipt for insurance claims. For after-hours medical requirements, try **Hickey's**, a chain of pharmacies with extended opening hours.

Condoms were not freely available in Dublin or the rest of the Republic until 1993 but are now easy to obtain from pharmacies, vending machines in pub toilets or behind the counter at Spar outlets.

MEDICAL TREATMENT

Residents of countries in the European Union can claim free medical treatment in Ireland by getting a European Health Insurance Card (EHIC) before setting out. To avoid having to pay for any treatment, you will need to show your EHIC card and a form of identification, such as a driver's licence or passport. Also, be sure to let the doctor know that you want treatment under the EU's social security regulations. Travellers from outside the EU should either have their own accident and health insurance or be willing to pay for any treatment received.

DIRECTORY

USEFUL ADDRESSES

Police, Fire, Ambulance and Coastguard Services
Tel 999 or 112.

Hickey's Late Night Pharmacy
55 O'Connell St. ⏱ 7:30am–10pm Mon–Sat, 10am–10pm Sun.
Map D2. *Tel* 873 0427.
www.hickeyspharmacies.ie

Beaumont Hospital
Beaumont Rd, Dublin 9.
Tel 809 2714

Dublin Dental Hospital
Lincoln Place, Dublin 2.
Map E4. *Tel* 612 7200.

Pharmacy in the fashionable Temple Bar area

Banking and Currency

Banks in Dublin provide a very good service and will often exchange traveller's cheques without charging commission. They will also change currency, and many have a cash dispenser, or automated teller machine (ATM), for use outside banking hours. Most of the banks are VISA/Delta affiliated, so as long as you have a card bearing the VISA or Cirrus logo, you should be able to withdraw cash at these machines, although a fee may be charged. Outside the city you will find that the banks do not always have cash machines, and opening hours may vary from those in the city centre. Traveller's cheques are by far the safest way to carry money around, but credit cards are more convenient and are widely accepted in the city.

Drawing money from an Allied Irish Bank cash dispenser

USING BANKS

The seven retail banks in the Republic of Ireland are the Bank of Ireland, the Allied Irish Bank (AIB), the Ulster Bank, the National Irish Bank the Permanent-TSB Bank, Halifax and Postbank.

The usual banking hours in Dublin are Monday to Wednesday and Friday from 10am to 4pm and Thursday 10am to 5pm. In rural areas banks often stay open late on market day

instead. Some of the smaller branches further out of the city centre may shut at lunch time. Branches of the Permanent-TSB Bank remain open from 10am to 5pm Monday to Friday, but open at 10:30am on Wednesday. All the banks are closed on public holidays (see p29).

BUREAUX DE CHANGE

In addition to the banks, there are some private *bureaux de change* in Dublin. As with most other exchange facilities, *bureaux de change* open later than banks. However, rates of exchange vary considerably and commission charges can be high, so it's worth looking around before undertaking any transactions. Some department stores also offer *bureaux de change* facilities.

Thomas Cook on Grafton Street in central Dublin

CREDIT CARDS

Throughout Dublin you can pay by credit card in nearly all hotels, petrol (gas) stations, large shops and supermarkets. The hotels (see pp128–33) and restaurants (see pp136–45) listings indicate which establishments accept which credit cards. VISA and MasterCard (also known as Access) are the most widely accepted credit cards. Fewer businesses are also prepared to accept American Express and Diners Club cards. In more rural areas you may not always be able to use your credit card, so be sure to carry cash or traveller's cheques with you as an alternative.

Allied Irish Bank logo

National Irish Bank logo

TRAVELLER'S CHEQUES

Traveller's cheques are the safest way to carry around large amounts of money. These are best changed at one of the main banks but, failing this, many shops and restaurants accept them in place of cash although they usually charge commission. Hotel receptions are often willing to change cheques.

Traveller's cheques can be bought before setting out at American Express, Thomas Cook or at your own bank at home. In Ireland, traveller's cheques can be purchased at banks or from *bureaux de change*, which can be found in Dublin and other large towns, as well as at airports.

Façade of the Bank of Ireland on College Green in central Dublin

THE EURO

The Republic of Ireland was one of those twelve countries taking the Euro in 2002, with the original currency phased out by 9th February of that year. EU members using the Euro as sole official currency are known as the Eurozone. Several EU members, including the UK, have opted out of joining this common currency.

Euro notes are identical throughout the Eurozone countries, each one including designs of fictional architectural structures and monuments. The coins, however, have one side identical (the value side), and one side with an image unique to each country. Both notes and coins are exchangeable in each of the participating Euro countries.

Banknotes

Euro bank notes have seven denominations. The €5 note (grey in colour) is the smallest, followed by the €10 note (pink), €20 note (blue), €50 note (orange), €100 note (green), €200 note (yellow) and €500 note (purple). All notes show the stars of the European Union.

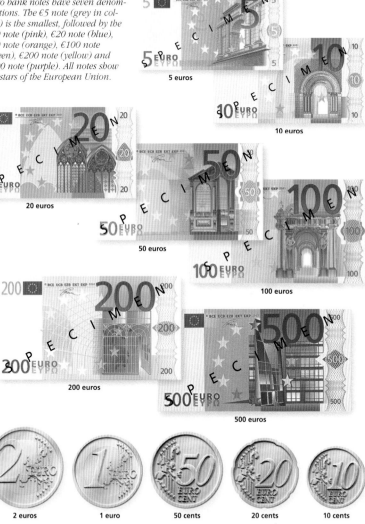

5 euros

10 euros

20 euros

50 euros

100 euros

200 euros

500 euros

2 euros

1 euro

50 cents

20 cents

10 cents

Coins

The euro has eight coin denominations: €1 and €2; 50 cents, 20 cents, 10 cents, 5 cents, 2 cents and 1 cent. The €2 and €1 coins are both silver and gold in colour. The 50-, 20- and 10-cent coins are gold. The 5-, 2- and 1-cent coins are bronze.

5 cents

2 cents

1 cent

Mail Services

Irish Post Office logo

In addition to the main Post Office branches that offer all the mail services available there are a large number of Post Office outlets throughout Dublin incorporated into newsagents and general stores. Although it is improving all the time, the mail service in the Republic is still quite slow; allow four days when sending a letter to Great Britain or anywhere else in Europe and at least six days for North America and other destinations. Sending mail by Swiftpost or Recorded Delivery costs about 5 euros extra but guarantees delivery in a specified number of days.

The modern St Andrews Post Office, in central Dublin

A typical post office in rural Ireland

MAILING A LETTER

Main post offices in Dublin are usually open from 9am to 5:30pm during the week and from 9am to 1pm on Saturdays. Some smaller post offices do not open on Saturdays and close for lunch on weekdays. The General Post Office on O'Connell Street *(see p71)* is well placed for tourist sights and is open at lunch-time on weekdays. It has extended opening hours of 8am to 8pm from Monday to Saturday and 10am to 6pm on Sunday. Standard-value stamps can also be bought from selected newsagents around the city. The Republic of Ireland has only one class of mail, with 90 per cent of

mail delivered within Ireland the next working day. The rate for mail to Great Britain and the rest of Europe is slightly higher than within Ireland and can take between two and six days, depending on whether the economy or priority service is used. All airmail letters (including ones heading for Great Britain) should carry a blue *Priority Aerphost* sticker, available at all post offices for no cost.

MAILBOXES AND POSTE RESTANTE

Mailboxes in the city and in the rest of the Republic are green. In Dublin, some have two slots, marked *Dublin Only* and *All Other Places*. Many of the Republic's mailboxes are quite historic. Some even carry Queen Victoria's monogram on the front, a relic from the days of British rule. Even the smallest towns have a mailbox, and the mail is collected regularly: anything from once to four times daily.

The easiest way to receive mail in Dublin is to have it sent to your hotel. Otherwise, a Poste Restante service is available at major post offices. In the city centre the General Post Office on O'Connell Street is the most convenient, with longer opening hours than any other post office.

List of the daily collection times

Monogram of Queen Victoria

A variety of standard issue Irish stamps

Standard mailbox

Rural mailbox

Communications

eircom phone booth

Eircom is the republic's national telephone company. Although it no longer has the monopoly on the telephone services in the country, the majority of the city's telephone booths are still controlled by eircom. Their modern, efficient service includes coin, card and credit card telephones, distinguished by the wording around the top of each phone booth. Eircom phonecards are available from newsagents, post offices, supermarkets and other retail outlets.

Another company, Smart Telecom, also provides coin and credit card phones. Calls on their phones cost the same as those on eircom phones and are charged at a fixed rate of approximately 40c for 2 minutes.

MAKING A PHONE CALL FROM DUBLIN

Cheap rate calls within the Republic and to the UK are from 6pm to 8am weekdays and all day at weekends. Off-peak times for international calls vary from country to country, but are generally as above. Calls from hotels are expensive at all times.

• To make a call within the Dublin area, dial the seven-digit number, dropping the general Dublin area code 01.
• To make a call to an area outside Dublin, dial the area code which begins with a 0 and then the local number.
• To call Northern Ireland, dial 048, then the area code, followed by the number.
• To call other countries, dial 00, followed by the country code (for example, 44 for the UK), the area code (minus the leading 0), then the number.

USING AN EIRCOM PHONE

1 Lift the receiver and wait for the dial tone.

2 Insert your phone card into the slot or deposit any of the following coins: 10c, 20c, 50c, €1 or €2. The minimum amount is 30c. Dial the number and wait to be connected.

3 The display indicates how much credit you have left. A rapid bleeping noise means your credit has run out. Insert more coins or another card.

4 If you want to make a further call and you have credit left, do not replace the receiver, press the follow-on-call button instead.

5 To redial the number you have just called, press the button marked "R".

6 After you have replaced the receiver, retrieve your card or collect your change. Only wholly unused coins are refunded.

eircom phone card, available in various amounts

ACCESSING THE INTERNET

Dublin, like most major cities, has plenty of public access to computers and the Internet. All libraries have computers and free Wi-Fi, but you may have to book in advance. One way to access the Internet is at one of the many Internet cafés found all over Dublin and throughout the country in major towns and cities. They generally charge by the hour or half-hour for computer use, so costs build up quickly. Many cafés and bars, however, have free Wi-Fi. Bear in mind that UK-style three-pronged plugs are used in Ireland; adaptors may be needed.

Coffee and computers at the Central Cyber Café

TRAVEL INFORMATION

Aer Lingus Airbus in flight

As Dublin becomes an increasingly popular tourist destination, the city becomes even easier to get to, with extremely frequent flights from the UK and good connections from elsewhere in the world. Ferry services are an alternative method of travel from the UK, docking at Dun Laoghaire harbour or Dublin Port. From both the airport and the harbours it is a short ride by car or bus into central Dublin. If you are planning to stay in the centre, it is not necessary to rent a car – most of the sights are within easy walking distance of one another, and the roads in the city centre can become very congested, particularly O'Connell Street. Should your feet require a rest, the bus services are frequent, and there are plenty of taxis available.

The modern exterior of Dublin International Airport

FLYING TO DUBLIN

Flights from most of the main cities in Europe arrive at **Dublin Airport**, which is the Republic of Ireland's busiest airport. Regular services to Dublin depart from all five of the London airports (Heathrow, City, Gatwick, Luton and Stansted) and from 15 other cities in Britain, such as Leeds and Manchester, as well as the Isle of Man and the Channel Islands.

The major airline operating scheduled flights from Britain to Dublin is Ireland's national airline **Aer Lingus**. However since deregulation, their low-cost rival **Ryanair** has grown fast, with cheap fares from several airports in Britain and around Europe. From the United States, Aer Lingus and **Delta Air Lines** fly direct to Dublin Airport. However, there are no direct flights to Dublin from Australia and New Zealand, so popular connecting points used by travellers include London, Singapore and Amsterdam.

AIR FARES

Airlines offer a host of options on air fares to Ireland from Britain. Usually, the amount you pay is determined by how flexible you are prepared to be and how far in advance you book your flight. The best bargains tend to be on flights for which the dates are not changeable. Flights from the United States can double in price in the summer and around Christmas when the fares are most expensive. Mid-week flights are often cheaper than weekend ones. The cheapest place to fly from in the UK is usually London, although the low-cost airline Ryanair flies from other locations in the UK and occasionally has very competitive deals. Ticket prices from the UK are generally fairly consistent throughout the year except at Christmas and during the summer when there are comparatively few discounted fares available. During these periods, due to the increased demand by visiting friends and relatives – usually referred to by airline companies as "VFR" – seats are taken well in advance so it is advisable to book as early as possible if you are intending to travel at these times. Many airlines offer discounts to those under 25, while USIT *(see p164)* and other agencies specializing in student traval often have cheaper rates for students and under-26s.

Airport sign in English and Gaelic

GETTING TO AND FROM THE AIRPORT

An express service, the Airlink bus, runs between Dublin Airport and the city's main rail and bus stations, from early morning to midnight. Tickets are purchased on board. The number 16A and 41 city buses, which run to the city centre, are a cheaper alternative. Also, an efficient DART and bus connection runs via Howth Junction. Ask at your DART station for details. There is a taxi stand outside the airport and car rental companies inside. If you are flying from Dublin and wish to leave your car there or are collecting someone, there are long- and short-stay parking facilities.

The frequent-running Airlink bus

Irish Ferries ship loading up in the harbour

FERRIES TO DUBLIN AND DUN LAOGHAIRE

There is a good choice of ferry services from Wales to Ireland. **Irish Ferries**, the country's largest shipping company, sails on the Holyhead-Dublin route and has two crossings a day on the conventional ferry, which takes about 3¼ hours to reach Dublin Port. They also operate the Jonathan Swift high-speed service, which takes 1 hour 49 minutes. Irish Ferries does not operate on Christmas Day and St Stephen's Day (26 Dec).

The service from Holyhead to the south Dublin suburb of Dun Laoghaire – traditionally the busiest port in Ireland – is served by **Stena Line**'s Stena HSS (High-speed Sea Service). The HSS has the same pas-senger and vehicle capacity as conventional ferries but its jet-engine propulsion gives it twice the speed, cutting journey times in half. Vehicle loading and unloading times on the Stena HSS are also

Directions for ferry passengers

shorter than on other ferries – the loading time for cars is about 20 minutes as opposed to a minimum of 30 minutes with most other ferries. Passengers requiring special assistance at ports or on board the ship should contact the company they are booked with at least 24 hours before the departure time. Like most other ferry companies, Irish Ferries and Stena Line take bicycles for a charge, and this should be mentioned when you make a reservation. The fast ferries may not run in rough weather. Stena Line's conventional ferries run from Dublin Port.

The **Isle of Man Steam Packet Company** operates the SeaCat Rapide service once a day between Liverpool and Dublin. The crossing takes four hours. Their Isle of Man crossing takes two hours, forty-five minutes.

PORT CONNECTIONS

All of Ireland's ports have adequate bus and train connections. At Dublin Port, available buses (with an extra fare) take ferry passengers into the city centre. From Dun Laoghaire, DART trains run into Dublin every 10 to 15 minutes, calling at Pearse Street, Tara Street and Connolly stations. These depart from the railway station near the main passenger concourse. Buses also run from outside Dun Laoghaire DART station to the city centre every 10 to 15 minutes. At all ports, taxis are readily available to meet arriving passengers.

DIRECTORY

USEFUL NUMBERS

Dublin Airport
Tel 814 1111.
www.dublin-airport.com

Aer Lingus
Tel 0818 365 000 or 886 8844.
Tel 0845 084 4444 (UK).
www.aerlingus.com

British Airways
Tel 1890 626747.
Tel 0870 850 9850 (UK).
Tel 1800 403 0882 (US).
www.ba.com

British Midland
Tel 407 3036.
Tel 01332 854000 (UK).
www.flybmi.com

Cityjet
Tel 870 0300.
Tel 0345 445588 (UK).
www.airfrance.com

Delta Air Lines
Tel 1800 768080.
Tel 0800 414767 (UK).
Tel 1800 221 1212 or 1800 241 4141 (US).
www.delta.com

KLM
Tel 08705 074074 (UK).
Tel 1800 447 4747 (US).
www.klm.com

Manx Airlines
Tel 260 1588.
Tel 08457 256256 (UK).
www.manx-airlines.com

Qantas
Tel 407 3278.
Tel 02 6913636 (Australia).
www.qantas.com.au

Ryanair
Tel 0818 303030 or 609 7800.
Tel 0871 246 0000 (UK).
www.ryanair.com

Isle of Man Steam Packet Company
Tel 1800 805055.
Tel 01624 661661 (Isle of Man).
www.seacat.co.uk

Irish Ferries
Tel 1890 313131 or 661 0715.
Tel 08705 171717 (UK).
www.irishferries.com

Stena Line
Tel 204 7777.
Tel 08705 707070 (UK).
www.stenaline.ie

Stena HSS on the Dun Laoghaire to Holyhead crossing

Getting Around Dublin

Dublin is a fairly easy city to get around. The centre is relatively compact, so most of the sights are within walking distance of one another, and much of it, particularly south of the Liffey, is pedestrianized. If you are travelling into the city centre there is an excellent bus service and the local DART railway runs an efficient, if crowded, service to three city centre stations. The Luas line links the north and south of the city, the main railway stations and the centre to the suburbs. If you prefer to be driven around, taxis are available but are fairly expensive.

Dublin Bus at College Green, passing the Bank of Ireland

GETTING AROUND BY BUS

Dublin Bus runs all the bus services in central Dublin and the Greater Dublin area. Bus stops for Dublin Bus are blue or yellow, and the numbers on them indicate which buses stop there. Buses in the city centre run approximately every 10 to 20 minutes from about 6am until 11:30pm, but do allow plenty of time if you have an appointment as they can run late. There is also a night bus service called Nitelink, which departs every hour from 12:30am to 2am Mon to Wed, 12:30am to 4.30am Thurs to Sat. If you are using the bus three or four times in a day, it is worth getting a one-day pass,

costing around 5 euros. There are also four-day, weekly and monthly passes. The main bus station is **Busáras** in Store Street, a short walk from O'Connell Street. You can catch the buses operated by **Bus Éireann** from here to destinations all over the country.

DART SERVICE

The convenient local electric rail service in Dublin known as the **DART** (Dublin Area Rapid Transit) serves 30 stations between Malahide in County Dublin and Grey-stones in County Wicklow with several stops in

Dublin city centre. A Three Day Bus and Rail ticket costs 15 euros and allows three consecutive days' travel on DART trains and also covers Dublin Bus and local subur-ban rail. A Day Rambler ticket covers the same methods of transport but just for one day and costs around 8 euros. Family tickets for two adults and up to four children under the age of 16 are very good value. Tickets can be pur-chased at any of the DART stations. Major works have been carried out along the DART line, including extensions northwards to Malahide and southwards to Greystones.

There are some spectacular views along the southern section, particularly at Killiney and from Bray to Greystones.

The DART is very crowded and to be avoided at peak times during the week. The rush hours are between 7am and 9am and 5pm and 7pm.

LUAS

Luas, the Irish word for speed, is the new on-street light rail network, the first stage of which was completed in June 2004. The network will provide an easy and conven-ient way to reach areas of the city and the suburbs previously only connected to the city centre by

DART station sign

bus. The first phase of the project saw the completion of two new tram lines. One runs west from Connolly Station along the north side of the Liffey. It then heads south at Heuston and terminates further south and west at Tallaght. The other line starts at St Stephen's Green and runs south to Sandyford. The **Luas** lines will eventually inter-sect with the DART and pro-posed Metro line, providing Dublin with an efficient and comprehensive transport system.

Logo on Bus Éireann local and express buses

TAXIS IN DUBLIN

In Dublin, cruising taxis are around but the best places to find cabs are at taxi stands, hotels and rail or bus stations. Prices are based on metered mileage and the minimum charge is around 4 euros. There are a whole range of taxi companies in the city. If you want any information about taxis, the **Irish Taxi Federation** is happy to supply details and information about taxi companies.

Taxis lined up outside the arrivals building at Dublin Airport

FARES AND TICKETS

In the Republic, long-distance buses are about half the price of the equivalent rail journey. If you are making the return trip on the same day, ask for a day-return ticket, which is much cheaper than the normal return fare. Also, between Monday and Thursday you can buy a "mid-week" return ticket for the price of a single journey. Under 16s pay half the adult fare. Students with a Travel-save stamp *(see p164)* get a 30 per cent reduction. For those intending to do a lot of travelling it is cheaper to buy a "Rambler" ticket. This allows unlimited bus travel throughout the Republic for a certain number of days in a set period, for example, 15 days' travel out of 30 consecutive days.

BUS TOURS

Bus Éireann and some local companies run half- and one-day excursions in Dublin. Dublin Bus (Bus Átha Cliath) runs the Dublin City Tour, which leaves from O'Connell Street Upper and takes in the city's most famous sights, including St Stephen's Green, the Bank of Ireland and the Parliament as well as some more obscure sights, such as Oscar Wilde's home. The witty commentary alone makes the tour well worth doing.

DRIVING

If you do not take your own car, there are plenty of car rental firms to choose from. Car rental can be expensive in peak season and the best rates are often obtained by booking in advance. Broker companies, such as **Holiday Autos**, use the major rental companies and will shop around to get the best dea Car rental usually includes unlimited mileage plus passenger indemnity insurance and

The distinctively marked Dublin City Tour bus

cover for third party, fire and theft, but not vehicle damage.

To rent a car, you must show a full driver's licence, which you have held for two years without violations. Cars are usually rented only to those aged between 23 and 70, but some companies may make exceptions. For a list of suggested car rental companies in Dublin see page 177.

PARKING

Dublin has "pay and display" areas, parking meters and car parks. Parking on the street is allowed, although a single yellow line along the edge of the road means there are some restrictions (there should be a sign nearby with permitted parking times). Double yellow lines indicate no parking at any time.

Disc parking – a version of "pay and display" – also operates in Dublin. Discs can be bought from local newsagents, petrol (gas) stations, tourist offices and many small shops.

DIRECTORY

USEFUL CONTACTS

Bus Éireann
Tel 836 6111.
www.buseireann.ie

DART & Irish Rail
Tel 836 6222. www.irishrail.ie

Dublin Bus Information
Tel 873 4222.
www.dublinbus.ie

Holiday Autos
Tel 872 9366.
www.holidayautos.co.uk

Irish Taxi Federation
Tel 836 4166 or 855 1487.

Luas
Tel 1800 300 604. www.luas.ie

A busy Hertz car rental desk at Dublin Airport

Travelling Outside Dublin

One of the best ways to see the magnificent scenery in the countryside around Dublin is by car. The roads have improved greatly in the last few years but the number of cars has also increased. One of the quickest ways to get to more distant destinations is by train. Ireland's national rail network is fast and efficient and also provides an ideal way to see the country's dramatic landscape. Alternatively, you can enjoy the countryside at your own pace by touring on a bicycle, although a certain degree of fitness is advisable if you are going to tackle the beautiful Wicklow Mountains.

Rural petrol pump

Purchasing a rail ticket at a station ticket office

TRAIN SERVICES IN IRELAND

The two main rail stations in Dublin are Connolly, for trains to the north, northwest and Rosslare; and Heuston, which serves the west, midlands and southwest. These two stations are connected by the red Luas and the No. 90 bus service, which runs every 10 to 15 minutes and takes a quarter of an hour, but can take about 30 minutes at rush hour. Irish Rail (Iarnród Éireann) operates a service out of Dublin to most

large cities and towns. Going by rail is probably the fastest and most convenient way of travelling to other major places. Most trains have standard and super-standard (first-class) compartments. Bicycles can be taken on trains for a supplement of around 10 euros.

TICKETS AND FARES

Throughout Ireland, train tickets are generally quite expensive, but there are lots of good-value incentive and concessionary passes. Most of these include bus travel, so you can travel to virtually anywhere in Ireland on just one ticket.

The most comprehensive ticket available, the Emerald Card, can be used on Irish Rail, Dublin Bus and Bus Éireann services. For around 180 euros it gives eight days' unlimited travel in a 15-day period. An 8-day Irish Explorer ticket is slightly cheaper and is valid on all Irish Rail and Bus Éireann transport. The Irish Rover ticket can also be good value. It is valid on all rail and bus journeys from three days within an 8-day period. For 15 euros

Yield (give way) road sign in Gaelic

GÉILL SLÍ

students can buy a National Student Travelcard for a discount on all Irish Rail single and return journeys, as well as on DART and Dublin Bus services. Older travellers can get Inter Rail Plus 26 cards costing 7 euros.

DRIVING YOUR OWN CAR

If you intend to use your own car, check your insurance to find out how well you are covered. To prevent a comprehensive policy being downgraded to third-party cover, ask your insurance company for a Green Card. Carry your insurance certificate, Green Card, proof of ownership of the car and, importantly, your driver's licence. If your licence was issued in the UK, bring your passport with you for identification.

Membership of a reputable breakdown service is advisable unless you are undaunted by the prospect of breaking down in remote countryside. Non-members can join up for the duration of their holiday only. Depending on the type of cover you have, breakdown organizations may offer only limited services in Ireland so check before you travel.

If you are renting a car, make sure the insurance cover meets your needs. You will need to show your driver's licence – if you are a US citizen you will need an International Driving Permit, available from the **AAA**.

Platform of Heuston Station in Dublin

RULES OF THE ROAD

Even for those unused to driving on the left, driving in Ireland is unlikely to pose any great problems. For many visitors, the most difficult aspect of driving on Ireland's roads is getting accustomed to passing other vehicles on the right and giving way to traffic on the right at roundabouts. The wearing of safety belts is compulsory for drivers and for all passengers whether they are sitting in the front or rear seats. All children must be secured with a suitable restraint system. Motorcyclists and their passengers are obliged by law to wear crash helmets.

Junction ahead	**Unprotected quay or river ahead**

Dangerous bends ahead	**Children or school ahead**

ROAD SIGNS

Most road signs in Ireland are in both Gaelic and English. Most are also now in kilometres although some signs may still appear in miles. The sign "Yield" is the same as the UK "Give Way". Brown signs with white lettering indicate places of historic or cultural interest.

BUYING FUEL

Unleaded fuel and diesel fuel are available just about everywhere in Ireland. Although prices vary, fuel is relatively cheap by European standards. Almost all the petrol (gas) stations accept VISA and MasterCard, though check before filling up, particularly in rural areas.

View of Dun Laoghaire from the road around Killiney Hill *(see p91)*

SPEED LIMITS

The maximum speed limits in Ireland, which are shown in kilometres, are similar to those in Britain:
• 50 km/h (30 mph) in built-up areas.
• 100 km/h (60 mph) outside built-up areas.
• 120 km/h (70 mph) on highways.
On certain roads, which are marked, the speed limits are 60 km/h (40 mph) or 80 km/h (50 mph). Where there is no indication, the speed limit is 100 km/h (60 mph). Vehicles towing caravans (trailers) must not exceed 90 km/h (55 mph) on any road.

CYCLING

The quiet roads of Ireland help to make touring by bicycle a real joy. **Belfield Bike Shop** and **Cycleways** are good rental outlets in Dublin. If you are venturing further afield, local tourist offices will give you details of bike rental in their area. You can often rent a bike in one town and drop

Road signs in the Republic in Gaelic and English

it off at another for a small charge, or put it on the train. Many dealers also provide safety helmets, but bring your own waterproof clothing to help cope with the weather.

DIRECTORY

CAR HIRE COMPANIES

Argus Rent-a-Car
Tel 490 4444.
www.argusrentals.com

Avis
Tel 1890 405060.
www.avisworldwide.com

Budget
Tel 844 5150.
www.budgetcarrental.ie

Dan Dooley
Tel 677 2723.
www.dan-dooley.ie

Hertz
Tel 844 5466.
www.hertz.ie

Murrays Europcar
Tel 812 0410.
www.europcar.ie

BREAKDOWN/ INSURANCE SERVICES

American Automobile Association (AAA)
www.aaa.com

Automobile Association
Tel 1800 667 788 *(freephone)*.
www.aaireland.ie

Royal Automobile Club
Tel 1800 535 005 *(freephone)*.
www.rac.ie

BICYCLE-HIRE SHOPS

Belfield Bike Shop
Tel 716 1697.

Cycleways
Tel 873 4748.

Street Finder Index

KEY TO THE STREET FINDER

▦ Major sight	🚏 Coach station	✚ Church
▦ Place of interest	🚖 Taxi rank	⊠ Post office
▦ Railway station	Ⓟ Main car park	═ Railway line
DART station	ℹ Tourist information office	One-way street
Luas stop	✚ Hospital with casualty unit	Pedestrian street
Main bus stop	Police station	

0 metres   200

0 yards   200

1:11,500

KEY TO STREET FINDER ABBREVIATIONS

Ave	Avenue	**E**	East	**Pde**	Parade	**Sth**	South
Br	Bridge	**La**	Lane	**Pl**	Place	**Tce**	Terrace
Cl	Close	**Lr**	Lower	**Rd**	Road	**Up**	Upper
Ct	Court	**Nth**	North	**St**	Street/Saint	**W**	West

A

Abbey Street Lower	D2
Abbey Street Middle	D2
Abbey Street Old	E2
Abbey Street Upper	C2
Abbey Theatre	D2
Adair Lane	D3
Adelaide Hospital	C4
Amiens Street	F1
Anglesea Row	C2
Anglesea Street	D3
Anne Street South	D4
Anne Street North	B2
Anne's Lane	D4
Ardee Street	A4
Arran Quay	A3
Arran Street East	B2
Asdill's Row	D3
Ash Street	A4
Aston Place	D3
Aston Quay	D3
Aungier Place	C5
Aungier Street	C5

B

Bachelors Walk	D3
Back Lane	B3
Baggot Street	F5
Baggot Street Lower	F5
Baggot Rath Place	E5
Ball's Lane	B2
Bank of Ireland	D3
Bass Place	F4
Beaver Street	F1
Bedford Row	D3
Bella Place	E1
Bella Street	E1
Bell's Lane	E5
Benburb Street	A2
Beresford Lane	E2
Beresford Place	E2
Beresford Street	B2
Bewley's Oriental Café	D4
Bishop Street	C5
Blackhall Parade	A2
Blackhall Place	A2
Blackhall Street	A2
Blackpitts	B5
Bolton Street	B1
Bonham Street	A3
Borris Court	B3
Bow Lane East	C4
Bow Street	A2
Boyne Street	F4
Brabazon Row	A5
Brabazon Street	A4
Bracken's Lane	E3
Braithwaite Street	A4
Bride Road	B4
Bride Street	C4

Bride Street New	C5
Bridge Street Lower	A3
Bridge Street Upper	A3
Bridgefoot Street	A3
Britain Place	D1
Brown Street North	A2
Brown Street South	A5
Brunswick Street North	A2
Buckingham Street Lower	F1
Bull Alley Street	B4
Burgh Quay	D3
Busáras	E2
Butt Bridge	E2
Byrne's Lane	C2

C

Camden Place	C5
Camden Row	C5
Camden Street Lower	C5
Capel Street	C2
Carman's Hall	A4
Carmelite Church	C4
Castle Market	D4
Castle Steps	C3
Castle Street	C3
Cathal Brugha Street	D1
Cathedral Lane	B5
Cathedral Street	D2
Cathedral View Court	B5
Chamber Street	A5
Chancery Lane	C4
Chancery Place	B3
Chancery Street	B3
Chapel Lane	C2
Charles Street West	B3
Chatham Row	D4
Chatham Street	D4
Christ Church Cathedral	B3
Christchurch Place	B4
Church Avenue West	B2
Church Lane South	C5
Church Street	B3
Church Street New	A2
Church Street Upper	A2
Church Terrace	B2
City Hall	C3
City Quay	F2
Clanbrassil Street Lower	B5
Clarence Mangan Road	A5
Clare Lane	E4
Clare Street	E4
Clarendon Row	D4
Clarendon Street	D4
Clonmel Street	D5
Coke Lane	A3
Coleraine Street	B1
College Green	D3
College Lane	E3
College Street	D3
Commons Street	F2
Constitution Hill	B1

Convent Close	F5
Connolly	F1
Cook Street	B3
Coombe Court	A4
Cope Street	D3
Copper Alley	C3
Cork Hill	C3
Cork Street	A5
Corporation Street	E1
Cow's Lane	C3
Crane Lane	C3
Creighton Street	F3
Crown Alley	D3
Cuckoo Lane	B2
Cuffe Street	C5
Cumberland Street North	D1
Cumberland Street South	F4
Curved Street	C3
Custom House	E2
Custom House Quay	E2

D

D'Olier Street	D3
Dame Lane	C3
Dame Street	C3
Dawson Lane	D4
Dawson Street	D4
Dean Street	B4
Dean Swift Square	B4
Denzille Lane	F4
Diamond Park	E1
Digges Lane	C4
Digges Street Upper	C5
Dominick Lane	C1
Dominick Place	C1
Dominick Street Lower	C1
Dominick Street Upper	B1
Donore Road	A5
Dorset Street Upper	C1
Dowlings Court	F3
Drury Street	D4
Dublin Castle	C3
Dublin Civic Museum	D4
Dublinia	B4
Dublin Writers' Museum	C1
Duke Lane	D4
Duke Lane Upper	C1
Duke Street	D4

E

Earl Place	D2
Earl Street North	D2
Earl Street South	A4
Earlsfort Terrace	D5
Ebenezer Terrace	A5
Eden Quay	D2
Ellis Quay	A3
Ely Place	E5
Erne Place Lower	F3
Erne Street Upper	F4
Erne Terrace Front	F3

Essex Quay	C3
Essex Street East	C3
Essex Street West	C3
Eustace Street	C3
Exchange Street Lower	C3
Exchange Street Upper	C3
Exchequer Street	D4

F

Fade Street	C4
Father Matthew Bridge	A3
Father Matthew Square	B2
Fenian Street	F4
Fishamble Street	B3
Fitzwilliam Lane	E4
Fitzwilliam Square	E5
Fitzwilliam Square North	E5
Fitzwilliam Square West	E5
Fitzwilliam Street Lower	F5
Fitzwilliam Street Upper	F5
Fleet Street	D3
Foley Street	E1
Foster Place	D3
Fountain Place	A2
Four Courts	B3
Fownes Street	D3
Francis Street	B4
Frederick Street South	E4
Frenchman's Lane	E2
Friary Avenue	A2
Fumbally Lane	B5

G

Garden Lane	A4
Garden of Remembrance	C1
Gardiner Street Lower	E1
Gardiner Street Middle	D1
Gate Theatre	D1
General Post Office	D2
Geoffrey Keating Road	A5
George's Dock	F2
George's Hill	B2
George's Lane	A2
George's Quay	E2
Gloucester Diamond	E1
Gloucester Place	E1
Gloucester Street South	E3
Glovers Alley	D4
Golden Lane	C4
Grafton Street	D4
Granby Lane	C1
Granby Place	C1
Granby Row	C1
Grangegorman Upper	A1
Grant's Row	F4
Grattan Bridge	C3
Gray Street	A4
Greek Street	B2
Green Street	B2

H

Hagan's Court — F5
Halston Street — B2
Hammond Street — A3
Hammond Street — A5
Hanbury Lane — A4
Hanover Lane — B4
Hanover Street — A4
Hanover Street East — F3
Ha'penny Bridge — D3
Harbour Court — D2
Harcourt Street — D5
Hawkins Street — E2
Haymarket — A2
Hendrick Lane — A2
Hendrick Street — A2
Henrietta Lane — B1
Henrietta Place — B2
Henrietta Street — B1
Henry Place — D2
Henry Street — D2
Herbert Lane — F5
Herbert Street — F5
Heytesbury Street — C5
High Street — B3
Hill Street — D1
Hogan Place — F4
Holles Place — F4
Holles Row — F4
Holles Street — F4
Hugh Lane Municipal
  Gallery of Modern Art — C1
Hume Street — E5

I

Inner Dock — F2
Inns Quay — B3
Irish Whiskey Corner — A2
Island Street — A3
Iveagh Gardens — D5

J

James Joyce Cultural
  Centre — D1
James Place — F5
James's Place East — F5
Jervis Lane Lower — C2
Jervis Lane Upper — C2
Jervis Street — C2
John Dillon Street — B4
John's Lane East — B3
John's Lane West — A4
John Street North — A3
John Street South — A5
Johnson Court — D4

K

Kevin Street Lower — C5
Kevin Street Upper — B5
Kildare Street — E4
Killarney Street — F1
Kings Inns — B1
Kings Inns Park — B1
Kings Inns Street — C1
King Street North — A2
King Street South — D4
Kirwan Street — A1

L

Lad Lane — F5
Lamb Alley — B3
Leeson Lane — E5
Leeson Street Lower — E5
Leinster House — E4
Leinster Street South — E4
Lemon Street — D4
Liberty Lane — C5
Liberty Park — E1
Liffey Street Lower — D2
Liffey Street Upper — C2
Lincoln Place — E4
Linenhall Parade — B1
Linenhall Street — B1
Linenhall Terrace — B1
Lisburn Street — B2
Little Britain Street — B2
Little Green Street — B2

Litton Lane — D2
Loftus Lane — C2
Lombard Street East — F3
Long Lane — B5
Longford Street Little — C4
Longford Street Great — C4
Lord Edward Street — C3
Lotts — D2
Luke Street — E3
Lurgan Street — B2

M

Mabbot Lane — E1
Madden Road — A5
Magennis Place — F3
Malpas Street — B5
Mansion House — D4
Mark Street — E3
Mark's Alley West — B4
Mark's Lane — E3
Marlborough Street — D1
Marshall Lane — A3
Marsh's Library — B4
Mary's Lane — B2
Mary Street — C2
Mary Street Little — B2
Matt Talbot Memorial
  Bridge — E2
May Lane — A2
Mayor Street Lower — F2
Meade's Terrace — F5
Meath Hospital — B5
Meath Place — A4
Meath Street — A4
Meetinghouse Lane — C2
Meeting House Square — C3
Mellowes Bridge — A3
Memorial Road — E2
Mercer Street Upper — C5
Merchant's Quay — B3
Merrion Row — E5
Merrion Square — F4
Merrion Square East — F5
Merrion Square North — E4
Merrion Square South — E4
Merrion Square West — E4
Merrion Street Lower — F4
Merrion Street Upper — E5
Michael's Terrace — A5
Millennium Bridge — C3
Mill Street — A5
Molesworth Place — D4
Molesworth Street — D4
Montague Place — C5
Montague Street — C5
Moore Lane — D1
Moore Street — D2
Morning Star Avenue — A1
Moss Street — E2
Mount Street Lower — F4
Mount Street Upper — F5
Mountjoy Street — C1
Mountjoy Street Middle — B1

N

Nassau Street — D3
National Gallery — E4
Natural History Museum — E4
National Library — E4
National Museum — E4
New Row South — B5
New Street North — A3
New Street South — B5
Newman House — D5
Newmarket — A5
Nicholas Street — B4
North Wall Quay — F2
North Great George's
  Street — D1

O

O'Carolan Road — A5
O'Connell Bridge — D2
O'Connell St Upper — D1
O'Connell Street Lower — D2
O'Curry Avenue — A5
O'Curry Road — A5
O'Donovan Bridge — B3
O'Rahilly Parade — D2

Oliver Bond Street — A3
Oriel Street Upper — F1
Ormond Quay Lower — C3
Ormond Quay Upper — B3
Ormond Square — B3
Ormond Street — A5
Oscar Square — A5
Oxmantown Lane — A2

P

Palmerston Place — B1
Parliament Street — C3
Parnell Place — D1
Parnell Square East — D1
Parnell Square West — C1
Parnell Street — C2
Patrick Street — B4
Pearse Station — F3
Pearse Street — E3
Pembroke Lane — E5
Pembroke Row — F5
Pembroke Street Lower — E5
Peter Row — C4
Peter Street — C4
Peterson's Court — F3
Phibsborough Road — C1
Phoenix Street North — A3
Pimlico — A4
Pleasants Street — C5
Poolbeg Street — E3
Poole Street — A4
Powerscourt Townhouse — D4
Prebend Street — B1
Preston Street — F1
Price's Lane — D3
Prince's Street North — D2
Prince's Street South — D2

Q

Queen Street — A2
Quinn's Lane — E5

R

Railway Street — E1
Rath Row — E3
Redmonds Hill — C5
Reginald Street — A4
River Liffey — A3
Ross Road — B4
Rotunda Hospital — D1
Royal Hibernian Academy — E5
Rutland Place — D1
Rutland Street Lower — E1
Ryder's Row — C2

S

Sackville Place — D2
Sampson's Lane — D2
Sandwith Street Upper — F4
Sandwith Street Lower — F3
Schoolhouse Lane — E4
Schoolhouse Lane West — B3
Sean Mac Dermott Street
  Lower — E1
Sean Mac Dermott Street
  Upper — D1
Sean O'Casey Bridge — F2
Setanta Place — E4
Seville Place — F1
Seville Terrace — F1
Shaw Street — E3
Shelbourne Hotel — E4
Sheriff Street Lower — F1
Ship Street Great — C4
Ship Street Little — C4
Smithfield — A2
Spring Garden Lane — E3
St Andrew's Street — D3
St Ann's Church — E3
St Audoen's Church — B3
St Augustine Street — A3
St Kevin's Avenue — B5
St Patrick's Cathedral — B4
St Patrick's Close — B4
St Patrick's Park — B4
St Cathedral Lane East — A4
St Mary's Abbey — B3
St Mary's Pro-Cathedral — D1
St Mary's Terrace — C1

St Michael's Close — B3
St Michael's Hill — B3
St Michan's Church — A2
St Michan's Street — B2
St Paul Street — A2
St Stephen's Green — D5
St Stephen's Green East — E5
St Stephen's Green North — D4
St Stephen's Green South — D5
St Stephen's Green West — D5
St Werburgh's Church — B4
St Thomas Road — A5
South Great George's Street — C4
Stable Lane — A3
Stanhope Street — A1
Stephen Street Lower — C4
Stephen Street Upper — C4
Stephen's Lane — F5
Stirrup Lane — B2
Stephens Place — F5
Stokes Place — D5
Stoneybatter — A2
Store Street — E2
Strand Street Great — C3
Strand Street Little — B3
Strong's Court — D1
Suffolk Street — D3
Summerhill — E1
Susan Terrace — A5
Swift's Alley — A4
Swift's Row — C3
Sycamore Street — C3

T

Tailors Hall — B4
Talbot Place — E2
Talbot Street — D2
Tara Street — E3
Temple Bar — C3
Temple Bar Square — D3
Temple Cottages — B1
Temple Lane North — D1
Temple Lane South — C3
The Coombe — A4
Thomas Court — A4
Thomas Court Lane — A4
Thomas Davis Street South — B4
Thomas Street West — A4
Thomas's Lane — D1
Townsend Street — E3
Trinity College — E3
Trinity Street — D3

U

Usher Street — A3
Usher's Island — A3
Usher's Quay — A3

V

Vicar Street — A4

W

Wards Hill — B5
Watkins Buildings — A4
Weaver's Square — A5
Weavers Street — A4
Wellington Quay — C3
Werburgh Street — C4
Western Way — B1
Westland Row — F4
Westmoreland Street — D3
Wexford Street — C5
Whitefriar Place — C4
Whitefriar Street — C4
Wicklow Street — D3
William Street South — D4
William's Place South — B5
Williams Row — D2
Windmill Lane — F3
Windsor Place — E5
Winetavern Street — B3
Wolfe Tone Park — C2
Wolfe Tone Street — C2
Wood Quay — B3
Wood Street — C4

Y

York Street — C4

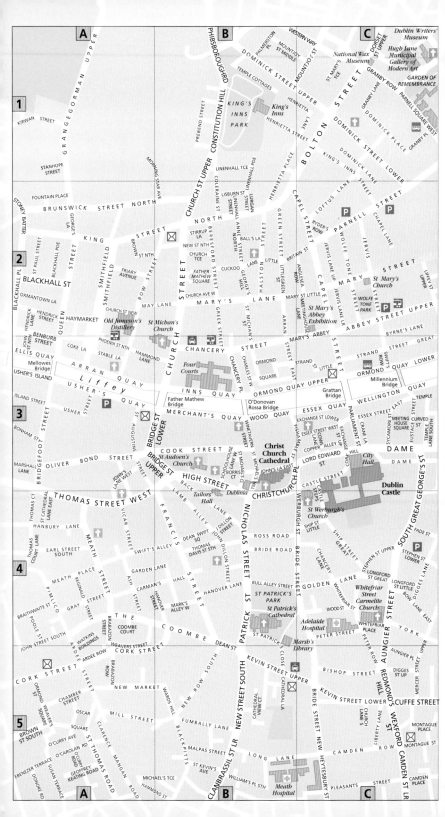

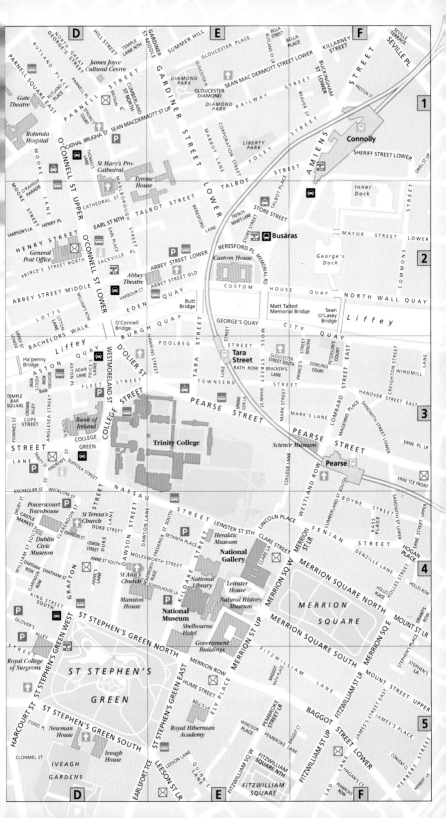

General Index

Page numbers in **bold** type refer to main entries.

A

Abbey Theatre 9, 69, **70**, 158
Abbeys see Monasteries and abbeys
Accommodation
  general information 126–7
  see also Bed & breakfast;
  Guesthouses; Hotels
Act of Supremacy (1541) 14
Act of Union (1800) 16
Admission charges 164
Aer Lingus 172, 173
Agricola 13
Ahern, Bertie 19
Ahmad Shaikh 57
Air travel **172**, 173
Airports **172**, 173
All-Ireland Football Final 28
All-Ireland Hurling Final 28
Ambulances 167
American Express 168
An Óige 127
An Taisce 62
Anglo-Irish 101
Anglo-Irish Treaty (1921) 18
Anglo-Normans 14, 53
Anna Livia International Opera Festival 28
Antiques
  Irish Antique Dealers' Fair 28
  shops **149**, 151
Aqueduct, Leinster 104
Áras an Uachtaráin 80
Archbold's Castle (Dalkey) 97
Ardee, hotels 133
Ardgillan Demesne 101, 102, **116–17**
Ardilaun, Lord 41
The Ark 159
Art galleries see Museums and galleries
Arthurstown
  hotels 133
  restaurants 145
Ashtown Castle 80
Ath Cliathe 13
August Bank Holiday 29
Australian Embassy 165
Autumn in Dublin 28
Avoca Handweavers 113
Avondale Forest Park 109
Avondale House 102, **109**
The Axis 158, 159

B

Bacon, Francis 73
Baily Lighthouse (Howth) 8, 90
Ballsbridge **85**
Bank of Ireland 34, **36**
Banking **168–9**
Banville, John 22
Barnard, Lambert 14
Barralet, James 85
Barret, George the Elder, A View of Powerscourt Waterfall 50

Barry, James 50
Bars **146–7**
  in hotels **156**, 157
  see also Pubs
Beattie, Olivia 47
Beaumont Hospital 167
Beckett, Samuel 22, **23**, **38**, 94
Bed & breakfast 126
Beer
  Arthur Guinness **83**
  The Brewing of Guinness **82–3**
  Guinness Storehouse **82**
Behan, Brendan 94, 95
  grave of 89
  McDaid's 25
  The Quare Fellow 18
Beit, Sir Alfred 108, 109
Beit Art Collection 108
Bellamont, Charles Coote, 1st Earl of 51
Belvedere, 1st Earl of 123
Belvedere House (Mullingar) 123
Benedictine order 76
Berkeley Library, Trinity College 39
Bernard, St 118
Bernini, Gian Lorenzo 115
Bewley's Café Theatre 158, 159
Bewleys Hotels 126, 127
Bicycles see Cycling
Black Death 14, 63
Blanche, Jacques Emile, Portrait of James Joyce 72
Blessington 109
Bloody Sunday (1920) 18
Bloody Sunday (1972) 19
Bloom, Leopold and Molly 72
Bloom in the Park 26
Bloomsday 27
Blues music **155**, 157
Boats
  cruising and sailing 161
  Dublin's Canals 85
  ferries 173
  National Maritime Museum (Dun Laoghaire) 90
Bog of Allen Nature Centre 104
Bolton, Thomas 86
Bonet 113
Book of Durrow 39
Book of Kells 8, **40**
Book shops **148–9**, 151
Boyne, Battle of the (1690) 15, 101, **119**
Boyne, River 119, 122
Boyne Valley 101, **119**
Brain Ború 13
Bray **116**
Brazen Head 93, 146, 147
  Dublin's Best Pubs 24
Breakdown services **176**, 177
Breakfast 134, **146**, 147
The Brewing of Guinness **82–3**
Bridges
  Father Matthew Bridge 93
  Ha'penny Bridge **77**
Brigid, St 104

British Airways 173
British Embassy 19, 165
British Midland 173
Brown, Capability 122
Brown Thomas 36–7, 150, 151
Browne's Hill Dolmen **109**
Brueghel, Pieter the Younger, Peasant Wedding 51
Budget restaurants 134–5
Buite, St 117
Bureaux de change **168**
Burgh, Thomas 62
Burke, Edmund 15, 22
  Trinity College 38
Burke, Phyllis 36
Burke family 14
Bus Éireann 174, 175
Buses **174**, 175
  airport 172
  fares and tickets 175
  ports 173
  tours 175
Butler family 14
Butterstream Gardens 123
Button Factory 58, 155, 157
Byrne, Patrick 63

C

Cafés **146**, 147
Canadian Embassy 165
Canals **85**
  Waterways Visitors' Centre **85**
Caravaggio, The Taking of Christ **49**, 51
Carlingford **118**
  hotels 133
Cars
  breakdown services **176**, 177
  driving 175, **176–7**
  hiring **175**, 177
  parking 175
  petrol 177
  rules of the road 177
  speed limits 177
Castiglione 50
Castle, Richard 15
  Belvedere House (Mullingar) 123
  Conolly's Folly 107
  Iveagh House 42
  Leinster House 46
  Newman House 42
  Powerscourt House 114
  Rotunda Hospital 68, 72
  Russborough House 108
  Tyrone House 71
Castles
  Ardgillan Demesne 101
  Dalkey Castle & Heritage Centre 97
  Dublin Castle 16, 54, **56–7**, 93
  Howth Castle 90
  King John's Castle (Carlingford) 118
  Malahide Castle **89**
  Slane Castle 122, 155
  Trim Castle 122
Castletown House 16, 103, **106–7**

Cathedrals
Christ Church Cathedral 54, **64–5**, 93
Glendalough 110
St Brigid's Cathedral (Kildare) 104–5
St Mary's Pro-Cathedral 69, **71**
St Patrick's Cathedral 9, **61**, 93
St Patrick's Cathedral (Trim) 123
Catholic University of Ireland 42
Cavendish, Lord 80
Celebrated visitors and residents **22–3**
Celts 13
Hill of Tara 101, **122**
Cemeteries
Glasnevin Cemetery **88–9**
Huguenot Cemetery 95
Central Fisheries Board 161
Ceramics
shops **149**, 151
What to buy in Dublin 153
Chain hotels 127
Chambers, Sir William
Marino Casino 88
Trinity College 38
Charlemont, Lord 73, 88
Cheeses **137**
Chelminski, Jan, *A Group of Cavalry in the Snow* 51
Chemists 167
Chester Beatty, Sir Alfred 57
Chester Beatty Library 57
Chesterfield, Lord 80
Chief O'Neill's Viewing Tower **74**
Children
Four Great Days in Dublin 9
in restaurants 134
theatre 159
Children of Lir (Kelly) 73
China shops **149**, 151
Christ Church Cathedral 54, **64–5**, 93
Christchurch, A 45-Minute Walk Around 93
Christianity 13
Christmas 29
Churches
Reefert Church (Glendalough) 111
St Ann's Church 34, **37**
St Audoen's Church **62–3**, 93
St Audoen's Roman Catholic Church 63
St Mary's Church **77**
St Mary's Church (Glendalough) 110–11
St Michan's Church **76**
St Teresa's Church **36**
St Werburgh's Church 54, **62**, 93
Temple-na-Skellig (Glendalough) 111
Whitefriar Street Carmelite Church **60**, 95
Cinema *see* Film
Cistercian order
Mellifont Abbey 118

Cistercian order (cont.)
Moore Abbey 104
St Mary's Abbey 76
Citizen's Information Board 127
City Hall 54, **57**, 93
Cityjet 173
Civic Theatre (Tallaght) 159
Civil War 18–19
O'Connell Street 71
Clara 112
Clare, Lord 91
Clare, Richard de *see* Strongbow
Clarendon 61
Clery's department store 71, 150, 151
Clontarf, Battle of (1014) 13
Clothing
fashion shops **150**, 151
What to buy in Dublin 152
Coastguard Service 167
Cobbe, Archbishop Charles 116
Cobbe family 116
Coffee and cakes **146**, 147
Coliemore Harbour (Dalkey) 96
Collins Barracks *see* National Museum at Collins Barracks
Collins, Michael 18
grave of 79, 89
National Museum at Collins Barracks 86
Colours Boat Race 26
Comedy 155, 157
Comhaltas Ceoltóirí Éireann 90
Comyn, Archbishop John 61
Connolly, James 17, 81
Conolly, Katherin 107
Conolly, William 106
Conolly's Folly 107
Constantinople School 51
Consulates 165
Contemporary Music Centre 58
Convent Garden, Brittany (Leech) 50
Cooley, Thomas 57
Cooley Peninsula 118
Corrigan, Dominic 96
Council of Ireland 77
Country houses
Ardgillan Demesne **116–17**
Avondale House **109**
Belvedere House (Mullingar) 123
Killruddery House **113**
Newbridge Demesne 101, **116**
Russborough House **108–9**
Country music **155**, 157
County Museum (Dundalk) 118
County Wicklow Gardens Festival 27
Covered Market 55
Cow's Lane 58
Crafts shops **149**, 151
Cramillion, Bartholomew 72–3
Credit cards **168**
in shops 148
Crime **166**
Croke Park 8, 28

Cromwell, Oliver 15, 117
Crown Alley 58
Cruising 161
Crystal
shops **149**, 151
What to buy in Dublin 153
Cúchulainn 71
Cultivate Sustainable Living Centre **59**
Culture Night 159
Cumin, Archbishop John 64, 65
Curragh 105
Currency 168–9
Custom House 16, 18, 66, 69, **70**
Customs and excise 164
Cycling **160**, 161, 177
Maracycle 27

D

Dáil Éireann 18, **46**
Leinster House 46
Mansion House 41
Dalkey **91**
A 90-Minute Walk Around Dalkey 96–7
Dalkey Island 96
Danby, Francis 50
Dance
classical **155**, 157
traditional **155**, 157
DART service **174**, 175
Davy Byrne's 37, 95, 146, 147
Dawson, Joshua 41
De Valera, Eamon
Catholic University of Ireland 42
Civil War 18, 19
Fianna Fáil 19
Garden of Remembrance 73
grave of 89
Kilmainham Gaol 81
as President 19
Deane, Sir Thomas 37, 44, 46
Declaration of Rights (1782) 16
Deerfield 80
Degas, Edgar, *Sur la Plage* 73
Delaney, Edward 41
Delta Air Lines 172, 173
Dentists 167
Devil's Glen 113
Dialling codes 171
Disabled travellers 165
in hotels 127
sports 161
Discalced Carmelite Fathers 36
Distilleries
Locke's Distillery (Kilbeggan) 123
Old Jameson Distillery **75**
Diving 161
Docklands Maritime Festival 27
Dodder, River 85
Douglas Hyde Gallery, Trinity College 39
Dowland, John 97
Dowth **119**
Doyle, Roddy 22, 135
Draíocht Theatre (Blanchardstown) 159

Driving in Dublin 175
Drogheda 117
  Earls of 104
Dublin, Battle of (919) 13
Dublin Airport 172, 173
Dublin Bus 174, 175
Dublin Bus Ghost Tour 156, 157
Dublin Castle 16, 54, **56–7**, 93
Dublin City Hall 57
Dublin City Marathon 28
Dublin Crystal 149, 151
Dublin Dental Hospital 167
Dublin Exhibition (1853) 17
Dublin Fringe 28, 158, 159
Dublin Horse Show 27
Dublin Literary Pub Crawl 9, 156, 157
Dublin Theatre Festival 28, 158, 159
Dublin Tourism 127, 154, 160, 164, 165
Dublin Toy and Train Fair 28
Dublin Writers' Museum 9, **73**
Dublin Zoo 9, 80, **81**
Dubliners 25
Dublinia 9, 54, **63**
Dun Laoghaire 78, **90**
  ferries 173
Dun Laoghaire Shopping Centre 148, 151
Dundalk **118**
Dundrum Shopping Centre 148, 151
Dunnes 150, 151
Duty-free goods 164

E
Easter 29
Easter Rising (1916) 17
  Garden of Remembrance **73**
  General Post Office 68, **71**
  Kilmainham Gaol 81
  O'Connell Street 68, 71
  Royal College of Surgeons 41
Edwards, Hilton 72
Egan, Felim 50
Eida, Minoru 105
Eida, Tassa 105
Eircom 171
Elizabeth I, Queen of England 14–15, 38
Ely Place **42**
Emancipation Act (1829) 16
Embassies 165
Emergency services 167, 171
Emmet, Robert 16, **57**
  Grafton Street 37
  Kilmainham Gaol 81
Enniskerry 113
Enright, Anne 22
Ensor, John 46, 72
Entertainment **154–61**
  booking tickets **154**, 157
  cinema **156**, 157
  classical music, opera and dance **155**, 157
  comedy **155**
  hotel bars **156**, 157

Entertainment (cont.)
  listings 154
  nightclubs **154–5**, 157
  outdoor activities **160–61**
  pub crawls and tours **156**, 157
  rock, jazz, blues, salsa and country **155**, 157
  theatre **158–9**
  traditional music and dance **155**, 157
Equestrian Holidays Ireland 160, 161
Essex Gate 93
Ethnic restaurants 134
Eurocheques 148
European Community 19
Euros 169
Events 26–9

F
Faber 51
Fáilte Ireland 126, 127, 160, 164
Famine (1845–48) 16, 17
  Merrion Square 47
Fashion shops **150**, 151
Fast food 135
Father Matthew Bridge 93
Feis Ceoil 26
Ferries 173
Festival of World Cultures (Dun Laoghaire) 27, 158, 159
Festivals **26–9**
  theatre **158–9**
Fianna Fáil 19
Field, John 62
Figure of Justice 56
Film **156**, 157
  Irish Film Centre **59**
  Jameson International Film Festival 59
Fine Gael 19
Fire services 167
Fish and chips 135
Fishing **160**, 161
  Salmon and Sea Trout Season 29
Fitzgerald, Lord Edward 62
Fitzgerald, "Silken" Thomas 14, 63, 77
Fitzgerald family 14
Fitzgibbon, Marjorie, statue of James Joyce 69
Fitzwilliam Square 94
Foley, John
  monument to Daniel O'Connell 69
  statue of Edmund Burke 38
  statue of Henry Grattan 36
Fontana, Prospero 51
Food and drink
  cafés **146**, 147
  coffee and cakes **146**, 147
  Dublin's Best Pubs **24–5**
  fast food 135
  Flavours of Ireland 136–7
  Malahide Food and Drink Affair 29
  pizza and pasta **146**, 147

Food and drink (cont.)
  in pubs 135, **146**, 147
  shops **150**, 151
  traditional food **146**, 147
  vegetarian meals 135, **146**, 147
  What to buy in Dublin 153
  whiskey **75**
  see also Breakfast; Restaurants
Football, All-Ireland Football Final 28
For the Road (Yeats) 48
Four Courts 16, 18, **76**
Four Great Days in Dublin 8–9
Francini, Paolo and Filippo 15
  Castletown House 107
  Newman House 42
  Russborough House 108
  Tyrone House 71
Friel, Brian 70
Fry, Cyril 89
Fry Model Railway **89**
Fuel 177

G
Gaelic Athletic Association 17
Gaiety Theatre 158, 159
Gainsborough, Thomas 50
Galilei, Alessandro 106
Galleries *see* Museums and galleries
Gallery of Photography **59**
Gandon, James
  Bank of Ireland 36
  Custom House 16, 70
  Four Courts 16, 76
  King's Inn 74
  Slane Castle 122
Garden of Remembrance **73**
Gardens *see* Parks and gardens
Gardiner, Luke 70
Garthorne, Francis 65
Gate Theatre 9, 68, **72**, 158
Gay and Lesbian Theatre Festival 158, 159
Genealogical Office **37**
General Post Office 68, **71**
George II, King of England 62
George IV, King of England 90
Georgian Dublin 16
  A 90-Minute Walk Through Literary and Georgian Dublin 94–5
Gérôme, Jean-Léon, *Guards at the Door of a Tomb* 50, **51**
Gibson, Mel 122
Gifford, Grace 81
Glaslough, hotels 133
Glasnevin Cemetery **88–9**
Glasson, restaurants 145
Glassware
  shops **149**, 151
  What to buy in Dublin 153
Glencree 112
Glendalough **110–11**, 112
Glenmacnass 112
Goat Castle (Dalkey) 97
Gogarty, Oliver St John 95
  James Joyce Tower 91

Gogarty, Oliver St John (cont.)
  Oliver St John Gogarty pub 25,
  146, 147
Goldsmith, Oliver 38
Gonne, Maud *see* MacBride, Maud
  Gonne
Good Friday 29
Good Friday Agreement (1998) 19
Gourmet restaurants 134
Government buildings **43**
Goya, Francisco de 51
Grafton Street 34, **36–7**
Grand Canal 16, **85**, 94, 104
Graphic Studio Gallery 58
Grattan, Henry 16
  statue of 36
Great Famine (1845–48) 16, 17
  Merrion Square 47
Great Sugar Loaf Mountain 112,
  114
Greater Dublin, map 11
El Greco 51
Gregory XVI, Pope 60
Gregory, Lady 70, 72
Gresham Hotel 71, 131
Griffith, Arthur 17
Gris, Juan 51
  Pierrot 48
A Group of Cavalry in the Snow
  (Chelminski) 51
Guards at the Door of a Tomb
  (Gérôme) 50, **51**
Guerin, Veronica 19
Guesthouses 126–7
Guinness
  The Brewing of Guinness **82–3**
  Guinness Storehouse **82**
Guinness, Arthur 16, **83**
  Guinness Storehouse 82
  St Mary's Church 77
Guinness, Sir Benjamin 61
Guinness, Desmond 62
Guinness family 41
  Iveagh House 42
  St Werburgh's Church 62

H

Habermel, Erasmus 86
Hall-Walker, William 105
Hallinan, Martin 105
Hallowe'en 28
Hamilton, Hugh Douglas 50
Handel, George Frederic **22**, 65
  Messiah 15
  St Michan's Church 76
Hanly, Daithí 73
Ha'penny Bridge **77**
Health **167**
Heaney, Seamus 22
Heineken Green Energy Festival
  155, 157
The Helix 158, 159
Henry II, King of England 14
Henry VIII, King of England 74
  1534 rebellion 77
  Act of Supremacy 14
  Christ Church Cathedral 65
  declared King of Ireland 15

Henry, Paul 50
Heraldic Museum **37**
Heritage Service 165
High Crosses, Monasterboice 117
Hill of Slane 122
Hill of Tara 101, **122**
Historical Walking Tour 156, 157
History **13–19**
Hobbema, Meindert 51
Hogan, John 36
Hogan's 146, 147
  Dublin's Best Pubs 24
Hogarth, William 50
Holidays, public 29
Holy Trinity Heritage Centre
  (Carlingford) 118
"Home Rule" 17
Hone, Evie 43
Hone, Nathaniel the Elder 50
Hopkins, Gerard Manley 95
  Catholic University of Ireland 42
  grave of 89
Hopper, Thomas 122
Horse racing **105**
  Irish Champion Hurdle 29
  Laytown Beach Races 26
  Leopardstown Races 29
  National Stud 105
Horse riding **160**, 161
  Dublin Horse Show 27
  Smithfield **74–5**
Hospitals 167
Hotels **126–33**
  bars **156**, 157
  beyond Dublin 133
  booking 127
  disabled travellers 127
  further afield 131–3
  North of the Liffey 131
  prices 127
  Southeast Dublin 128–30
  Southwest Dublin 130–31
  tipping 127
House of Ireland 150, 151
Howth 8–9, **90**
Howth Head 8, **90**
Howth Music Festival 26
Hugh Lane Municipal Gallery of
  Modern Art 9, **73**
  concerts 155, 157
Huguenots 61, 95
Hurling, All-Ireland Hurling Final
  28
Hyde, Douglas 37, 61

I

Iarnród Éireann (Irish Rail) 176
Inniscorrig (Dalkey) 96
Insurance 166
  cars 176
International Puppet Festival 158,
  159
Internet access 171
Internet cafés 171
IRA *see* Irish Republican Army
Ireland's Eye 8–9, 90
Irish Antique Dealers' Fair 28
Irish Celtic Craftshop 149, 151

Irish Champion Hurdle 29
Irish Citizen Army 41
Irish Federation of Sea Anglers 161
Irish Ferries 173
Irish Film Institute **59**, 146, 147,
  156, 157
Irish Free State 18, 46
Irish Georgian Society 106
Irish Hotels Federation 127
Irish language 165
Irish Museum of Modern Art **84**
Irish Parliament **46**
  Bank of Ireland 36
  Leinster House 46
  Mansion House 41
Irish Rail *see* Iarnród Éireann
Irish Republican Army (IRA) 17
  bombs Nelson's Column 19
Irish Sailing Association 161
Irish Taxi Federation 175
Irish Underwater Council 161
Irish Volunteers 17, 18
Irish Welcome 126, 127
Irish Wheelchair Association 161
Iron Age 122
Isle of Man Steam Packet
  Company 173
Isolde's Tower 93
Iveagh, Rupert Guinness, 2nd Earl
  of 42
Iveagh Gardens 9, **42**
Iveagh House **42**

J

James II, King of England 86
  Battle of the Boyne 15, 89, 119
  Christ Church Cathedral 65
James Joyce Cultural Centre 68,
  72
James Joyce Tower **91**
Japanese Gardens (Tully) 105
Jazz **155**, 157
Jervis Shopping Centre 148, 151
Jesuits 42
Jewellery
  shops **149**, 151
  What to buy in Dublin 152
John Paul II, Pope 19
  Papal Cross 80
Johnson, Esther 61
Johnston, Denis 72
Johnston, Francis
  Dublin Castle 56
  King's Inns 74
  Powerscourt Townhouse 60
  Slane Castle 122
Johnstown, restaurants 145
Jordaens, Jacob 50
Joyce, James **23**, 94, 95
  Bloomsday 27
  Catholic University of Ireland 42
  James Joyce Cultural Centre 68,
  72
  James Joyce Tower 91
  Portrait of James Joyce (Blanche)
  72
  statue of 41, 69
  Ulysses 72, 95, 97

Judith with the Head of Holofernes
(Mantegna) **49**, 51
June Bank Holiday 29

K

Kavanagh, Patrick 94, 95
  statue of 85
Kelly, Oisín, *Children of Lir* 73
Kenmare, Michael 72
Kennedy, John F. 18
Kevin, St **111**
  Glendalough 110–11
Kilbeggan **123**
Kildare **104–5**
Kildare, 8th Earl of 14, 61, 65
Kildare, 9th Earl of 14
Kildare, 19th Earl of, monument
54
Kilkenny, Statutes of (1366) 14
Killiney **91**
Killruddery House & Gardens **113**
Kilmainham Gaol 17, **81**
King John's Castle (Carlingford)
118
King's Inns **74**
KLM 173
Knitwear shops **150**, 151
Knowth **119**
Koralek, Paul 39

L

Lacy, Hugh de 122
Lambert Puppet Theatre (Dun
Laoghaire) **90**, 159
Land League 12
Lane, Sir Hugh 73
Lanfranco, Giovanni 50
Language **165**
Lanyon, Sir Charles 38
Larkin, James, statue of 68, 71
Laughter Lounge 155, 157
Lawless, Matthew James, *The Sick
Call* 49
Laytown Beach Races 26
Le Fanu, Joseph 94, 95
Leech, William, *Convent Garden,
Brittany* 50
Leinster, Duke of 46
Leinster Aqueduct 104
Leinster House 15, 35, **46**
Lennox, Lady Louisa 106–7
Leopardstown 105
Leopardstown Races 29
Lever Brothers 54
Liberty Hall Theatre 158, 159
Libraries
  Berkeley Library, Trinity College
  39
  Chester Beatty Library **57**
  Marsh's Library **61**
  National Library 35, **46**
  Old Library, Trinity College 39
Liffey, River 13, 53, 109
Liffey Swim 28
Linen
  shops **150**, 151
  What to buy in Dublin 153
Liszt, Franz 72
Livingstone, Dr David 43

Locke's Distillery (Kilbeggan)
123
Long Hall 55, 146, 147
Lost property 166
Lowrey, Dan 60

M

Mac Liammóir, Mícheál 72
MacBride, Maud Gonne, grave of
89
McCormack, John 71, 104
McDaid's 95, 146, 147
  Dublin's Best Pubs 25
Mack, Robert 60
Maclise, Daniel, *The Marriage of
Strongbow and Aoife* 14
MacMurrough, Dermot, King of
Leinster 14
Macreddin Village
  hotels 133
  restaurants 145
Magazines 165
Maginni, Profesor Dennis J 72
Mail services 170
Malachy, St 118
Malahide Castle **89**
Malahide Food and Drink Affair
29
Mallin, Michael 41
Malone, Molly, statue of 36
Mangan, James Clarence 95
Mansion House 34, **41**
Mantegna, Andrea, *Judith with the
Head of Holofernes* **49**, 51
Manx Airlines 173
Maps
  A 45-Minute Walk Around
  Christchurch 93
  A 90-Minute Walk Around
  Dalkey 96–7
  A 90-Minute Walk Through
  Literary and Georgian Dublin
  94–5
  Around O'Connell Street street-
  by-street 68–9
  Celebrated Visitors and
  Residents **22–3**
  Dublin transport map *see* Back
  endpaper
  Dublin's Best Pubs 24–5
  Exploring Beyond Dublin 102–3
  Further afield 79
  Glendalough 110
  Greater Dublin 11
  Ireland 10–11
  North of the Liffey 67
  Phoenix Park 80
  Southeast Dublin 33, 34–5
  Southwest Dublin 53, 54–5
  Street Finder 178–81
  Temple Bar 59
  Three Guided Walks 92–6
  Tour of the Military Road 112
Marathon 28
Marino Casino **88**
Markets
  Covered Market 55
  Moore Street Market 68

Markievicz, Countess Constance
  Easter Rising 17, 41
  elected as MP 18
  grave of 89
*The Marriage of Strongbow and
Aoife* (Maclise) 14
Marsh, Archbishop Narcissus 61
Marsh's Library **61**
Martello towers 90
  James Joyce Tower **91**
Mason, James 72
Mathew, Father Theobald 16
  statue of 71
Matisse, Henri 91
Mattock, River 118
Maturin, Charles 95
May Day 26, 29
Meath, Earls of 113
Medical treatment 167
Medieval Trust 63
Meeting House Square **58**
Meeting of the Waters 113
Mellifont Abbey **118–19**
Merchants' Arch 58
Merrion Square 9, 32, **46–7**, 94
Metrication 165
Military Road 113
  Tour of the Military Road 112
Mill Theatre (Dundrum) 159
Millbank Theatre (Rush) 159
Millmount Museum (Drogheda) 117
Milltown, Joseph Leeson, Earl of
108
Minot, Archbishop 61
Monasterboice **117**
Monasterevin **104**
Monasteries and abbeys
  Glendalough 110–11
  Mellifont Abbey **118–19**
  Monasterboice **117**
  Moore Abbey 104
Monet, Claude 51
Money **168–9**
Monument of Light 68, 71
Mooney, Patrick 63
Moore, Henry 38
  memorial to WB Yeats 41
Moore, Thomas 113
Moore Abbey 104
Moore Street Market 68
Moroni, Giovanni Battista 51
Mosse, Dr Bartholomew 72
Mount Usher Gardens **111**
Mountaineering Council of Ireland
160, 161
Muiredach's Cross 117
Mullingar **123**
Murillo, Bartolomé Esteban 51
Museums and galleries
  admission charges 164
  Ardgillan Demesne 117
  Beit Art Collection 108
  Bog of Allen Nature Centre 104
  cafés in **146**, 147
  Chester Beatty Library 57
  County Museum (Dundalk) 118
  Douglas Hyde Gallery, Trinity
  College 39

Museums and galleries (cont.)
Dublin Writers' Museum 9, **73**
Dublinia 9, 54, **63**
Gallery of Photography **59**
Graphic Studio Gallery 58
Guinness Storehouse **82**
Heraldic Museum **37**
Holy Trinity Heritage Centre (Carlingford) 118
Hugh Lane Municipal Gallery of Modern Art 9, **73**, 155, 157
Irish Museum of Modern Art **84**
James Joyce Cultural Centre 68, **72**
James Joyce Tower **91**
Locke's Distillery (Kilbeggan) 123
Malahide Castle 89
Millmount Museum (Drogheda) 117
National Gallery 9, **48–51**
National Maritime Museum (Dun Laoghaire) 90
National Museum (Archaeology) 8, 35, **44–5**
National Museum at Collins Barracks **86–7**
National Photographic Archive **59**
National Stud 105
National Transport Museum (Howth) 9, **90**
Natural History Museum **43**
Newbridge House 116
Number 29 **47**
Old Jameson Distillery **75**
Original Print Gallery 58
Royal Hibernian Academy 42, **47**
St Mary's Abbey Exhibition **76–7**
Science Gallery **47**
Shaw's Birthplace **84**
Temple Bar Galley and Studios 58
Trinity College 39
Yeats Museum 48
Music
Anna Livia International Opera Festival 28
Button Factory 58, 155, 157
classical music, opera and dance **155**, 157
Contemporary Music Centre 58
Howth Music Festival 26
Music in Great Irish Houses 27
music pubs 146, 147
Opera Ireland **28**
Oxygen 27
rock, jazz, blues, salsa and country **155**, 157
Scurlogstown Olympiad Celtic Festival 27
shops **149**, 151
Summer in Dublin Festival 27
traditional music and dance **155**, 157
Music Hall of Fame 156, 157
Musical Pub Crawl 156, 157

N
National Botanic Gardens 16, **88**
National Concert Hall 9, 155, 157
National Disability Board 165
National Gallery 9, **48–51**
Baroque Gallery 50
British School 50
café 146, 147
floorplan 48–9
French School 50–51
Irish School 50
Italian School 51
Northern European Schools 51
Spanish School 51
Visitors' Checklist 49
National History Museum **43**
National Library 35, **46**
National Maritime Museum (Dun Laoghaire) 90
National Museum (Archaeology) 8, 35, **44–5**
café 146, 147
National Museum at Collins Barracks **86–7**
National Photographic Archive **59**
National Stud 105
National Transport Museum (Howth) 9, **90**
Nature reserves
Bog of Allen Nature Centre 104
Ireland's Eye 8–9, 90
Nelson Pillar 19
Neolithic period 13, 119
New Theatre 158, 159
New Year's Eve 29
Newbridge Demesne 101, **116**
Newgrange **120–21**
Newman, Cardinal John Henry **42**, 97
Newman House 15, **42**, 95
Newspapers 165
Newton, Lord 37
Nightclubs **154–5**, 157
Nolde, Emil 51
Normans 14
castles 101
North of the Liffey **67–77**
area map 67
Around O'Connell Street street-by-street map 68–9
hotels 131
restaurants 142–3
Northern Ireland 19
Number 29 **47**

O
O2 Theatre 155, 157
O'Brien, Flann 42, 94, 95
O'Brien, William Smith 87
O'Carolan, Turlough 61
O'Casey, Sean 72
Abbey Theatre 70
St Mary's Church 77
O'Connell, Daniel 17
Catholic Emancipation Act 16
Glasnevin Cemetery 89
Hill of Tara 122

O'Connell, Daniel (cont.)
Merrion Square 47
monument by John Foley 69, 71
St Audoen's Roman Catholic Church 63
O'Connell Street **70–71**
Street-by-Street map 68–9
O'Connor, James Arthur 50
O'Conor, Roderic 50
October Bank Holiday 29
O'Donoghue's 146, 147
Dublin's Best Pubs 25
traditional music and dance 155, 157
O'Donovan Bridge 18
Old Jameson Distillery **75**
Oliver St John Gogarty 146, 147
Dublin's Best Pubs 25
Olympia Theatre 55, 58, **60**, 155, 157, 158, 159
O'Neill's 146, 147
Dublin's Best Pubs 25
Opening hours 165
post offices 170
pubs 135
restaurants 134
shops 148
Opera **155**, 157
Opera Ireland 28
Original Print Gallery 58
Ormonde, Duke of 80
Ormonde, Earl of 61
Osbourne, Danny, statue of Oscar Wilde 46
O'Toole, St Laurence
Christ Church Cathedral 65
St Mary's Pro-Cathedral **71**
Outdoor activities **160–61**
Oxygen 27

P
Pale 101, **108**
Dundalk 118
Trim 122
Palestrina Choir 71
Pantomime season 29
Papal Cross 80
Papworth, George 60
Parking 175
Parks and gardens
Ardgillan Demesne 102, 117
Avondale Forest Park 109
Avondale House 102
Butterstream Gardens 123
County Wicklow Gardens Festival 27
Dillon's Park (Dalkey) 97
Dublin Garden Festival 26
Garden of Remembrance 73
Howth Castle 90
Iveagh Gardens 9, **42**
Japanese Gardens (Tully) 105
Killruddery House & Gardens 113
Merrion Square **46–7**
Mount Usher Gardens **111**
National Botanic Gardens 16, **88**
People's Park (Dun Laoghaire) 90

Parks and gardens (cont.)
Phoenix Park 9, **80–81**
Powerscourt **114–15**
St Fiachra's Gardens (Tully) 105
St Stephen's Green 34, **41**
Slane Castle 122, 155
Slieve Foye Forest Park 118
Sorrento Park (Dalkey) 97
Parliament *see* Irish Parliament
Parnell, Charles Stewart 12
Avondale House 109
grave of 89
"Home Rule" campaign 17
Kilmainham Gaol 81
Parnell Monument 68, 71
Parnell Square **72–3**
Passage graves
Dowth **119**
Knowth **119**
Newgrange **120–21**
Passports 164
Patrick, St 13
Hill of Slane 122
Hill of Tara 122
St Patrick's Cathedral 61
Pavilion Theatre (Dun Laoghaire) 159
Payne-Townsend, Charlotte 84
Peacock Theatre 158
Pearce, Edward Lovett 36
Pearse, Patrick 17, 71
Peasant Wedding (Brueghel) 51
Penal Laws 15, 16
Pencz 51
People's Garden (Phoenix Park) 80
Personal security **166**
Pharmacies 167
Phoenix Column 80
Phoenix Park 9, **80–81**
map 80
Phonecards 171
Photography
Gallery of Photography **59**
National Photographic Archive **59**
People's Photographic Exhibition 27
Picasso, Pablo 51
Picnics 135
Pierrot (Gris) 48
Pissaro, Camille 51
Plague 14
Plunkett, Joseph 81
Plunkett, Oliver 117
Poddle, River 13, 53
Poetry Now Festival 26
Police 166, 167
Pomodoro, *Sphere within Sphere* 35, 39
Pony trekking **160**, 161
Portrait of James Joyce (Blanche) 72
Ports 173
Post offices 170
Postal services **170**
Poste restante 170
Poulaphouca Reservoir 109

Poussin, Nicolas 50
Powerscourt 15, **114–15**
Powerscourt, Viscounts 60, 114
Powerscourt Townhouse 55, **60**
Powerscourt Townhouse Shopping Centre 60, 148, 151
Powerscourt Waterfall 112
Project Arts Centre 58, 158, 159
Protestant Ascendancy 15, 16
Protestantism 14
Public holidays 29
Pubs **146–7**
Dublin's Best Pubs **24–5**
food in 135, **146**, 147
music pubs **146**, 147
opening hours 135
pub crawls and tours **156**, 157
traditional pubs **146**, 147
Punchestown 105
Puppets
International Puppet Festival 158, 159
Lambert Puppet Theatre (Dun Laoghaire) **90**, 159

Q

Quantas 173

R

Racing *see* Horse racing
Radio 165
Raeburn, Henry 50
Railways *see* Trains
Rainfall 28
Reefert Church (Glendalough) 111
Reinagle, Philip 50
Religious services 165
Rembrandt 51
Renting
bicycles 177
cars **175**, 177
Republic of Ireland 19
Restaurants **134–45**
beyond Dublin 145
budget dining 134–5
eating out 134
Flavours of Ireland 136–7
further afield 143–5
gourmet and ethnic dining 134
Irish eating patterns 134
North of the Liffey 142–3
Southeast Dublin 138–40
Southwest Dublin 141–2
vegetarian food 135
see also Food and drink
Reynolds, Sir Joshua 50
Richard II, King of England 14
Riding **160**, 161
Road signs 177
Roberts, Thomas 47
Robertstown **104**
Robinson, Sir William
Marsh's Library **61**
Royal Hospital Kilmainham 84
St Mary's Church 77
Rock music **155**, 157
Rodin, Auguste 73

Roman Catholic Church 15
Romantic movement 50
Rotunda Gardens 15
Rotunda Hospital 68, **72–3**
history 15, 16
Roundwood 112
Royal Canal **85**, 123
Royal College of Science 43
Royal College of Surgeons **41**
Royal Dublin Hotel 71, 131
Royal Dublin Society (RDS) 15
concerts 155, 157
Leinster House 46
National Library 46
Royal Dublin Society Showgrounds (RDS) 85
Royal Hibernian Academy **47**, 95
Gallagher Gallery 42
Royal Hospital Kilmainham (Irish Museum of Modern Art) 15, **84**
concerts 155, 157
Rubens, Peter Paul 50, 51
Rugby, Six Nations Rugby Tournament 29
Rules of the road 177
Russborough House **108–9**
Russell, AE 94, 95
Ryanair 172, 173
Rynhart, Jean 36

S

Sailing 161
St Ann's Church 34, **37**
St Audoen's Church **62–3**, 93
St Audoen's Roman Catholic Church 63
St Brigid's Cathedral (Kildare) 104–5
St Fiachra's Garden 105
St James's Hospital 167
St Mary's Abbey Exhibition **76–7**
St Mary's Church **77**
St Mary's Church (Glendalough) 110–11
St Mary's Pro-Cathedral 69, **71**
St Michan's Church **76**
St Patrick's Cathedral 9, **61**, 93
St Patrick's Cathedral (Trim) 123
St Patrick's Day 26, 29
St Patrick's Day Celtic Winners Show 26
St Stephen's Day 29
St Stephen's Green 9, 34, **41**, 95
St Stephen's Green Shopping Centre 148, 151
St Teresa's Church **36**
St Vincent's Hospital 167
St Werburgh's Church 54, **62**, 93
Sales tax 148
Sally Gap 112, 113
Salmon and sea trout season 29
Salsa 155, 157
Samuel Beckett Centre 158, 159
Science Gallery 47
Scurlogstown Olympiad Celtic Festival 27
Seanad Éireann **46**

Security **166**
Semple, George 116
Shannon, River 123
Shaw, George Bernard **84**
  National Gallery 48
  Shaw's Birthplace **84**
  Torca Cottage (Dalkey) 97
Sheares, Henry 76
Sheares, John 76
Shelbourne Hotel 9, 35, 41, 95, 130
Sherbourne, Bishop 14
Shopping **148–53**
  antiques **149**, 151
  books **148–9**, 151
  cafés in shops **146**, 147
  china, crystal and glassware **149**, 151
  crafts **149**, 151
  fashion **150**, 151
  food and drink **150**, 151
  Grafton Street 36–7
  how to pay 148
  jewellery **149**, 151
  knitwear and tweed **150**, 151
  linen **150**, 151
  music **149**, 151
  sales tax and refunds 148
  shopping centres **148**, 151
  What to buy in Dublin 152–3
  when to shop 148
  where to shop 148
The Sick Call (Lawless) 49
Simnel, Lambert 14, 65
Sinn Féin 17
  Civil War 18, 19
  Custom House 70
Sirr, Major Henry, tomb of 62
Sisley, Alfred 51
Sitric the Silkbeard, King 13, 65
Six Nations Rugby Tournament 29
Slane **122**
Slane Annual Rock Festival 155, 157
Slane Castle 122
Slattery's, Dublin's Best Pubs 24
Slazenger family 114
Slieve Foye Forest Park 118
Smithfield 8, **74–5**
Smock Alley Theatre 158, 159
Smyth, Edward
  Custom House 69, 70
  Dublin Castle 56
  King's Inns 74
Sorrento Point (Dalkey) 97
Southeast Dublin **33–51**
  area map 33
  hotels 128–30
  National Gallery **48–51**
  National Museum **44–5**
  restaurants 138–40
  Street-by-Street map 34–5
  Trinity College **38–40**
Southwell, James 62
Southwest Dublin **53–65**
  area map 53
  Christ Church Cathedral **64–5**

Southwest Dublin (cont.)
  Dublin Castle **56–7**
  hotels 130–31
  restaurants 141–2
  Street-by-Street map 54–5
  Temple Bar **58–9**
Souvenirs, What to buy in Dublin 152–3
Speed limits 177
Sphere within Sphere (Pomodoro) 35, 39
Sports **160–61**
Spréacha Festival 159
Spring in Dublin 26
Stag's Head 146, 147
  Dublin's Best Pubs 24
Stapleton, Michael
  Ely Place houses 42
  James Joyce Cultural Centre 72
  Powerscourt Townhouse 60
  Trinity College 38
Statues
  Daniel O'Connell 69, 71
  Edmund Burke 38
  Father Theobald Mathew 71
  Figure of Justice 56
  Henry Grattan 36
  James Joyce 41, 69
  James Larkin 68, 71
  Oscar Wilde 46
  Parnell Monument 68, 71
  Strongbow Monument 64
Stena Line 173
Stewart, Richard 62
Stoker, Bram **22**, 94, 95
  St Ann's Church 37
Stone Age 101, 122
Strongbow (Richard de Clare) 14, 53
  Christ Church Cathedral 64
Student information 164
Summer in Dublin 27
Sunlight Chambers 54
Sunshine 27
Sur la Plage (Degas) 73
Sweetman, John 36
Swift, Jonathan 15, **22**, **61**, 94
  Marsh's Library 61
  St Patrick's Cathedral 61
Synge, JM 94
  Abbey Theatre 70
  Playboy of the Western World 17
Synod Hall 63, 65

T

Tailors' Hall 62
The Taking of Christ (Caravaggio) **49**, 51
Talbot Castle 123
Talbot family 89
Tara *see* Hill of Tara
Tara, High Kings of 13, 122
  Newgrange 120
Taxes, VAT 148
Taxis 175
Tay, Lough 112
Telephones **171**
Television 165
Temperatures 29

Temple, William 58
Temple Bar 9, 19, 52, 53, **58–9**
  map 59
  Street-by-Street map 55
Temple Bar Tradfest 26
Temple Bar Gallery and Studios 58
Temple Bar Information Centre 58
Temple Bar Square 58
Temple Bar Cultural Trust Summer Programme 27, 58, 156, 159
Temple-na-Skellig (Glendalough) 111
Textile shops **150**, 151
Theatre **158–9**
  children's 159
  Dublin Fringe 28, 158, 159
  Dublin Theatre Festival 28, 158, 159
  festivals 158–9
  information sources 158
  see also individual theatres by name
Thomas Cook 168
Ticketmaster 154, 157
Tickets
  buses 175
  for entertainments **154**, 157
  trains 176
Time zone 165
Tipping, in hotels 127
Titian 51
Tivoli Theatre 158, 159
Tombs
  Dowth **119**
  Knowth **119**
  Newgrange **120–21**
Tone, Wolfe 16, 89, 90
  monument on St Stephen's Green 41
  St Ann's Church 37
  St Mary's Church 77
  Tailors' Hall 62
Torca Cottage (Dalkey) 97
Tour of the Military Road 112
Tourism Ireland 164, 165
Tourist Information 164
Town and Country Homes 126, 127
Toy and Train Fair 28
Traditional food **146**, 147
Traditional music and dance **155**, 157
Traditional pubs **146**, 147
Trains
  DART service **174**, 175
  Fry Model Railway **89**
  outside Dublin 176
  ports 173
  tickets and fares 176
Tramyard (Dalkey) 96
Travel **172–7**
  air **172**, 173
  buses **174**, 175
  cars 175, **176–7**
  cycling 177
  Dublin transport map *see* Back endpaper
  Exploring beyond Dublin 103

Travel (cont.)
  ferries 173
  Getting around Dublin **174–5**
  North of the Liffey 67
  outside Dublin **176–7**
  Southeast Dublin 33
  Southwest Dublin 53
  taxis 175
  trains **174**, 175, 176
Traveller's cheques **168**
  in shops 148
Trevor, William 22
Trim **122–3**
  restaurants 145
Trim Castle 122
Trinity College 8, 14–15, 35,
  38–40, 94
  Book of Kells 8, **40**
  floorplan 38–9
Tully 105
Turner, Richard 88
Tweed shops **150**, 151
Tyrone, Marcus Beresford, Earl of
  71
Tyrone House **71**

U
U2 58
Uccello, Paolo 51
Uden, Lucas van 51
Ulster 18
United Irishmen 16
United Kingdom
  tourist information 165
  UK Embassy 165
United States
  tourist information 165
  US Embassy 165
Universities
  Catholic University of Ireland
  42
  Trinity College **38–40**
  University College Dublin, Royal
  College of Science 43
USIT 165

V
Valdré, Vincenzo 56
Vale of Avoca 113
Vale of Clara 112
Valentine, St 60
Van Dyck, Anthony 51
Vanhomrigh, Hester 61
Vartry, River 111
Vegetarian food 135, **146**, 147
Velázquez, Diego de 51
Vermeer, Jan 51
Vernet, Joseph 108
Victoria, Queen of England 17,
  18
A View of Powerscourt Waterfall
  (Barret) 50
Vikings 13
  Christ Church Cathedral 65
  Dublinia 63
  Glendalough 110
  Viking Splash Tours 9, 156, 157
  Wood Quay 53, 54
Visas 164

W
The Walk Macabre 156, 157
Walking **160**, 161
  Three Guided Walks 92–6
Walpole, Edward 111
Ware, Sir James, tomb of 62
Water sports 161
Waterfalls
  Devil's Glen 113
  Powerscourt Waterfall 112
Waterways Visitors' Centre
  85
Wavertree, Lord 105
Weather 26–9
Welles, Orson 72
Wellington, Duke of **22**
  birthplace 47
  Grafton Street 37
  Ha'penny Bridge 77
  Wellington Testimonial 80
Wheatley, Francis 50
Whichcraft Gallery 149, 151

Whiskey **75**
  Locke's Distillery (Kilbeggan) 123
  Old Jameson Distillery **75**
Whitefriar Street Carmelite Church
  60, 95
Whyte, Samuel 37
Wicklow Mountains 101, **113**
  Tour of the Military Road 112
Wicklow Way 113
Wide Street Commission 16
Wilde, Oscar 22, **23**, 72, 94, 95
  Merrion Square 47
  statue of 46, 94
William III, King of England
  Battle of the Boyne 15, 119
  Dublin Castle 56
  Mellifont Abbey 118
  National Museum at Collins
  Barracks 86
Williams, Richard 116
Windsor, John 77
Windsurfing 161
Winter in Dublin 29
Wood Quay 53, 54
World War I 17
World War II 19
Wyatt, James 122

Y
Yeats, Jack B 50
  For the Road 48
  Yeats Museum 48
Yeats, John B 50
Yeats, William Butler 22, **23**, 94,
  95
  Abbey Theatre 70
  Easter Rising 71
  Henry Moore's memorial to 41
  Merrion Square 47
  Yeats Museum 48
Youth hostels 127
Yverni, Jacques 50

Z
Zárata, Doña Antonia 51
Zoos, Dublin Zoo 9, 80, **81**
Zurbarán, Francisco 51

Acknowledgments

Dorling Kindersley would like to thank the following people whose contributions and assistance have made the preparation of this book possible.

Main Contributor
Tim Perry, from Dungannon, County Tyrone, writes on travel and popular music for various publishers in North America and the British Isles. He was also a contributor to the *Eyewitness Travel Guide to Ireland*.

Editorial and Design Assistance
Gillian Allan, Douglas Amrine, Lydia Baillie, Claire Baranowski, Des Berry, Tessa Bindloss, Jo Blackmore, Vivien Crump, Nicola Erdpresser, Fay Franklin, Annette Jacobs, Kathryn Lane, Nonie Luke, Therese McKenna, Caroline Mead, Ian Midson, Christina Park, Victoria Peel, Polly Phillimore, Mani Ramaswamy, Lee Redmond, Sands Publishing Solutions, Andrew Sanger, Meredith Smith, Rachel Symons.

Maps
Richie Toomey (ERA-Maptec Ltd, Dublin, Ireland)
Map Co-ordinator David Pugh

Indexer
Hilary Bird.

Proofreader
Stewart Wild.

Additional Picture Research
Monica Allende, Brigitte Arora, Rachel Barber, Rhiannon Furbear, Anna Grapes, Ellen Root.

Additional Illustrations
Joy Fitzsimmons.

Additional Photography
Peter Anderson, Ian O'Leary, Clive Streeter.

Special Assistance
Particular thanks to Niall Kennedy at Dublin Tourism for his invaluable help throughout this project.

Thanks also to everyone at the National Museum, especially Dr Felicity Devlin, Damien Debarra and Aoife O'Shea, to Adrian le Harivel at the National Gallery, to Telecom Eireann and the General Post Office.

Photography Permissions
The Publisher would like to thank all those who gave permission to photograph at various cathedrals, churches, museums, restaurants, hotels, shops, galleries and other sights that are too numerous to list individually.

Picture Credits
tl = top left; tc = top centre; tr = top right; cla = centre left above; ca = centre above; cra = centre right above; cl = centre left; c = centre; cr = centre right; clb = centre left below; cb = centre below; crb = centre right below; bl = bottom left; bc = bottom centre; br = bottom right.

The Publisher would like to thank the following individuals, companies and picture libraries for permission to reproduce their photographs:

AER LINGUS/AIRBUS INDUSTRIE: 172t; AKG LONDON: 14cb, 22c; ALAMY IMAGES: AA World Travel Library 9br; Caro/Sorge 167cla; David Sanger Photography 95bc; Peter Horree 92bl; irishphoto 93tr; Barry Mason 94bl; mediacolor's 137c; nagelestock.com 96bl; Profimedia International s.r.o./Alzbeta Bajgartova 92cl; Robert Harding Picture Library Ltd/G. Richardson 8cl; Neil Setchfield 95ca; Peter Titmuss 137tl, 174cl; AN POST, THE IRISH POST OFFICE: 170bl; AXIS ARTS CENTRE: 158cb.

BORD FAILTE/IRISH TOURIST BOARD: 120tr, 120tl; Brian Lynch 19t, 29clb; BRUCE COLEMAN LTD: George McCarthy 112tl; BUS EIREANN: 174b.

CENTRAL BANK OF IRELAND: 169; CENTRAL CYBER CAFÉ, DUBLIN: Finbarr Clarkson 171br; CHESTER BEATTY LIBRARY, DUBLIN: 57t; COLLECTIONS: Image Ireland 26t, 85b; Slide File 30crb; CORBIS UK LTD: Bettmann/Reuters 19b; Julian Calder 9tr; Jack Fields 136cl; Werner Forman 8tc; Hulton-Deutsch Collection 23t, 23crb; Library of Congress 22bl; National Gallery, London 22t.

DALKEY CASTLE & HERITAGE CENTRE: 97bc; DAVISON & ASSOCIATES LTD, IRELAND: 65cra; DUBLIN THEATRE FESTIVAL: 159tl; DUBLIN TOURISM: 164tc; DUNBRODY COUNTRY HOUSE HOTEL & RESTAURANT: 127bl.

EIRCOM: 171tl, 171bl, 171bc; MARY EVANS PICTURE

LIBRARY: 7c, 13c, 15c, 17tr, 31c, 57cl, 70b, 125c, 162c.
GUINNESS IRELAND LTD: 82bc, 82br, 83bl, 83tl, 83tr, 83br.

HULTON GETTY: 18bc, 38bl, 99t.

THE IRISH ANTIQUE DEALERS FAIR: Louis O'Sullivan 28cr; THE IRISH PICTURE LIBRARY: 15t; IRISH RAIL (LARNROD EIRANN) 176BL; IRISH TIMES: 114br.

JAROLD COLOUR PUBLICATIONS: 38bc.

LAUGHTER LOUNGE: 155c.

TIMOTHY KOVAR: 58b.

MANSELL/TIME INC: 65bl.

HUGH McKNIGHT PHOTOGRAPHY: 85t.

JOHN MURPHY: 104cb; JOHN MURRAY: 29c, 80c.

LILLIE'S BORDELLO: 154cr; LONELY PLANET IMAGES: Oliver Strewe 25crb.

THE MERMAID CAFÉ: 134bl; MORRISON HOTEL: 127tc.

NATIONAL GALLERY OF IRELAND, DUBLIN: 61tr, 73b, 84cr, 108b; For the Road, JB Yeats 48cl; *The Houseless Wanderer*, JH Foley 48tl; Pierrot, Juan Gris 48tr; *Judith with the Head of Holofernes*, Andrea Mantegna 49crb; *The Castle of Bentheim*, Jacob van Ruisdael 49c; *The Sick Call*, Matthew James Lawless 49b; *The Taking of Christ*, Caravaggio 49tr; *Convent Garden, Brittany*, c. 1913, William John Leech, ©DACS, London 2006 50ca; *A View of Powerscourt Waterfall*, George Barret the Elder 50bl; *A Group of Cavalry in the Snow*, Ernest Meissonier 51tl; *Virgin and Child Hodigitria*, Constantinople 51cra; *Guards at the Door of a Tomb*, Jean-Léon Gérôme 51cla; *Peasant Wedding*, Pieter Brueghel the Younger 51br; *Portrait of James Joyce*, Jacques Emile Blanche ©ADAGP, Paris and DACS, London 2006 72bl; NATIONAL MUSEUM OF IRELAND, DUBLIN: 21tl, 35crb, 44tr, 44cl, 44b, 45c, 45tr, 45bc, 45crb, 86clb, 87tl, 87cra, 87cr; NATIONAL LIBRARY OF IRELAND: 6/7, 12, 111t, 119t; NORTON ASSOCIATES: 54clb.

OFFICE OF PUBLIC WORKS, IRELAND: 120cl, 121cr, 121t, 122b; OLYMPIA THEATRE: Linda Farrelly 158cl.

PAPHOTOS: PA Archive/Niall Carson 8br; PHOTOSHOT/NHPA: Jean-Louis Le Moigne 96tr; POWERSCOURT ESTATE: 115tl; PUNCHSTOCK: Brand X Pictures 134c.

RETROGRAPH ARCHIVE LTD: Martin Ranicar-Breese 46c; REX FEATURES: 22b.

SAMSARA CAFE: 135tl; SHELBOURNE HOTEL, DUBLIN 95tr, 156tl; SINNOTT HOTELS: 126cra; SLIDE FILE: 18br, 19cl, 26crb, 26bl, 27ca, 28cl, 28b, 29b, 62tl, 105c, 112cl, 112b, 118t, 122t, 154t; JENNIFER SMITH-MAYO: www.photographersdirect.com 155tl; STENA LINE: 173b; STREET PERFORMANCE WORLD CHAMPIONSHIP: 154bc; CINDY STRUNZE: www.photographersdirect.com 97tr; THE SUGAR CLUB: 155br.

TEMPLE BAR PROPERTIES: 58c; BROWN THOMAS: Kieran Harnett 34t; TIPPERARYPHOTOS.COM: 167CL, 167TL; TRINITY COLLEGE, DUBLIN:, 39cr, 40c, 40b, 40crb, 40cra; *The Marriage of Princess Aoite and the Earl of Pembroke*, Daniel Maclise 14t; TRIP ART DIRECTORS: 110c; ROD TUACH: www.photographersdirect.com 93bl.

VIKING SPLASH TOURS: 156bl.

WHELANS: 135bl.

JACKET
Front – DK IMAGES: Magnus Rew clb; GETTY IMAGES: Photographer's Choice. Back – DK IMAGES; Magnus Rew bl, tl; Alan Williams cla, clb. Spine – DK IMAGES: Alan Williams b; GETTY IMAGES: Photographer's Choice t.

All other images are © Dorling Kindersley. For further information see www.dkimages.com

SPECIAL EDITIONS OF DK TRAVEL GUIDES

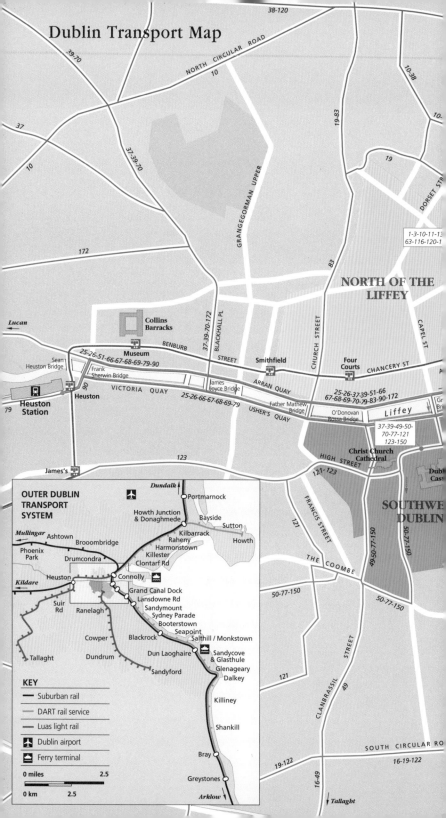